Creative Writing and Stylistics

Creative and Critical Approaches

Jeremy Scott

First published 2013 by
PALGRAVE MACMILLAN

Palgrave Macmillan in the UK is an imprint of Macmillan Publishers Limited,
registered in England, company number 785998, of 4 Crinan Street,
London N1 9XW.

Palgrave® and Macmillan® are registered trademarks in the United States,
the United Kingdom, Europe and other countries.

ISBN 978–1–137–01066–7   hardback
ISBN 978–1–137–01065–0   paperback

This book is printed on paper suitable for recycling and made from fully
managed and sustained forest sources. Logging, pulping and manufacturing
processes are expected to conform to the environmental regulations of the
country of origin.

A catalogue record for this book is available from the British Library.

A catalog record for this book is available from the Library of Congress.

Typeset by MPS Limited, Chennai, India.

Printed and bound by CPI Group (UK) Ltd, Croydon, CR0 4YY

For Lily, of course

Contents

Contents ix

Acknowledgements

The author and publishers wish to thank the following for permission to reproduce copyright material: "(listen)// this a dog barks and". Copyright © 1963, 1991 by the Trustees for the E.E. Cummings Trust, from COMPLETE POEMS: 1904–1962 by E.E. Cummings, edited by George J. Firmage. Used by permission of Liveright Publishing Corporation; Excerpt by Susan Howe, from EUROPE OF TRUSTS, copyright ©1990 by Susan Howe. Reprinted by permission of New Directions Publishing Corp; "Questions of Travel" from THE COMPLETE POEMS 1927–1979 by Elizabeth Bishop. Copyright © 1979, 1983 by Alice Helen Methfessel. Reprinted by permission of Farrar, Straus and Giroux, LLC; "Italics" by Roger McGough from *Gig* (© Roger McGough 1973) is printed by permission of United Agents (www.unitedagents.co.uk) on behalf of Roger McGough; Tom Leonard for "The Six O'clock News"; Nancy Gaffield for "Belle Isle"; Janklow & Nesbit Associates for "Ma" from *Collected Stories* by Leonard Michaels, reprinted by permission of the author's estate; "Thing Language" from *My Vocabulary Did This To Me* © 2008 by the Estate of Jack Spicer. Reprinted by permission of Wesleyan University Press; "What is Poetry" from HOUSEBOAT DAYS by John Ashbery. Copyright © 1975, 1976, 1977, 1999 by John Ashbery. Reprinted by permission of Georges Borchardt, Inc., on behalf of the author; "What is Poetry" from *Selected Poems* by John Ashbery. Copyright © 1988, 1998 by John Ashbery. Reprinted by permission of Carcanet Press; "The Christmas Present" from *Creative Editing* © 1995 Mary Mackie. Reprinted by permission of The Orion Publishing Group, London, Mary Mackie and Juliet Burton Literary Agency; 'Old House' from *Collected Poems* © 2012 Peter Redgrove. Reprinted by permission of David Higham Associates.

I would also like to thank my dear colleague Nancy Gaffield, for solidarity, support, input, advice and wisdom beyond measure; Patricia Debney, for her voices of reason; my friends and colleagues from the Poetics and Linguistics Association for cogency, insight, encouragement and drink; Graeme Harper, for taking me on; Lucinda Knight at Palgrave Macmillan for her diligence and massive assistance and all students, past, present and future, who have/will have taken our module 'Creative Writing: A Stylistics Approach' at the University of Kent and emerged, stylised, on the other side. Writeandread on.

Every effort has been made to trace all the copyright holders, but if any have been inadvertently overlooked, the publishers will be pleased to make the necessary arrangements at the first opportunity.

Introduction: Style, Composition, Creative Practice

The idea for this book came from an observation: that some 'traditional' approaches to creative writing in the academy still seemed to hang on the two thousand-year old advice of Plato in *The Republic*:

> The poet is an airy thing, winged and holy, and he is not able to make poetry until he becomes inspired and goes out of his mind.
>
> (Leitch 2001: 35)

In other words, the writer all but abandons the critical faculty with which he or she has been inculcated elsewhere when studying texts and devotes all energy to self-expression. The assumption often (but not always) appears to be that beginning writers (or any writer at all) will write well if pushed in at the deep end and asked to produce full stories and poems, or to 'just write'. While, self-evidently, this may well produce good results in some cases, I wondered whether there was not something to be drawn from more critical, theoretical approaches to the discipline – especially, as so often, when it is being practised in an academic context.

An analogy could be drawn with learning to paint: would your first experience of an art class be to sit down and paint a still life in oils? Continuing this analogy: is there not an argument for complementary approaches to creative writing that view the subject in a similar way; that is, that a writer has available to him or her a set of tools and techniques, in the same way that an artist has a range of colours on his or her palette and a spread of different-sized brushes in the china pot next to the easel? Where we might learn to lighten a deep red by adding a drop of white paint, so a writer might benefit from learning how a particular mood in a piece of writing can be 'foregrounded' by careful selection of particular lexical fields, or by repetition, or parallelism. Just as a painter learns to use shading to create the illusion of depth, so can a writer learn to use fracturing syntax, creative punctuation and linguistic deviation to convey the illusion of being inside the mind of a character.

Of course, approaching the art of creative writing from the perspective of 'craft' is not a new idea. In dialogue with Plato, Aristotle's *Poetics* constitutes the first rigorous categorisation of the form of verbal art. *Poetics* is a scientific anatomisation, in opposition to Plato's obsession with 'inspiration',[1] just as can be found in Aristotle's work on classifications of the natural world, and as such anticipates the ambition of stylistics to provide rigorous accounts of the form of literary discourse. During the Renaissance, it was treated as a rulebook or manual for literary composition, and can be seen as the first work of true literary criticism, putting down the roots which grew into Neoclassicism, Russian Formalism and the New Criticism. Note, then, that at the dawn of the discipline we find an interest in the processes of *composition*, not textual analysis. *Poetics* is a technical manual. In their exploration of the twin concepts of **mimesis** and **diegesis**, the work of classical poetics sets out one of the key dichotomies to be discussed in this book.

So, the idea of approaching creative writing from the perspective of technique is not new; approaching it from the perspective of a discipline rooted in linguistics, I believe, is. The discipline I am referring to is that of (literary) stylistics,[2] and if this book has a manifesto, it is this: that stylistics has an enormous amount to offer the practising writer by virtue of its widening of his or her understanding of the 'expressive mechanics' of language. There is an intense debate around whether creative writing should be taught in an academic context creatively, and by practitioners, or technically, with emphasis on craft and critical theory. I do not wish this book in any way to suggest that a firm choice has to be made in one direction or the other; in fact, I think we can have our cake and eat it. There are many different ways to approach the subject, each with their own strengths and weaknesses. I view this contribution to the discipline as an augmentation rather than a replacement of any existing methodologies – as a new, complementary perspective. I would add, further, that intense and rigorous awareness of the stuff of language can in and of itself lead to creativity (or, if you prefer, inspiration). Creativity can arise from within language, and not only from sources external to it; in other words, inspiration often comes from and within the act of writing itself. As Carter and Nash (1990: 176–7) make clear, a great deal can be learned about the relationships between language and creativity through writing games, wherein language itself provides the creative stimulus which might normally be expected to come from an extra-linguistic source (William Empson, in work which anticipates the growth of stylistics, also defined this incarnation of creativity as one of his seven types of ambiguity (1995)). Creativeness, it must surely be agreed, is directly accessible *through* language, and thus to everyone. As such, this book has little to say in answer to that perennial question of 'where do ideas come from?', other than: 'often, from creative use of language itself'.

However, this book is not only about creative writing; it is also about 'doing stylistics from the inside'. Thus, it will be of benefit to those studying stylistics as a whole, as well as language, linguistics and literature more generally. The goal of 'doing stylistics' will become exactly that: a practical exploration of the tenets of the discipline.

What is stylistics?

For readers coming to this topic with little or no knowledge of stylistics, it will be useful now to provide a brief summary of the subject. This is no easy task, however, as modern stylistics is a broad and diverse church. Put as simply as possible, stylistics explores how readers interact with the language of texts in order to explain how we understand, and are affected by, texts when we read them. The goal of this book, as should by now be clear, is to travel in the other direction through that paradigm: from writer to text to reader. A short history of the discipline's development and influences should help clarify this goal.

Stylistics as an academic discipline stands on the border between language and literary studies, and has feet in both camps. However, it is, at heart, a sub-discipline of linguistics, combining the use of linguistic analysis with what psychologists have uncovered about the cognitive processes involved in reading. Despite its roots in linguistics[3], stylistics is in many ways a logical extension of the classical poetics of both Plato and Aristotle, and moves within literary criticism early in the twentieth century to concentrate on studying texts rather than their writers: in Western Europe and America, Practical Criticism, and in Eastern Europe and Russia, Formalism. In England, the literary critic I.A. Richards and his student, William Empson, dismissed the nineteenth-century critical obsession with authors and their social contexts in favour of criticism that took as its object the literary text itself and how readers read it, an approach which became known as Practical Criticism (closely related to New Criticism in the US). These scholars were interested primarily in the language of texts, and describing how appropriately trained and acute critics such as themselves were affected by them. Arguably, this approach to studying literature still predominates in schools and universities in Europe and the US. Students write essays in which they assert a point about a particular text and their reading of it, and then discuss a short excerpt from that text in order to back that reading up. A stylistician would assert that this approach is inadequate when arguing for a particular view of text, especially when that view is based on textual analysis or close reading. Intuition is not enough; we should both analyse the text in detail and take account of what we understand about how people read when arguing for particular views of texts. Nevertheless, the stylistics approach to literature certainly grows from the inferences of Practical Criticism and New Criticism: that the proper object of study is the text itself.

There is another important strand in the development of stylistics (in which Roman Jakobson was involved) that comes from Eastern Europe and Russia. In the early years of the twentieth century, the members of the Linguistic Circle in Moscow (usually called the Russian Formalists), like Richards and Empson, also rejected undue concentration on the author in literary criticism in favour of an approach which favoured the analysis of the language of the text in relation to psychological effects of that linguistic structure. The group contained linguists, literary critics and psychologists, and they (along with the Prague Linguistic Circle, with whom Jakobson was associated) began to develop what became a very influential aspect of textual study in later stylistics, called **foregrounding theory**. This view suggested that some parts of texts had more effect on readers than others in terms of interpretation, because the textual parts were linguistically deviant or specially patterned in some way, thus making them psychologically salient (or 'foregrounded') for readers. In short, an unusual linguistic usage would be foregrounded against the 'background' of standard language, and thus would stand out.[4] The Russian Formalists were, in effect, the first stylisticians. Another important scholar connected to Formalism is Mikhail Bakhtin, whose work on the narrative 'voices' of the novel and their relationships to the diversity and conflicts within language in its totality should be of great interest to both the stylistician and the creative writer.

Jakobson himself became one of the most influential linguists of the twentieth century, and the reason for his considerable influence on stylistics was because he wove the various threads of linguistics together, seeing, for example, the poetic function of language as fundamental to *all* language use, not just to that which we customarily view as 'literary'.

He left Moscow after the revolution and moved to Prague, where he became a member of the Prague Linguistic Circle, whose members were also exploring the same themes: how the language of texts affects readers. Subsequently, after the invasion of the then-Czechoslovakia by the Soviet Union, he moved to the US, bringing with him the approach to the study of literary texts which later became called stylistics. His work was taken to heart by those who wanted to push Practical and New Criticism in more precise, analytical directions.

As well as classical poetics, Western European Practical Criticism/ American New Criticism and the Russian Formalists, any potted history of stylistics must also mention **narratology**, a discipline which has myriad applications to creative practice and which was also influenced by both classical poetics and Russian Formalism. Stylistics has many interconnections with narratology (Shen 2007), and together they give an intricate account of narrative function and effect on two levels: that of *story* and of *discourse*, corresponding to the Formalist distinction between *fabula* and *syuzhet* (Propp 1968; Shklovsky 1965). From the first, we gain insight into plot structure (e.g. the simple linear plot of exposition, complication, climax, resolution) and simple versus complex structures (the ways in which the time of the discourse need not correspond to the time of the story it mediates; more on this shortly). The second level explores the complex interrelationships between authorial voice, narrator voice and character voice, the various methods of representing discourse (speech, thought, writing), and also the essential distinction between point of view (who tells) and focalisation (who sees).

Initially, narratology was associated with structuralism (due to its attempt to model the underlying patterns of narrative universally), but has now become more 'catholic' in its ambitions, having applications to disciplines as diverse as psychology (e.g. the study of memory), anthropology (e.g. the evolution of folk traditions) and even philosophy (especially ethics). Narratologists such as Propp (1928), Todorov (1977), Genette (1980) and Greimas (1983) deconstructed the machinery of narrative with a view to putting together a narrative 'grammar' which would be as rigorous and universal as, say, accounts of syntax in linguistics. However, some modern theorists have argued that this formal grammar of narrative now seems a little 'clunky' and 'unnecessarily scientific' (Van Loon 2007: 19). The questions it explores are highly relevant to the writer, though. What drives the machinery of narrative? What makes reading compelling? How can we as writers apply the insights of narratology to the act of creating narrative fiction (and, indeed, poetry)?

As a summarising justification for the approaching of creative practice via and through stylistics and narratology, it will be useful to turn to Michael Toolan (1998: ix) for support:

> [One of the] chief feature[s] of stylistics is that it persists in the attempt *to understand technique, or the craft of writing.* ... Why these word-choices, clause-patterns, rhythms and intonations, contextual implications, cohesive links, choices of voice and perspective and transitivity etc. etc., and not any of the others imaginable? Conversely, can we locate the linguistic bases of some aspects of weak writing, bad poetry, the confusing and the banal?
>
> Stylistics asserts we should be able to, particularly by bringing to the close examination of the linguistic particularities of a text an understanding of the anatomy and functions of the language. ... Stylistics is crucially concerned with excellence of technique.
>
> [My emphasis]

What applications might the stylistics toolkit have in the *production* of the literary text, not just in its analysis by academic critics 'post-event'? Of course, the most obvious answer to that question is: during the editorial phase of the creative process, that is, during re-reading and re-writing. Stylistics, as Toolan suggests, can help identify and, crucially, account for moments of 'excellence' as well as parts of the work which are less successful. However, I would like to suggest that the stylistics 'toolkit' and the insights it provides into literary process *can become an integral part of creative practice itself.* Its precepts can inform the way you write, *as* you write.

Stylistics also has the potential to complement and augment current creative writing pedagogy in the academy (and beyond) by providing a detailed and rigorous critical taxonomy with which to describe the key issues of both craft and reader reception that come up for discussion time and time again in creative writing workshops. I have lost count of the number of times I have sat in or led writing workshops, or been a part of reading groups, to find a particular technical or reading issue comes up which participants struggle to articulate clearly. I find myself thinking, 'Stylistics has a word for this...'.

A note of caution, though. As I have already hinted, it is no way the intention of this book to suggest that creative writers *must* engage with stylistics. Such a proposition would be patently absurd. You do not need to understand stylistics to be a good writer. My hope, though, is to point to the various ways in which a practical exploration of stylistics through writing rather than just reading can benefit both the creative writer and the student of stylistics, or anyone with an interest in the mechanics of language; indeed, I would venture that anyone with a desire to write creatively must have, by definition, an interest in these things. Rather than showing the only way to write well, combining stylistics and creative writing provides opportunities to explore how you *can* write, to avoid certain common pitfalls of the beginning writer, and, at the very least, to consider in depth the question posed by Toolan above: why *these* words, and not others?

The structure of this book

The book is divided into nine chapters, with an appendix at the end. Each chapter is sub-divided several times according to theme, so you can if you wish home in on the particular theme that interests you without reading through the book as a whole. There is some inevitable overlap between the chapters, as it is often difficult to separate the various aspects of stylistics and narratology neatly from one another, and the relevance of one aspect for creative writers may be similar in vein to the relevance of another. However, where this overlap is unavoidable, every attempt has been made to cross-reference to other chapters where similar topics are discussed. Each chapter will also contain exercises, some in the course of the chapter itself but most at the end. Some exercises are 'standalone' explorations of the particular topic under discussion, while others can be applied to work in progress – a creative project that you are working on already, or one that you start with the book. **The book aims to address the writing of both narrative fiction *and* poetry**; as such, many of the stylistic principles and exercises will be relevant and applicable to both genres (indeed, there are many obvious and fruitful interfaces between them). However, where a section or exercise is aimed explicitly at one or the other, this should be apparent.

1 Seeing through Language

1.1 Overview

It will useful to begin by stating the obvious. The literary text[1] is, inescapably, built from two essential materials: language, and the world that language creates in the mind of the reader. Of course, to encompass the creative process from both 'ends', we should say that the creative writer creates a world which he or she attempts to express through language; the reader reads that language, and creates (or envisions) a world in response. It bears clarifying that these two worlds are extremely unlikely to be the same; that is part of the beauty and mystery of the process. And, of course, the worlds created will vary from reader to reader, even though the language from which they are built is identical. This is why reading is a performance; no two readings are ever the same.[2] Reading is, inevitably, an act of rewriting. Communication is taking place (as stylistics terms it, a **discourse world** ensues[3]), involving the creative writer and the reader, who are (usually) unknown to one another, and not in direct face-to-face contact. The situation is portrayed (by Rimmon-Kenan 1986; see also Booth 1983) as follows:

> Real author – implied author – narrator – (narratee) – implied reader – real reader

The real author (you, as you write creatively) writes text which the real reader reads (can also be you, as you re-read your own work or this book, or it can be the person who reads your work once it is finished[4]). The real reader sees you as the implied author. You see the real reader as the implied reader. In other words, both of the agencies that participate in this discourse world have an imagined, conventionalised idea of each other; the creative writer writes with an imagined reader in mind, a reader reads with an imagined creative writer in mind. The crucial point is that, right across this cline, there is interactivity between its various agencies, and the literary text cannot exist or function (despite the protestations of structuralism and what followed it) without all of these agencies being in play. There is little point (some, perhaps, but not very much) in writing a story that no one else will ever read. You can read your own work with (it is hoped) pleasure, but surely it is possible to argue that the true literary experience, the experience of what Keith Oatley (2003) has christened **writingandreading** in all its messy, vivacious glory, must involve both a writer and a reader.

> 'Writingandreading' is not an English word. It should be. We tend to think of its two parts as separate. Pure writing is possible. One may just write an email, careless of syntax and spelling, then press a key, and off it goes into the ether. Pure reading is also possible: one can absorb, if that is an apt metaphor, the information in a newspaper article with almost no thought except what the writer has supplied. More usually, we writeandread. As I write this chapter, I am also reading it, and I will read it again, and re-write and re-read. Even in my first draft I have made four or five changes to the previous sentence, though only two (so far) to this one.
>
> (2003: 161)

So, writers are also readers. During creative practice, writers engage in the act of reading, prefiguring the subsequent reading practice of their eventual readers, and so on. And readers are also creative writers. The two activities are, to all intents and purposes, inseparable. A stylistics-based approach to creative practice must have an appreciation of this notion at the forefront throughout. The reasons for this are quite complex, but sit at the heart of this book in its attempt to make what for want of a better term we could call 'stylistic self-awareness' a central aspect of creative practice, part of the act of writing, and not just a 'post-event' editorial mechanism.

Now for a less obvious point. To return to the writer side of Rimmon-Kenan's cline: it is not strictly (or not always) correct to say that the creative writer imagines a world and then expresses that world through language. Indeed, it is possible to argue, as Derrida (1976) has done, that the text refers to nothing at all outside of itself: that its 'meaning' resides at the centre of an unattached web of words with no external anchoring. Contrary to this, Abrams (1953) proposes that we *can* mediate both material and interior (mental) worlds through language, but that this is not the primary purpose of art. Rather, verbal art focusses and directs attention. Unlike Hamlet's 'mirror held up to nature', it should not reflect; nor should it simply 'imitate', a function of verbal art that Plato disparages in *The Republic*. Rather, it should illuminate like a lantern. Joyce's fictional alter-ego, Stephen Dedalus, pronounces as

much in *Stephen Hero* (1991), appealing for a 'transparency' of mediation, and an end to the medium's transfiguration of the message:

> The ancient method investigated law with the lantern of justice,
> morality with the lantern of revelation, art with the lantern of tradition.
> But all these lanterns have magical properties; they transform and dis-
> figure. The modern method examines its territory by the light of day.
>
> (1991: 190)

It is easier, probably, for most writers to accept the assertions of Abrams
and Joyce than those of Derrida. However, while it is self-evidently useful for the creative writer to reflect upon the representational aims of the
text that she or he is writing and its essential interrelationship with the
'real world' (wholly fictitious, semi-autobiographical, science-fictional,
fantastical, objective, subjective, self-aware), it is also an interesting
thought experiment – if nothing else – to dwell for a moment on Derrida's
infamous pronouncement that '*Il n'y a pas de hors-texte*'. The process of
translating this phrase into English has (appropriately enough) proved
to be a contentious one. '*There is nothing outside the text*' is often used,
but disputed (see, for example, Deutscher 2009). For our purposes here,
it will be sufficient to render it as 'There is no such a thing as out-of-the-
text', or, more arguably, 'There is no such thing as context'. I introduce
the concept to build on our previous discussion of the ways in which
creative writing uses language to mediate between an imaginary world
and a reader. Creative language use need not always spring from this
process or from an imagined context; *creativity can arise from within
language itself.* The two processes of imagining a world and mediating it
through language are not necessarily antecedent one to the other. Often,
it is in the very act of writing (and, as we have already hinted, reading),
that is, through creative practice, that the imaginary world is created.
The process of world creation can take place as part of creative practice,
and need not be a priori or, indeed, a posteriori. It is through the (often-
playful) use of language that verbal art emerges.

> It is possible to learn a great deal about the relationship between lan-
> guage and creativeness by devising writing games in which language
> itself provides the creative stimulus which we might normally expect
> to come from an extra-linguistic source. ... Some games reverse the
> ordinary supposition, that a context of reference is mapped onto lan-
> guage, and invite the player to infer, from the rudimentary linguistic
> map, a plausible terrain.
>
> (Carter and Nash 1990: 176–7)

And if literature is a verbal art (which it is, inescapably) then, surely, the insights of disciplines which make language the object of their study (such as stylistics, drawing as it does on linguistics) will be invaluable in understanding how the process of literary creativity functions. Language is at the base of all that we do as creative writers, even to the extent that the worlds which we create can arise from within it rather than in some sense from beyond or above it. Creative writing 'happens' in the interplay between language and world, but also within language itself. From the one, we gain access to the other, and the two are interdependent – if not one and the same.[5] To borrow again from Carter and Nash (1990), we *see through language*. Crucially, and obviously, this happens whether we are writers or readers. Those who are hoping to read through this book are presumably – inescapably? – both. We think in sentences. And the way we think is the way we see.

Of course, the process of seeing through language to the fictional world contained within can take place in many different ways, and exploring this assertion opens the door to a range of available techniques within fiction and poetry. It will be useful now to focus on some examples.

Here are three texts, through which the reader 'sees' in fundamentally different ways. In keeping with the ambitions of stylistics as discussed in the introduction to this book, I have provided no information about the author or the title or the genre (although this information appears in the notes and bibliography). For now, just read these texts and think about the various ways in which the language that they use and the worlds that they create in your imagination are related – inextricably, inexorably – to one another.

Text 1

> No sweat, we'll never win; other choirs sing about Love, all our songs are about cattle or death!

> Fionnula (the Cooler) spoke that way, last words pitched a little bit lower with a sexyish sideways look at none of the others. The fifth-year choir all laughed.

> Orla, still so thin she had her legs crossed to cover up her skinniness, keeked along the line and says, When they from the Fort, Hoors of the Sacred Heart, won the competition last year, they got kept down the whole night and put up in a big posh hotel and ... everything, no that I want that! Sooner be snogged in the Mantrap.

Know what the Hoor's school motto is? Fionnula spoke again, from the longest-legs-position on the wall. She spoke louder this time, in that blurred, smoked voice, It's 'Noses up ... knickers DOWN'!
The Sopranos all chortled and hootsied; the Seconds and Thirds mostly smiled in per-usual admiration.[6]

Text 2

It was when she ate that Lin was most alien, and their shared meals were a challenge and an affirmation. As he watched her, Isaac felt the familiar trill of emotion: disgust immediately stamped out, pride at the stamping out, guilt desire.

Light glinted in Lin's compound eyes. Her headlegs quivered. She picked up half a tomato and gripped it with her mandibles. She lowered her hands while her inner mouthparts picked at the food her outer jaw held steady.
Isaac watched the huge iridescent scarab that was his lover's head devour her breakfast.[7]

Text 3

(listen)

this a dog barks and
how crazily houses
eyes people smiles

faces streets
steeples are eagerly

tumbl
ing through wonder
ful sunlight

– look –
selves,stir:writhe
o-p-e-n-i-n-g

are(leaves;flowers)dreams

,come quickly come

run run
with me now
jump shout(laugh
dance cry sing)for

it's Spring
– irrevocably;
and in
earth sky trees
:every
where a miracle arrives

(yes)

you and I may not
hurry it with
a thousand poems
my darling

but nobody will stop it

With All The Policemen
In The World[8]

Text 4

riverrun, past Eve and Adam's, from swerve of shore to bend of bay, brings us by a commodius vicus of recirculation back to Howth Castle and Environs.

Sir Tristram, violer d'amores, fr'over the short sea, had passencore rearrived from North Armorica on this side the scraggy isthmus of Europe Minor to wielderfight his penisolate war: nor had topsawyer's rocks by the stream Oconee exaggerated themselse to Laurens County's gorgios while they went doublin their mumper all the time: nor avoice from afire bellowsed mishe mishe to tauftauf thuartpeatrick: not yet, though venissoon after, had a kidscad buttended a bland old isaac: not yet, though all's fair in vanessy, were sosie sesthers wroth with twone nathandjoe. Rot a peck of pa's malt had Jhem or Shen brewed by arclight and rory end to the regginbrow was to be seen ringsome on the aquaface.[9]

These texts all illustrate, with various methods and through various genres, different ways in which we see through language into the imaginary world beyond – or, in the terms of the discussion earlier in this section, how creative writers create worlds from language itself. Before you read my own comments on the differences (and similarities) between them, take the time to note down your own thoughts on the matter.

- Who is 'witnessing' the imagined world in each case (i.e. from who's perspective – if anyone's – do we see the world)?
- Whose voice is telling the reader about the world? Does that voice have any idiosyncratic qualities?
- Some of the texts draw more attention to their use of language than others. Which ones, and why do they do it? What is the effect on the way you see the imaginary world depicted?

It is beyond the scope of this book to discuss each of the texts in detail. However, I will talk about them briefly to illustrate the kinds of observations you could have been making about the language of the texts, and about how this language influences your 'ways of seeing'. Compare these notes to your own.

When reading text 1 (the opening of a novel), presumably you envisaged a relatively quotidian situation, something one might see every day: a group of schoolgirls (members of a school choir about to enter a competition) sitting on a wall, talking together. Note, however, that none of this information is 'told' to you directly. So how do you know it? There is no description of the wall; it is introduced with a definite article, 'the', signalling that the story begins *in media res* ('in the midst of things') and thus we are drawn into the story world straightaway. The use of 'the' assumes a shared mental space (compare the effect if we substitute 'the' for 'a') – a world in common. We picture schoolgirls because of the character names, the references to the 'Hoors of the Sacred Heart' (another school) and the phrase 'fifth-year choir'; the term 'fifth year' is culturally specific to the UK and, as it happens, now obsolete. We also picture a Catholic School (from its name, and from the Irish-origin girls' names: Fionnula, Orla), and the use of 'hoors' (whores) signals an all-girls school. Where does the action take place? The names signal Ireland, but the language – and this becomes abundantly clear as the novel proceeds – signals Scotland (the use of 'keeked', 'hootsied' and 'hoors'). Thus, we as readers also infer a particular place, culture and time, from very little information. How does this miraculous process take place? Cognitive linguistics provides the answer through its development of schema theory; we will look at this topic in detail in Chapter 6.

We have already drawn attention to the narrative voice of text 1, which is clearly not standard English[10]; neither does it follow the conventions for presenting direct speech (inverted commas). Thus, the voices of the characters and the voice of the narrator appear to function on an equal plane, separated neither orthographically nor in terms of register. The narrative voice is third-person, but uses a spoken register more akin to a first-person voice[11] (as well as the dialect words, notice the demotic use of 'longest-legs' and 'per-usual' as adjectives, which sounds like the voice of a teenage girl). The effect is to allow the narrator to remain much closer to the characters, adopting their language and perspective, rather than appearing to speak on their behalf from a point somewhere above and beyond them. We see through the language to a world beyond, but at the same time both the particular detail of that world and our view into it are conditioned fundamentally by the distinct attributes of the narrative voice. In short, the narrative voice of the text is linguistically 'other' than standard English, and thus stands out (it is also 'other' when compared to the 'traditional' third-person voice,[12] which tends to be in standard English). The world being described by it, however, is familiar, and ordinary.

By comparison, the narrative voice of text 2 is standard English. There is nothing especially deviant about its use of words or grammatical structures, although the syntax of the opening sentence does foreground itself. Compare 'It was when she ate that Lin was most alien' to the (arguably) more usual 'Lin was most alien when she ate'. The act of eating is the focus in the original, rather than the fact that Lin is non-human. The syntax has the dual effect of drawing the reader's attention to the act (which is the focus of the rest of the paragraph), and also of maintaining suspense. We engage with the everyday act of eating food *before* we come to the realisation that Lin is 'other' than Isaac. The form of the sentence used in the extract is more effective in expressive terms, pointedly so, than its more 'normalised' version. The point of view is also third-person here, as in text 1, but in this case aspires towards a kind of 'transparency': we see through the discourse into the world of the story without becoming unduly interested in the language use itself (in opposition to the situation in text 1, where the demotic cadences, lack of speech marks and slang words draw attention to themselves; they *foreground* the narrative discourse). The narrative discourse is standard in terms of language and point of view, but describes scenes and characters that are anything but matter-of-fact: a human character, Isaac, sharing food with his alien lover, Lin, who has a scarab – complete with mandibles – for a head. In text 1, the discourse is foregrounded while the story world is matter-of-fact. In text 2, the discourse is matter-of-fact but the story world is fantastical.

You will almost certainly have judged text 3 to be a poem. On what grounds have you made that judgement? The look on the page? The fact that it is 'difficult' to read?[13] This introduces a key feature of the poetic text: that the voice is often not 'transparent' in the way that we might expect the voice of a piece of narrative fiction to be, but foregrounds language using linguistically deviant forms of expression. What 'world' (if any) do you 'see' through this language? Or do you just see language? The text is clearly very open to interpretation. Why is it more so than the two excerpts from fiction? If a text deviates from most common linguistic and textual norms, what is its status as creative writing?

When it comes to text 4, I will leave the discussion to you. However, I will return to this text briefly in section 1.3.

The various features of these texts and the contrasts between them help to introduce one of the central paradigms underpinning this book's approach to the topic: that if the reader of a novel, short story or poem is in a very real sense 'seeing through language' then it will benefit the creative writer to take account of the processes involved, and become attuned to the nuances of language and technique which mediate the imaginary world. It is helpful to envisage a cline between 'standard' discourse, which aspires towards transparency, and more self-conscious, linguistically *deviant* modes of expression, which draw attention to themselves rather than to the world which they mediate.[14] In the former, we are seeing as if through a clear, flawless window pane to a world beyond (as in text 2, say); in the latter, the pane is cracked, or stained, or distorted (as it undoubtedly is in texts 3 and 4). Some might argue that creative writing of the latter, more opaque type is considered by many to be somehow more 'literary', although this is a contentious point to make. In any case, the creative writer may situate his or her narrative discourse at either end of this cline, or, much more commonly, at a point somewhere along it, or even fluctuating back and forth across it. The choice is a crucial one, though, and consideration of these choices should automatically become an aspect of creative practice. We will continue to explore these various 'ways of seeing' in the remainder of this chapter, and, indeed, throughout the book.

1.2   Worlds from words: Mimesis and diegesis

There is a fundamental quality of human language, then, that separates it from all other forms of communication across the natural world. Chimpanzees have been taught to sign, and to press, correctly, buttons inscribed with various messages and requests for their human trainers. The clicks and clucks of dolphins have also been shown to communicate specific messages: danger, food here, come this way. Pet owners can learn to distinguish between and decode the various meows and barks of their pets. However, there is one crucial difference between these kinds of communication and the kinds of interchange that are possible through human language: *the capacity of human language to refer to situations, contexts and even worlds that are 'other' than the here-and-now of the communicative situation.* The chimpanzee can ask for food because it is hungry *now*, but (as far as we know) it cannot describe the food it had yesterday, or the food it would prefer to have tomorrow. The clicks of dolphins can warn of an approaching killer whale in the present moment, but (again, as far as we know – although I feel this one is a fairly safe bet) cannot subsequently tell the story of what happened to friends later on the same day. In short, human language creates worlds in the mind of the listener/reader that are different to and other than the present moment in which the exchange takes place. We do this all the time: every time we tell a joke, tell someone about our day, recount a traumatic experience or sketch out our hopes and dreams for the future. We are using language to evoke a world that does not exist in the here and now. To be portentous for a moment: we are using language to try and capture, to pin down, the irrevocably ephemeral and mutable stuff of life.

Recent developments within the fields of stylistics, particularly within what is commonly referred to as 'the cognitive turn', have explored how this process works from a linguistic perspective.[15] We will discuss some of its insights and how they are relevant to the creative writer in Chapter 6. For now, though, it will be sufficient to acknowledge that language creates these worlds in the reader's imagination through a combination of two distinct but intimately connected functions, which in creative writing parlance are often referred to as 'showing' and 'telling'. Worlds are created in the mind of the reader by using language both to *show* and to *tell*.

To take some examples, which is more effective in each case?

(1) *She was very angry so she left the room.*
    She left the room, slamming the door behind her.
(2) *As he walked into the café, several pairs of eyes looked up to follow his progress. He walked towards a table at the far end of the room, nodding at the five people already there waiting for him. They*

smiled as he approached. A book protruded from the back pocket of his jeans. As he passed my table, I could see it was Jeremy Scott's 'Creative Writing and Stylistics'.

He was handsome, popular, intelligent, and had excellent taste.

This issue is familiar to all students of creative writing. It is nearly always better to aim to *show* an emotion, a reaction or a character trait than to describe it. The reasons that this is so are complex, but, again, the cognitive turn of stylistics goes a long way towards explaining them in terms of schema theory (Lakoff 1987; Bartlett 1995) and the concept of foregrounding (Haber and Hershenson 1980); in my view it will pay the creative writer to take account of these concepts and, again, we will return to them in Chapter 6.

In keeping with the ambitions of this book to assemble a more rigorous and replicable terminology with which to discuss the processes of creative writing, we will prefer the terms **mimesis** and **diegesis** to 'showing' and 'telling'. The cline between the two is a fundamental paradigm of this book's approach. In short, we 'see through language' via the twin effects of mimesis and diegesis. The terms are classical in origin, but their influence can be traced in the etymology of many current English words: to *mimic*, to *imitate*, to *mime* – all these words are concerned with the representation of reality through 'counterfeit' means. Indeed, it might be better to describe the *mediation* of reality through, say, language or paint or music or celluloid as the essence of mimesis in art. The use of the term with reference to creative writing is not unproblematic, though; *mimesis* is used by Plato and Aristotle in quite a specific way, as we shall see shortly. However, I also want to capture a little of its wider sense: the representation of an imaginary world through language (in the sense that mimesis is used by Auerbach (1953) to refer to the representation of reality in art). As we move through the rest of the book, we will try to anatomise the term more rigorously.

The discussion of poetry and the representative arts in general which makes up much of Plato's *Republic* Books III and X is, arguably, the first theorisation of the function and, indeed, the *point* of literary discourse. The theme of the dialogues in Book X is representational poetry and its mimesis of the world. Socrates, the dialogic sparring partner of the whole work, sees poetry as completely superfluous to the imaginary utopian society which he and the author discuss throughout the book. Poetry simply imitates. It does not create. And imitation is play, a mere sport, without use or merit. The dialogues of *The Republic* ignore craft or methodology completely, and focus instead on poetic inspiration:

> The poet is an airy thing, winged and holy, and he is not able to make poetry until he becomes inspired and goes out of his mind.
>
> (Leitch 2001: 35)

As we will discuss shortly, this out-of-mind state can be hard to achieve for those of us who are a little more corporeal, and not blessed with wings.

In Book III of *The Republic*, Plato goes on to distinguish between mimesis and diegesis, seeing the latter as representation of actions in the poet's own voice and the former as the representation of action in the imitated voices of characters. He uses Homer as an example, citing the opening scene of *The Iliad* where the Trojan Chryses asks Menelaus and Agamemnon to release his daughter for a ransom. The exchange is 'imitated' initially by the narrator (hence, diegesis) and then mimetically via the direct speech of the characters concerned. To illustrate his point even more clearly, Plato goes on to rewrite the scene diegetically, in the voice of the authorial narrator, transposing all direct speech into indirect speech[16] (so that 'Get back in that longboat!' becomes 'Agamemnon told Achilles to return to his longboat').

Building on Plato's ideas, Aristotle's *Poetics* constitutes the first rigorous categorisation of literary discourse. *Poetics* is a scientific anatomisation, just as can be found in Aristotle's work on classifications of the natural world, and as such anticipates the ambition of stylistics to provide rigorous accounts of the form of literary discourse. During the Renaissance, it was treated as rulebook or manual for literary composition, and can be seen as the first work of true literary criticism, putting down the roots which grew into Neoclassicism, Formalism and the New Criticism. Note, then, that at the dawn of the discipline of poetics we find an interest in the processes of *composition*, not textual analysis. *Poetics* is a technical manual.

Aristotle makes a distinction between objects which are 'natural' and those which are 'man-made'; for example, a tree and a chair. Poetry is made from language as a chair is made of wood. Thus poetry, *ποιείν*, is based on the verb 'to make'. Aristotle treats poetry as a *craft*, distancing himself from Plato's focus on inspiration. Alongside his well-known definition of tragedy, he spends a great deal of time discussing plot and its structures, anticipating the key concerns of story narratology. Central to this, again, is mimesis; the best plots must be plausible, and must imitate life (bringing to mind Henry James's appeal for 'solidity of specification').

To summarise: *The Republic* and *Poetics* pre-echo an important paradigm which still resonates in approaches to creative writing: between the way a text works (the mechanics of craft) and the way it is received in context by readers and by the culture at large (the mechanics of reading). Both of these should be of interest to creative writers. In addition, Plato and Aristotle begin the debate which still rages in and around the subject of creative writing in the academy: is it a craft with a set of rules (or guidelines) which can be taught, or is it primarily the result of personal creativity, talent and, dare I say it, inspiration?

There is an artificiality and brittleness to the division between mimesis and diegesis as proposed by Plato, and, as the novelist and literary critic David Lodge[17] (1990: 28) points out, it is not straightforward; neither is it a simple matter to distinguish between the two effects. Remember that for Plato, diegesis is representation of action 'in the poet's voice', while mimesis is representation of action in the 'voice(s) of characters'. However, as we shall see in Chapter 5, the taxonomy which stylistics proposes to categorise literary presentation of discourse[18] is more complex, ranging from Narration, pure diegesis ('She opened the door and walked into the room, seeing him standing by the window') to Direct Discourse, as close to a pure mimesis as written language can get ('Here she comes', he said). Thus, stylistics addresses Lodge's valid objection, mapping the distinction between mimesis and diegesis, and thus between showing and telling, more rigorously. This can only be of benefit to practice, allowing the creative writer to explore the extent to which mimetic process can enter into the diegetic narrative voice, so that the writer can 'show' as much as possible at the expense of 'telling'.

Look back at the examples of showing versus telling earlier in this section. Instead of 'She was very angry', we prefer 'She left the room, slamming the door behind her'. Why? To pre-empt some of the material of Chapter 6: the second mediation of the story event is closer to the 'psychic space' of the character. There is no external voice of mysterious provenance explaining what the character is feeling on her behalf. Rather, her behaviour speaks for itself. To be glib for a moment: actions speak louder than words. The description of a character's behaviour leaves space for the reader to interpret it, as he or she would in the actual world, based on the everyday familiarity with the kinds of mood that slamming a door indicates (in cognitive terms, the reader has a 'losing one's temper' schema which is activated by the slamming of the door; we've seen someone do this before, or, indeed, we've done it ourselves; we know why it happens, and we know what it signifies: anger). Straight diegetic description bypasses that space, enervating the reader's visualisation of the events of the text. Rather than seeing *through* language, the reader is *looking at* the narrative voice (or at best, seeing *via* it, with all the connotations of detouring that this word implies). In short, as cognitive approaches can demonstrate (Chapter 6), the narrative discourse should aim (unless there are very good reasons not to – and there may be) for proximity to the sphere of character rather than narrator.[19] We can also argue here for a connection to the **connotative** as opposed to **denotative** functions of language; mimesis corresponds to the former, while diegesis draws upon the latter.

Do not be mistrustful of this capacity in your reader. Do not 'lay the table' or 'manage the stage' too diligently, or in too much detail. Let the reader's imagination, their schema, do the work (this is particularly true of writing poetry, of course, and yet for some reason we are often happier to make room for creative, interpretative reading of poetry than when writing fiction). Much of interest can be gleaned from the gaps in texts, from ellipsis, from the unsaid, from the unexplained. The reading experience will be richer and more nuanced – more personal, more like writing ... And thus our discussion comes full circle. Creative practice and creative engagement with the output of that practice are two sides of the same coin. The processes are equiponderant, and reading is, in many important ways, the same as writing. Rather than simply writing or only reading, it helps to think of ourselves as writingandreading. Thus, we become both writers and readers simultaneously, each attuned to the needs and processes of the other.

1.3 Language and creativity

This is a burgeoning area of research within the academy (see Swann et al. 2010 for an excellent overview of current thinking on the topic), and its areas of exploration have obvious relevance to creative writing. As we have already averred, there is something fundamentally creative about the act of putting words together on the page. The act of creative writing need not (does not?) come about purely in response to some kind of primeval inspirational urge, as Plato suggested – a thunderbolt from the sky which sends us scurrying to fill the blank page. It can sometimes happen like that, I am sure, and if it happens like that for you, well, then, I am envious and you probably do not need this book. I would argue, rather, that creativity will often (always?) arise through practice itself.

I have already suggested that stylistics can help us perceive the ways in which the medium of language can distort, change or otherwise condition the message, and this assertion will be axiomatic throughout this book. However, what is hopefully new here is a second assertion: that creative practice itself is a valid way of exploring the discipline, and that creative practice itself is a fundamental source of creativity, rather than a response to pre-existing ideas or stimuli. As Carter and Nash (1990: 175) point out, there is a commonly held prejudice that creative writing involves more than just language, while the act of 'composition' (say, writing a letter or a press release) can be viewed in purely linguistic terms. Creative writing, rather, is seen as involving some quality or even another agency (Genius? Inspiration? A muse?) which has nothing (or little) to do with language. It should by now be abundantly clear to the reader that this book takes issue with that premise.

Firstly, it will be useful to return to Keith Oatley's concept of writingandreading as developed so far in this chapter. As I have already argued, reading in and of itself can and should be viewed as a creative activity – as a performance, if you wish. Creative writing, by its very definition, is already seen as such, and distinctly from mere composition. However, again, as I have already been asserting, the two processes of writing and reading are intertwined. It follows from this assumption that the act of creative writing is also based on our experience of reading. We learn to write, to compose, through reading, as children. Subsequently, we learn to write poetry through reading (and, certainly, listening to) other poetry. And we learn to write stories from reading (or, indeed, hearing) stories. It is my contention that the role of the reader is too often under-emphasised during the act of creative writing.

Swann, Pope and Carter (2010: 9) set out the interconnection between the two activities as follows, and pose an intriguing question:

> If all reading is in some sense a form of rewriting (recasting what one reads in one's own mind), and if much writing is a form of rereading (recasting the resources of the language and texts as found into what one makes of them), at what point can a really fresh reading or writing be said to appear?

If human creation is not from nothing (*ex nihilo*) but from something or someone else (*ex aliis*), is it all just about re-creation? (Swann et al. 2010: 9–10). Whole swatches of literary, linguistic and cultural theory have developed in an attempt to address this question, including the aesthetics of reception theory, reader response theory and, as I have mentioned, the insights of cognitive science, psychology and, indeed, physiology have been brought to bear to explore the influence of the reader. These issues were crystallised in Roland Barthes's now-infamous statement: 'the birth of the reader must be at the cost of the death of the author' (1977). Subsequently, modern theoretical approaches to writing and culture that embrace the idea of creative reading include feminism, Marxism, postcolonialism and, indeed, overtly deconstructive approaches to the text that exploit collage, hybrid texts (writing and image), graphology and multimodality (including online hypertext and narrative video games). More recently, the study of reading reception has taken place through analysis of discourses associated with the burgeoning number of reading groups that have sprung up in a wide range of environments in recent years (see, for example, Whiteley 2011). All of these theories and data, and the insights that they bring to understanding how, what (and even where) people read, should be of great interest to the creative writer.

What about the other side of the equation, though? If reading is by definition creative, then how does creativity arise through the act of writing? We could argue here for **linguistic** approaches to creativity, based on the assumption that, as Roman Jakobson argued (1960: 356), linguistic creativity (what he called 'the poetic function') is an integral part of human communication and can be found in the most quotidian utterances. Indeed, as David Crystal (1996) demonstrates, 'language play' is a key aspect of our linguistic development, and as children we indulge in it in the form of rhymes, morphological play, onomatopoeia, repetition, the echoing and re-echoing of each others' words, evocative language to invoke atmosphere and, of course, experimenting with taboo words (Carter 2004: 93). It could be argued, in fact, that the intricate phonological correspondences, linguistic deviation and wordplay of Joyce's *Finnegans Wake* (text 4 in section 1.1) are simply a more sophisticated literary development of this innate human propensity. For more examples, witness how applied linguistics (particularly sociolinguistics) has through investigating the links between culture and creativity managed to identify the creative processes involved in the ways in which different language communities shape linguistic resources rather than abiding by static, often centrally imposed rules and codes of language use and of what is 'correct' or 'standard'. Writers such as James Kelman, Irvine Welsh and Alan Sillitoe have found tremendous creative energy in their dissension from these norms (witness also the vast swathes of writing commonly classified as 'postcolonial' and its ambition to 'write back' against the language of the centre using the centre's own language[20]). In his model of transformational generative grammar, Noam Chomsky uses creativity as an example of language's 'productivity' (1964: 7–8); that is, the fact that speakers and listeners can produce and understand entirely novel sentences which they have never used or encountered before.

> The central fact to which any significant linguistic theory must address itself is this: a mature speaker can produce a new sentence of his language on the appropriate occasion, and other speakers can understand it immediately, though it is equally new to them ... the class of sentences with which we can operate fluently and without difficulty or hesitation is so vast that for all practical purposes ... we may regard it as infinite.

Indeed, some researchers would argue that *all* language use is by definition creative. Thus, creativity is a fundamental plank of the language system rather than being confined only to the 'literary' or 'poetic' (Swann et al. 2010: 12). As stylistics predicts and asserts, there are inescapable continuities between everyday linguistic creativity and literary language. As Carter puts it:

> Creativity is a pervasive feature of spoken language exchanges as well as a key component in interpersonal communication, and ... it is a property actively possessed by all speakers and listeners; it is not simply the domain of a few creatively gifted individuals.
>
> (2004: 6)

To return to a point made at the opening of this chapter, then, and implicit throughout it: creativity resides within language itself, and thus its resources are accessible to everyone. A lot can be learned about the relationships between language and creativity by using writing games (see section 1.5), with the raw material of language itself – its sounds, shapes, conventions, norms and varieties – providing the stimulus which, traditionally, we envisage as coming from some external, extralinguistic source. I am urging you, then, to see what happens when you invert the usual assumption: that 'a context of reference is mapped on to language' (Carter and Nash 1990: 166–7). The ideas needn't always come first. Sometimes, it's the words.

1.4   Summary

- To be a creative writer is to be a linguist ...
- When we read and write, we see (and show and tell) through language into a world beyond, exploiting language's innate capacity to refer to and create states and worlds other than the here and now.

- The strange and mysterious process by which we can 'see' through literary discourse (whether fiction or poetry) can, broadly, be split into two opposing tendencies of language and the ways in which it mediates between the human imagination and the actual world: **mimesis** (discourse which aims closely to mimic reality, as occurs, say, in direct speech) versus **diegesis** (narrative discourse, which sets out to describe the world of the text, as, for example, in descriptive narration; the reader is 'seeing' at one remove, as it were). The essential interaction between mimesis and diegesis equates to a useful degree with the common creative writing dichotomy between 'showing' (the former) and 'telling' (the latter).
- We should aim towards mimesis (showing) in our writing wherever possible, as this quality of language exploits and activates the almost-infinite range and capacity of the reader's imagination.
- Thus, the imaginative processes involved in writing and reading are equiponderant and interrelated: hence, *writingandreading*.[21]
- Creativity can (will) arise from within the resources language itself, and not just from extra-linguistic sources. Thus, creativity is universally accessible.

1.5   Practice

(1) Here is a situation.

A young couple is sitting outside a station café somewhere in a hot country. Surrounding the station and café are some hills, a few pieces of vegetation, and little else other than dust and aridity. A waitress appears in the doorway and the couple order drinks. The couple then have a conversation in which the man is trying to convince the woman to undergo a medical procedure.

Write the scene as a camera might have recorded it, that is, as transparently (covertly) as possible. What types of language have you used to create this effect of transparency? How effective is it? Are there any linguistic indicators of **mediation** within the text, that is, language that implies a point of view? The linguistic features to look out for are as follows (adapted from Short 1996: 286–7):

- value-laden expressions (hot, ugly, happy)
- ideologically slanted expressions (foreign, oriental, upper-class)
- deixis (here, then, now, yesterday, this, that – what about 'the'?)

- adjectives
- adverbs
- representations of a character's thoughts or internal perceptions.

You could also try mediating the world as a poem. Is it fair to say that a poem will *always* signal greater mediation, or lack of transparency (or, if you prefer, overtness) by virtue of its form, which by necessity draws attention to itself as a linguistic construct? Or can a poem mediate invisibly between world and mind? What about in the case of the prose poem?

It can surely be concluded that it is very difficult for language ever to be considered completely 'transparent', and that the narrator's 'ways of seeing' are central to the effect of a piece of creative writing. Is 'transparency' synonymous somehow with a *lack* of linguistic deviation? Could we argue that, in the examples in this chapter, the more 'standard' language of text 2 is more transparent than texts 1 and, 3 and 4, despite its fantastical subject matter?

The prompt for this exercise is taken from Ernest Hemingway's short story 'Hills Like White Elephants' (in the collection *Men Without Woman*; a version is also available online). If you can, compare your writing of the scene with the original. Famously, the narrative discourse of the story is 'terse', striving towards a strict objectivity. Did your version approach the task in a similar way? Is there something intrinsic to the subject matter which seems to suggest, or call for, this kind of approach? If so, reflect further on this relationship between 'world' and 'word' in the light of the discussion in this chapter.

(2) Here is are two lists, one of objects and one of actions:

   (A) Lipstick on the rim of a wineglass.

       Red stains on the tabletop.

       Six cigarette stubs in the ashtray.

       A blanket and cushions on the floor.

       A ring among the roses.

   (B) The river flows.

       Children play.

       Planes drone.

       Apples fall.

       The sky reddens.

Identity a situation in which these items could have played a role (there may be several possibilities) and then write a brief phrase or sentence at the end of the list that summarises what happened and gives coherence to the foregoing list of objects. Of course, it is more than possible that you may perceive symbolic as well as literal coherences – or detect a symbolism *in* and *through* the literal pattern of coherence. Note also that the perceptual inferences you make may depend on the order of the items, which you are free to change.

What did you write? Most people will have come up with 'a fight between lovers' or something similar. The way that you structure this last line could also be of interest. Have you automatically copied the type of noun phrase in the list (e.g. 'A quarrel between lovers'), or opted instead for a declarative sentence (e.g. 'Two people have broken off their engagement')? Why choose one structure over the other? Is the choice connected to poetic effect? If so, how? Have you suggested a change in the order of events? If so, to what end? Most people will agree that *a ring among the roses* needs to come last because the phrase suggests the last act of the drama, and also because of the allusion to the nursery rhyme. (Adapted from an exercise in Carter and Nash 1990: 177).

(3) Take an extract from your own poetry (i.e. work in progress) and attempt to identify the features within it which help its reader to *see* (or *observe*). The idea is to draw attention to the ways in which readers see through poetic texts in the same way as narrative fiction, focussing in this case on the mechanics of visual deixis (language that indicates a perspective). You should look for the following features: reference (definite referring expressions), the origo (the 'perceiving centre' of the poem), indicators of time and space, subjectivity, the text (all elements which orientate the text to itself for the reader/hearer) and, finally, grammatical features (for example, an interrogative will assume the presence of an addressee).

Now, with this linguistic data to hand, attempt a rewrite of the poem or extract which expunges all of these deictic features (i.e. which aims towards some kind of neutrality or transparency). Of course, the poem will alter fundamentally – perhaps even cease to function effectively as a poem at all. Does it still 'work' in the way you intended it to?

How does this exercise affect your assumptions about the differences between poetry and fiction? Do poems have to imply or contain a voice of some kind?

2 Building Blocks I: A Grammar of Creative Writing

2.1 Overview

The purpose of this chapter is to introduce you to the building blocks of the English sentence – the basic units from which your novel, short story or poem will eventually be built. We will also look at how literary style can be sub-divided into different categories or types, and pose an important and intriguing question which we touched on in the previous chapter: to what extent is it possible for the mediation of the *content* of text (its meaning or sense; its message, if you prefer) to be augmented or in some way enhanced through the 'form' of that text? For 'form' here, read 'linguistic structure' – both at the micro-level of the clause or sentence, and at the macro-level of the text, or discourse, as a whole (and of course, beyond that – to the level of genre).

It is rare, on the whole, for books about creative writing to focus on writing at the micro-level of linguistic detail.[1] However, at its most essential level, is this not where the real work of writing is done: through the painstaking process of putting one word next to another and on and on and on until the piece is deemed complete? I would propose that an understanding of the (reasonably) simple grammatical structures of the English language will aid the creative writer in many, fairly obvious, ways which probably do not need listing here. However, what is perhaps less intuitive is the fact that these structures can be manipulated creatively to great expressive effect. To take a very simple example, compare these two sentences:

> John Lennon was assassinated.
> Mark Chapman assassinated John Lennon.

The sentences describe the same actual-world event. However, the sentence structures are different; the first is passive, the second active.

In the first, the **agent** (or **subject**) of the sentence is missing. In the second, it is present ('Mark Chapman'). The first sentence emphasises the action; the second, the perpetrator of that action. The agent can be left out of the first sentence, or included:

John Lennon was assassinated by Mark Chapman.

However, again, the expressive effect is subtly altered. Lennon is still the focus due to the word's position in the sentence; it is **thematised** (i.e. brought to the front of the sentence), and, as the first word the reader reads, is foregrounded (Toolan 2001: 223). In short, the syntactic pattern of each sentence encodes and mediates subtly differing representations of the same real-world event (more on this in a moment). To return to the terms of the previous chapter: we are seeing through language in different ways. Indeed, to re-rehearse briefly the points made there, the manipulation of the essential underlying architecture of language is what contributes to the degree to which the reader 'sees' through the language of your writing to the world beyond, or whether they focus on the writing itself.

The purpose of the following section is to give an overview of some relatively simple grammatical terms that will be of use in understanding the discussions of Michael Halliday's (2003) functional grammar and transitivity which occur later in the chapter. If you are already comfortable with these terms, then please feel free to skip this section and continue to 2.3. The various phrase, sentence and clause types will be illustrated with examples from literary texts.

2.2 Basic components of grammar

(1) Among other public buildings in a certain town, which for many reasons it will be prudent to refrain from mentioning, and to which I will assign no fictitious name, there is one anciently common to most towns, great or small: to wit, a workhouse; and in this workhouse was born; on a day and date which I need not trouble myself to repeat, inasmuch as it can be of no possible consequence to the reader, in this stage of the business at all events; the item of mortality whose name is prefixed to the head of this chapter.

(2) As Oliver gave this first proof of the free and proper action of his lungs, the patchwork coverlet which was carelessly flung over the iron bedstead, rustled; the pale face of a young woman was

raised feebly from the pillow; and a faint voice imperfectly articulated the words, 'Let me see the child, and die.'

The surgeon had been sitting with his face turned towards the fire: giving the palms of his hands a warm and a rub alternately. As the young woman spoke, he rose, and advancing to the bed's head, said, with more kindness than might have been expected of him:

'Oh, you must not talk about dying yet.'

'Lor bless her heart, no!' interposed the nurse, hastily depositing in her pocket a green glass bottle, the contents of which she had been tasting in a corner with evident satisfaction. 'Lor bless her dear heart, when she has lived as long as I have, sir, and had thirteen children of her own, and all on 'em dead except two, and them in the wurkus with me, she'll know better than to take on in that way, bless her dear heart! Think what it is to be a mother, there's a dear young lamb, do.'

Apparently this consolatory perspective of a mother's prospects failed in producing its due effect. The patient shook her head, and stretched out her hand towards the child. The surgeon deposited it in her arms. She imprinted her cold white lips passionately on its forehead; passed her hands over her face; gazed wildly round; shuddered; fell back – and died. They chafed her breast, hands, and temples; but the blood had stopped for ever. They talked of hope and comfort. They had been strangers too long.

'It's all over, Mrs. Thingummy!' said the surgeon at last.

'Ah poor dear, so it is!' so it is, said the nurse, picking up the cork of the green bottle, which had fallen out on the pillow, as she stopped to take up the child. 'Poor dear!'

Above are two excerpts from the opening to Charles Dickens's *Oliver Twist* (1838). Look at excerpt 1, a single not-at-all-simple sentence. The fictional world described by this complex arrangement of words, phrases and clauses is centred on a building in a town. That is all we are told. Note that, despite the very deliberate non-specificity ('a certain town', 'it will be prudent to refrain from mentioning', 'on a date and date which I need not trouble myself to repeat', 'it can be of no possible consequence to the reader') a story world nevertheless begins to build in your imagination as you read.

The bare facts of this sentence could be presented like this:

- Oliver Twist is born
- In a town
- In a workhouse

Dickens could easily have chosen to write the sentence like this:

> Oliver Twist was born in a public workhouse in the town of Mudfog (70 miles north of London) on the 7th February 1825.

Why choose the original version out of the many possibilities which language presents? Arguably, at its heart, the communicative intent of each sentence – Charles Dickens's original and an alternative possibility – is the same: to set up and describe the story world in which the novel begins, and to mediate the facts listed above for the benefit of the reader. However, why does Dickens avoid naming specific features of his story world? When the novel was originally published the place was named as the (fictional) town of Mudfog, 70 miles north of London – corresponding, perhaps, to Northampton. Why was this information dropped from the version we are all familiar with? There must have been a good artistic reason for the change; something to do with making Oliver's past as mysterious as possible, perhaps. You are, of course, free to speculate further on why Dickens chose this form of language to tell his tale.

So: the sentences mediate the same story world, but the choice of one version over the other was made because one was deemed to be more effective (authentic, appropriate, fitting – whatever) than the other. Out of the many choices available, why these words and not others? This is the question that the stylistically self-aware creative writer should be asking of his or her work. At the risk of stating the obvious: the importance of the choices illustrates the ways in which our imaginative engagement with that story world is wholly dependent upon the language used to describe it. It is clear that story world and narrative discourse are intimately connected, and in some ways inseparable. However, it will help the creative writer at this stage to visualise the language and the world it describes (or, more properly, creates) separately (more on this in Chapters 3 and 4). How do the two interrelate? What expressive purpose does the non-specificity of Dickens's original serve?

Compare the language of the first extract to the one that follows it. This is more 'standard' in style and tone, and thus less foregrounded linguistically. The narrator has withdrawn (or at last, stepped back into the shadows; we will be discussing these shades of overtness and covertness in more detail in the next chapter), and confines himself to describing the scene in the past tense and in the third person. If you are reading perceptively, however, you will note that there are still injections of comment from the narrator: on the nurse's secret green bottle, on the unexpected (and muted) solicitousness of the surgeon and on the unfeeling exhortations of the nurse to Oliver's mother (which the narrator highlights somewhat ironically as a 'consolatory perspective of a mother's prospects'). Language is rarely, if ever, as neutral as it tries to appear. We will be using the many-headed hydra of an introductory sentence, contrasted with the more 'traditional' narrative prose of excerpt 2, to illustrate some basic grammatical concepts that will be of use in getting the most out of the discussion and analyses which follow throughout the rest of the book.

To reiterate (as this concept may well be unfamiliar to you): the purpose of introducing and clarifying these grammatical terms is to illustrate how certain approaches to stylistic analysis predict and assume a relationship between linguistic structure and meaning which functions above and beyond the purely semantic; that is, linguistic structure in and of itself encodes particular ways of seeing the world. In yet other words, language is a mimesis of cognitive functions. Thus, when it comes to the first extract from *Oliver Twist* you could argue that the rambling syntax, the constant qualification of noun phrases and the 'non-specificity' of the language mirror the ways in which the description seems to move away from the 'truth', from the real world – to embark upon the process of fictionalisation, of creating the imaginary world.

One grammatical model that attempts to capture the relationship between language and cognition is Halliday's model of Functional Grammar. Like most systemic grammars, this model assumes that language has various levels of organisation and is made up of 'meaningless' units of sound (**phonemes**) combined into 'meaningful' units (**morphemes** and **lexemes**[2]). These meaningful units can then be organised into larger, high-level structures (phrases, clauses, sentences, discourses/texts).

In most systems of syntax, including Halliday's functional model, grammatical units are arranged in an order according to their size. Human language can be viewed, then, as being made up various levels, beginning with units of sounds that do not in and of themselves carry meaning (phonemes and/or phonological features); these are then arranged to form units which *do* carry meaning (morphemes and words). These meaning-carrying units are then themselves arranged into higher-level structures (sentences, clauses, phrases etc.). Above this comes **discourse**, or text. To represent the levels in a different way, it might help to think of them running like this, from largest unit to smallest:

- (discourse)
- text
- sentence

- **clause**
- phrase
- word
- morpheme
- phoneme/grapheme

Note that this model does not directly address the issue of *meaning*, or semantics. This is because meaning is, in fact, a product of the interaction and effects of each of the other levels, including, as I have suggested above, the level of structure – or syntax. The discipline of pragmatics in particular has demonstrated that meaning is not dependent upon one particular systemic feature of language, but permeates the system as a whole (Jeffries and McIntyre 2010: 34); that is, it is the product of the interaction of *all* of the levels above. This is of obvious importance to the creative writer, and has bearing on our previous discussion of the opening of *Oliver Twist*. The linguistic choices and structures of the opening sentence of that novel greatly influence, even dictate, the ways in which the reader imagines the ensuing world. What appears highly fictionalised, mediated, distanced from the reader, could equally be seen as appealing to a 'truth' outside of the text ('I will refrain from mentioning details, in case the source is traced', as it were). The many related clauses meander away from the noun phrase which opens the sentence, so that the pattern of the syntax seems to mirror the sense of the sentence. The structure of the clauses constitutes an additional mimesis of the story world which they mediate.[3]

However, we need to be careful not to become caught up in the logical fallacy of circular reasoning, where we begin our thought processes and analysis at the point where we wish to end them.[4] This can be a problem in stylistic analysis/criticism if it is not carried out well. I refer to it as 'The Poem About Trees Fallacy'. The analyst reports something like this:

> Here, we have a poem called 'Oaks' which is about trees. I have carried out a careful stylistic analysis of the poem and found that it contains a lot of words connected to trees. Therefore, I have concluded that this is a poem about trees.

This is a classic example of a circular argument, and something we should avoid when bringing the insights of detailed linguistic analysis to bear both on our work and our creative practice. We need to be *instrumental* in our use of this material, and link it explicitly to expressive/artistic effect. We may even, as we shall see, be able to make qualitative judgements about good or bad writing (or at least effective and ineffective writing). Indeed, I would argue, at the risk of courting controversy, that stylistic analysis *of this very focussed, Hallidayan type* has even more to contribute to our understanding of the processes involved in creative writing that it does to the processes of producing interesting readings of extant literary texts. It inculcates an increased level of awareness during creative practice: an awareness of the ways in which we can exploit the many different shapes that sentences can take. To pursue this argument further, it will now be useful to examine the taxonomy that grammar systems use to describe these shapes.

2.2.1   The clause

The most important level for our purposes is that of the **clause**, and thus we will focus on that level in a little more detail. It is possible to distinguish between four basic elements of clause structure, which will be abbreviated as SPCA: **subject** (S), **predicator** (P), **complement** (C) and **adjunct** (A) (Simpson 2004: 10).

Here are some examples drawn from excerpt 2 above, modified slightly to fit the prototypical pattern. The fact that we can modify the clauses' structure from Dickens's originals shows, obviously enough, that there is an inbuilt flexibility in the system; there were other choices the writer could have made. Apart from the positions of subject and predicator, which are fixed, the other positions as stipulated here represent typical tendencies rather than hard-and-fast rules (Dickens has 'feebly from the pillow' for sentence 2, for example). The terms should be reasonably self-explanatory:[5]

	Subject	Predicator	Complement	Adjunct
1	The surgeon	rubbed	his hands	alternately.
2	The pale face of a young woman	was raised	from the pillow	feebly.
3	This consolatory perspective of a mother's prospects	failed	–	in producing its due effect.
4	The blood	had stopped	–	forever.
5	The surgeon	advanced	to the bed's head.	–
6	Mrs Thigummy	deposited	a green glass bottle	hastily.

2.2.2   The phrase

Notice in the table in 2.2.1 how the 'slot' for each element of clause structure can be taken up by a number of smaller units further down the scale ('had stopped', 'to the bed's head', 'The young woman'). Notice too (of course) that as long as the clause contains a subject and a predicator then it is adjudged to be complete and functioning ('The blood had stopped', 'The surgeon advanced'). However, within this flexibility, it is a characteristic of English grammar that the four basic elements of clause structure are normally made up of certain kinds of *phrase* rather than just one word. The subject will usually be a *noun phrase*; for example, 'The pale face of a young woman', 'This consolatory perspective of a mother's prospects' or, more obviously, 'The surgeon'. The complement of the clause, if it has one, is also usually another noun phrase (the 'object' of the verb) as in 1, 2, 3, 5 and 6, or it can be an *adjective phrase* (say, 'The young woman's lips were **cold and white**.') The adjunct slot will usually be filled by an *adverb phrase* or a *prepositional phrase*; the adjuncts of clauses 1, 2, 4 and 5 above are all adverb phrases. The adjunct of 3 is a prepositional phrase, which begins with a preposition ('in') and is finished by another noun phrase ('producing its due effect').

Identifying the various constituent parts of a clause is fairly straightforward and Simpson (2004: 11–12) suggests a very useful way of doing this as follows:

Finding the Subject	It should answer the question 'who' or 'what' placed in *front* of the verb.
Finding the Complement	It should answer the question 'who' or 'what' placed *after* the verb.
Finding the Adjunct	It should answer questions such as 'how', 'when', 'where' or 'why' placed after the verb.

So, in sentence 1: 'Who rubbed his hands?' produces 'the surgeon', correctly, as the subject. Subsequently, the question 'The surgeon rubbed what?' elicits 'his hands', the complement. Finally, 'The surgeon rubbed his hands how?' points to 'alternately' as the adjunct of the clause. Of course, it is important to point out that the basic SPCA pattern of clause structure is only one – often preferred – combination. Other types of patterning are possible, as we will see. However, this basic pattern does set up a kind of preferred norm which you as a writer will need to work with – or against...

Herein lies the central point of interest for the creative writer. The examples from the Dickens extracts need slight 'tinkering' in order to fit the model. In other words, the SPCA pattern functions as a standard model which haunts the background of English clauses; it can also be an indicator of *what might have been written, but was not*. As mentioned in 2.2, this sense of almost-infinite possibility – of the different word choices stretching into the distance on either side of the words you actually choose – should draw your awareness to the many different ways of mediating your story for the reader. Saussure (1995) described this as the **paradigmatic** axis of language. To illustrate this, look at some of the ways in which the various 'slots' of one of the sentences from *Oliver Twist* above could have been filled:

The surgeon	rubbed	his hands	alternately
The doctor	massaged	his fingers	one after the other
The man	scraped	his palms	against each other
The medic	banged	his fists	together

Obviously, we move further away from the sense of the original with each change. However, imagine the SPCA slots as the reels of a fruit machine. Each arrangement works and has meaning, but which is the one you want to use? This may sound to you like an unduly mechanistic approach to creative practice. Perhaps it is. However, as an exercise in exploring the structures and expressive capabilities of language it is of great use. Even more intriguingly: there is a very real sense in which the (almost) infinite array of choices along the paradigmatic axis ('surgeon', 'doctor', 'quack', 'sawbones', 'medical practitioner', 'medic') 'haunt' (to use that metaphor again) the choice that you happen upon in your text. Saussure refers to the way in which meaning of a word (a 'linguistic sign') is based upon difference, that is, through reference to other words (**signifiers**) rather than to its own meaning (**signified**).[6] So, a cat is a cat because it is not a bat, or a mat, or a hat, or a cap... We understand meaning, he says, by virtue of the paradigmatic axis – through reference to all the other words that *might* have filled that slot in the clause. On this intriguing proposition rests much of deconstructive theory; it is also worth considering word choice in detail, and thinking about the ways in which the words that you *didn't* choose can still infect the sense of the one that you did.

You can play around within the SPCA structure as a way of flexing your writing muscles, of warming up (as we will see in the exercises at the end of this chapter). Being able to recognise and identify the constituents of clauses will help tune the writing ear to the creative potential of the many variations possible (or the many possible variations). This structure is the bowstring against which your writing should gently, but firmly, tug.

2.3 Levels of style: language as cognitive code

As we have already mentioned, the structures of language can be viewed as a representation of the ways in which we think and interface with the world. Language mediates the world for us, not just in the semantic content of its words (the paradigmatic axis referred to in 2.2.2) but through its structures. Saussure (1995) terms this the **syntagmatic axis**: the way in which meaning comes about also by virtue of the chain of signifiers that make up a clause or sentence. In *Style in Fiction* (2007: 95), Leech and Short describe language as a 'cognitive code', that is, that it functions as a 'shorthand' for mental images and representations of the real world.

> Considered primarily as a means of spoken communication, language has been regarded, both traditionally and in modern linguistics, as a system for translating meanings in the speaker's mind into sounds or, conversely, for translating sounds into meanings in the hearer's mind.
>
> (2007: 96)

This approach has its limitations, though, as the authors point out. These are, briefly, as follows:

- The view of language as a 'code' (like a barcode on a supermarket package, carrying detailed information in a simple representational form) is limiting because it suggests a fixed set of rules within which language must operate. Language is used much more flexibly in reality and, indeed, many of the so-called effects of creative writing discourse come about through 'non-standard' use (as we shall see). Take a simple metaphor such as 'She was the apple of my eye.' This is now so common as to have become standard, what Leech and Short term 'an institutionalised part of language' (2007: 97). Compare this to 'Her face rooted itself in the centre of my eye,' for example. This is part of the process of linguistic creativity, and is connected to the concept of linguistic deviation which we introduced in Chapter 1.

- The view is also limiting because it oversimplifies the processes of encoding and decoding between speaker and hearer/writer and reader. Both activities are highly complex, and involve a broad array of cognitive processes which mean, as we will see in Chapter 6, that no two readings are likely to be the same. To return to Saussure: he proposed a model of communication now known as the 'talking heads' model (or, more formally, the dyadic model) which assumes just such an uncomplicated view of how linguistic messages are decoded. Even a cursory examination of the process will reveal its flaws. The 'message' you have in your head will almost certainly not be the message that ends up in the other person's head at the end of the conversation, despite the best efforts of both parties. Think about what is really going on next time you have a face-to-face conversation with someone and you will see some of the issues involved clearly.

Bearing these limitations in mind, the approach is still very useful when it comes to discussing the linguistic mechanics of the literary text, especially from the point of view of the creative writer. This book has proposed, in keeping with the premises of stylistics, that we 'see' through language into the world of the novel, story or poem. Thus, the words on the page do function in some ways like a code, in this case representing (or, perhaps more accurately, *building*) the world of the text.[7] For the writer, then, it helps to think of the words that you write as the keys that the reader will use to unlock your imaginary world. To reiterate the point made in 2.1: this is not to suggest that the form of your work (i.e. the language that you use) can be separated entirely from the content (the imaginary world).[8] It will help, though, to envisage 'code' and 'message' (for now) as irredeemably intertwined. Approach the idea as a kind of 'thought experiment' from which useful observations about the relationship between the 'code' of language and the story world it creates can be drawn.

Leech and Short (2007: 96–7) divide this code into four levels of organisation: **semantics** (concerned with meaning), **syntax** (broadly, sentence structure, which we have already been discussing), **phonology** (the sounds of words) and **graphology** (the 'look' on the page). This last category is inserted into the model specifically because the literary text tends to be read on the page, silently. Of course, poetry in particular is often read aloud in a performance, but I think it is safe to say that this is not the way in which it is most often encountered.

We will deal with each of these categories below, the last two in a cursory fashion for now given that they are treated in much more detail later in this book (Chapters 9 and 10 respectively). Unfortunately, we need to deal with another objection to this model before we move on. This is simple to state, but difficult to encompass in a book of this nature, and develops the point made about semantics in 2.2. Put as concisely as possible: the various levels of the model are not completely – or, arguably, not at all – independent from one another. We can speak of 'semantics' as the study of meaning but, of course, in most literary texts meaning taken as a whole is dependent on all of the four categories working together,[9] even the phonological (Jeffries and McIntyre 2010: 34). A simple example should serve to demonstrate this point:

> 'Twas brillig, and the slithy toves
> Did gyre and gimble in the wabe:
> All mimsy were the borogoves
> And the mome raths outgrabe.[10]

The individual lexemes of this poem ('brillig', 'slithy', 'toves', 'gyre', 'gimble' and so on) mean nothing in purely semantic terms (in isolation). Try looking them up in the dictionary. However, our imaginations will happily engage with this text and create a world in response to it. 'Toves' are creatures of some kind, aren't they? They are small and slithy creatures. 'Gyring' and 'gimbling' are movements, and toves make these movements. I think of 'gyrating' (doubtless because of the phonological correspondence between the two words). What does 'slithy' mean? To me, it is a cross between 'slimy' and an adjective built from the verb 'to writhe'; a kind of slimy writhing motion, then, encompassed in an adjective... To you it may well mean something slightly different, although I would suggest that your reading (or 'internal performance') of this stanza is broadly similar in essence and effect. The words' syntactic position is what 'simulates', or suggests, their meaning, along with a phonological correspondence to other words that we *do* know them meaning of. Thus, the meaning of this poem arises from an interplay of various aspects of its linguistic code, and not from a formal semantic relationship between its individual lexemes (which are made up by the poet) and a set of pre-agreed meanings. It still works, though.

It will be interesting now to look at another famous example which has almost the opposite effect. Look at the following sentence:

> Colourless green ideas sleep furiously.

It is grammatically correct. As I typed it, my computer's spellcheck/grammar facility had no problems with it. However, what does it mean?

We could understand each of its lexemes in another sentence, but what about when they are combined in this particular syntagmatic pattern? Each lexeme appears to contradict the next as the reader moves along the chain. Can something be colourless *and* green? Is it possible to have a green idea?[11] Do ideas sleep? How can something sleep furiously? This sentence, famously, was put together by Chomsky in his work on generative grammar, *Syntactic Structure* (1957), as an example of a sentence which is correct grammatically but nonsensical in semantic terms. His point was to highlight the difference between syntax and semantics. In almost direct opposition to the example poem above, we struggle to build an imaginative world in response to this statement – despite the fact that the words it uses *do* appear in the dictionary. It is possible to conclude that the linguistic structure – the 'form' – is in some circumstances more important than individual words – the 'content' – when it comes to a reader's imaginative response to a piece of writing. This is a highly counter-intuitive notion, but one which bears considering from the perspective of creative practice. To put it as simply as possible: 'meaning' as such flows from a combination of both 'form' and 'content'.

To summarise: the categories that go to make up linguistic code are to a large extent inseparable, and focussing on one at the expense of the other(s) can inevitably lead to simplification. With these objections in mind, however, we will look at each of the categories in turn, with examples.

2.3.1   Semantics

As demonstrated by the examples in section 2.2, to discuss meaning in isolation is no easy task, given the various ways in which the categories combine to create it. Imagine that you want to describe what is happening as a woman drives a car along a motorway. She starts to drive faster. You have a vast array of choices available to you to convey this information (to mediate the fictional world for the benefit of the reader).

(1)   She started to drive faster.
(2)   She gunned the car along the motorway.
(3)   Mark Chapman assassinated John Lennon.

The third example will have caused surprise. The point, of course, is that you could choose any sentence available within the English language. The reason you do not just choose any sentence is that, to return to Leech and Short:

> ... the vast majority of such sentences would either not fit into the story (message) meaningfully, or would alter the story to a greater or lesser degree. It would no longer be, in this particular, the same 'mock reality'.
>
> (2007: 101)

The word 'bike' will not work as an alternative to 'car'. The adverb 'slower' is not equivalent to 'faster'. 'Mark Chapman' is not equivalent to 'she' and 'John Lennon' is not a semantic alternative to 'car'. This is, of course, an obvious point; but, as mentioned several times already, the point of the exercise is to some extent to *defamiliarise* language to yourself, to put it under the microscope. So: particular stylistic choices match the events of the story world[12] in just the same way as users of language in all contexts, according to the model outlined above, encode often-abstract cognitive processes linguistically. The processes involved in creating worlds from writing are the same as we use in everyday discourse.

What, then, if you used the following sentence to describe the events of your story world?

(1)   Her foot pressed down on the accelerator.

You could also have written:

(2)   She pressed her foot down on the accelerator.

Why might you choose 'Her foot' as the subject (or agent) of the sentence and not 'She'? This is the kind of *semantic* choice that stylistics can help illuminate for you, as discussed in section 2.2 in relation to clause structure. The answer lies partly in the degree of *agency* suggested, which differs slightly in each sentence. In sentence 2, the character comes across as in control, and responsible for her actions. The use of the pronoun 'she' as subject of the sentence means that it is the character who performs the movement of pressing down on the pedal. In 1, however, the use of the noun phrase 'her foot' in subject position suggests something subtly different. Here, the character is less in control. It is almost as if the action of speeding up the car is carried out unconsciously. The character appears distracted, thinking of something other than the act of driving, her thoughts elsewhere. Note that all of this information is conveyed very economically, by a simple stylistic choice.

What about this?

(3) She floored the gas pedal.

This time, the verb is, to some extent, linguistically deviant as discussed in Chapter 1 (it could also be argued, in contrast, that it is demotic, and normalised; we will leave this discussion until later in the book). However, the sense is, again, different from 1 and 2. Here, the dynamism of the deviant/demotic verb *floor* as the clause's predicator suggests even more agency than 2; the character is evidently in control of what she is doing, and conscious of it. Indeed, the associations that the word 'floored' has with fighting (as in 'to floor an opponent' in boxing), or with intense surprise ('his new appearance floored me'), lend the action an aggressive, surprising edge. The use of 'gas pedal' and not 'accelerator' (British English), obviously, suggests a specific context (US English).

The crucial point to grasp here is that all three sentences can be interpreted as descriptions (or, to be rigorous, *encodings*) of the same event. However, the semantic effect of each sentence – its particular foregrounded lexemes – is different, and creates a subtly different cognitive engagement on the part of the reader in each case. As we have seen, semantic effect as a whole is, irredeemably, dependent upon all other levels of style in this model;[13] however, it is also, arguably, the most important of all for the writer to consider in detail. It is hoped that an integration of these kinds of semantic awareness into your creative practice can attune your writing brain to the significance of tiny alterations and the disproportionately large effect they can have on what the reader imagines when reading the text. We will explore this point further in the exercises at the end of the chapter, which include some textual intervention.

2.3.2 Syntax

One central point already made on several occasions in this chapter is so important that it bears repetition: shifts in semantics will also, often, involve differences of 'form', that is, syntax, phonology, graphology. However, it is perfectly possible to envisage sentences which, though differing in syntactic form, are equivalent in sense; that is, they are paraphrases (Leech and Short 2007: 104).

(1) The young woman raised her head from the pillow feebly.
(2) From the pillow the young woman feebly raised her head.
(3) Feebly the young woman raised her head from the pillow.

Although the action described by these three sentences is the same, the effect on the reader is different due to the syntactic variation. The most obvious difference is the word order. In 1 and 2, the thematised or foregrounded noun phrase is different. The noun phrase occupying the subject position in each clause varies, and thus, the first 'object' that the reader meets is different; so, the image the reader gets of the event described in each case is subtly altered in each case. Note that this is not a variation in transitivity terms[14]; in both sentences (and, indeed, in sentence 3), the young woman is the actor and the verb 'raise' is the process. However, in 1, the young woman is foregrounded; in 2, the pillow is foregrounded, and thus the fact that she is lying in bed. You could argue, then, that 1 foregrounds the character, while 2 foregrounds her situation. In 3, the adjunct comes first in the clause, and is foregrounded; thus, it is the *manner* in which the activity is performed which is emphasised. The focus of 3, then, is the woman's enfeebled condition. Note how 1, 2 and 3 emphasise different aspects of the story world while, in purely lexical semantic terms, their 'meaning' is the same. It should be pointed out also that sentence 2 would be unusual in that the complement comes first in the clause, lending the sentence a slightly awkward feel. However, this, of course, foregrounds the particular clause against the background of more standard usage and therefore is in itself an interesting stylistic effect.

In poetry, the issue of syntactic choice becomes even more significant, especially if the text attempts to adhere to a prosodic form or meter. Compare the original here with two syntactic variations:

(1) 'Twas brillig, and the slithy toves
    Did gyre and gimble in the wabe.
(2) Brillig it was, and the slithy toves
    In the wabe gyred and gimbled.
(3) In the wabe the slithy toves
    Gyred and gimbled, and it was brillig.

The issue is slightly different here as the lines are made up of two clauses joined by the conjunction 'and' (creating a compound sentence); also, 1 contains an extra word (the auxiliary verb 'did') and the verbs in 2 and 3 take the past form due to its omission. However, the importance of the choices the poet makes with regard to syntactic positioning is still clear. Variation 1 makes use of the traditional prosody structures of the iambic tetrameter,[15] with repeated consonants (/g/) creating alliteration in 'gyre' and 'gimble' and in the stop of 'brillig'. There is also a phonological aptness to the sibilance of 'slithy toves', foregrounded in all three versions; as already discussed, 'slithy toves' must be things that slither and hiss. Variations 2 and 3 lose the iambic meter, but 2 nevertheless seems to work, partly due to the inversion of subject and predicator in the first clause which creates a patterning (or parallel) effect through the running of the hard/g/ and /t/ stops of 'brillig' and 'it' (try saying them aloud). In the second line of 2, though, the effect of the alliteration of 'gyred and gimbled' in the original (1) is slightly less-ened due to the words' position later in the clause (avoided through the inversion of the second line of 1, which uses the auxiliary 'did' – thereby also introducing another hard consonant to add to the effect of the /g/ sounds). Variation 3 is probably the least preferred. The second clause (after 'and') appears clumsy, out on a limb. This awkwardness, which, of course, could well be successfully exploited in a different context, foregrounds itself and grabs the reader's attention, here detracting from the previous clause, particularly the effect of 'gyred' and 'gimbled'.

2.3.3   Graphology

The choice of the 'shape on the page' of a particular syntactic form is also important, as can be seen in the extracts from 'Jabberwocky' in 2.3.2. Let us revisit some of the examples from 2.3.2 with the 'look on the page' in mind.

(1)   The young woman raised her head from the pillow – feebly.
(2)   Feebly, the young woman raised her head from the pillow.

The sentences are divided into two sections by the punctuation marks, a dash and a comma. Making this choice has an effect on the reader's perception of the story world events. The manner of the action in 1 is given extra emphasis by the dash, and becomes more central to the sense of the sentence. In short, it is foregrounded. Indeed, conven-tion surrounding graphological features of style (such as punctuation, paragraph/line breaks, the use of different fonts and so on) becomes significant only as an example of deviation from the norm.

Here, Will Self (2006) uses italics to distinguish character voice from narrative voice:[16]

> *Tatty coaches full of carrot-crunchers up for the Xmas wallet-fuck,* pale-skined, rust-grazed Transit vans with England flags taped across their back windows, *boogaloo bruvvers in Seven Series BMWs,*

> *throw-cushion specialists in skateboard-sized Smart cars, Conan-the-fucking-Barbarian motorcycle couriers,* warped flat-bed trucks piled high with scrap metal, one-eyed old Routemaster buses… (27–8)

Famously, James Joyce enjoyed pushing hard against the conventions of graphology (as well as syntax and lexis, as we saw in the previous chapter, and much else besides), using deviations of this kind to represent uninterrupted streams of thought mixed with sounds and sensations, as in this example from Molly Bloom's monologue at the end of *Ulysses*:

> I wish hed sleep in some bed by himself with his cold feet on me give us room even to let a fart god or do the least things better yes hold him like that a bit of my side piano quietly sweeeee theres that train far away pianissimo eeee one more tsong
>
> (1986: 628)

The matter of graphology is even more important when it comes to poetry, of course. We could revisit the example from e.e. cummings in Chapter 1 in this connection (whose graphological representation of his own name is also foregrounded…).

2.3.4 Phonology

You might think intuitively that if a text is written down (as most literary texts will be), then it has no discernible phonological effect unless it is read aloud; however, the question of the 'sound' of language is enormously relevant to the creative writer (especially the poet, but writers of fiction need to address it to), and we will discuss it briefly here.[17] Of course, some poetry will be performed and read aloud, as, indeed, will some fiction; however, even if it is not, the 'implicit sound pattern' (Leech and Short 2007: 105) *will still be recognisable* to the silent reader (as it were, the 'reading aloud' takes place in the mind), and may well to a greater or lesser extent determine word and structure choice at the syntactic level, as we discussed in section 2.3.2 above.

Given that the English system of writing is to some extent a system for representing – however imperfectly and imprecisely – the sounds of speech, then graphology too can play an important role in attempting to capture the individual qualities of a character's (or narrator's) speech in fiction.[18] A brief example will serve to illustrate this, as we will return to the topic in detail in Chapter 5 when discussing representations of speech:

> Strange thing wis it stertit oan a Wedinsday, A mean nothin ever sterts oan a Wedinsday kis it's the day afore pey day an A'm ey skint.

Mibby git a buckshee pint roon the *Anchor* bit that's aboot it. Anywey it wis eftir 9 an A wis thinkin aboot gin hame kis a hidny a light whin Boab McCann threw us a dollar an A boat masel an auld Erchie a pint. The auld yin hid 2 boab ay his ain so A took it an won a couple a gemms a dominoes. Didny win much bit enough tae git us a hauf boattle a Lanny. Tae tell ye the truth A'm no fussy fir the wine bit auld Erchie'll guzzle till it comes oot his ears, A'm tellin ye. ... The auld cunt's a disgrace.

(Kelman 1995: 30)

The point here is that unorthodox spelling is used to represent a Glaswegian dialect. As Leech and Short point out, 'There is apparently no graphological device, whether spelling, punctuation, capitalisation, etc. that cannot be exploited for such purposes' (2007: 106). Capitals can be used to represent spoken emphasis, for example. It could be argued, though, that an overreliance on these kinds of written conventions can be construed as slightly mistrustful of the reader's innate capacity to imaginatively recreate the sounds of character voices with the minimum of guidance from the author.

The phonological level of style is, arguably, of more relevance to writers of poetry, however. Hence, a complete chapter will be devoted to the topic (Chapter 9) later in the book.

2.3.5   Summary

Our discussion of levels of style has aimed to present the creative writer with a sense of the quite simply vast range of possibilities available within the English language for the presentation of any given fictional world situation to the reader, from the reasonably simple and straightforward to the positively outlandish. It is to be hoped that these considerations can become part of creative practice, so that the creative writer, when faced with an already-written word, phrase, clause or sentence, will be able to ask: 'What else might I have written, and didn't?' The follow-up questions should be equally revealing: 'Why did I choose to write what I did? And does it have the most appropriate stylistic value for the job in hand?' Even the relatively simple manipulation of the sentence from Dickens in section 2.3.2 yielded subtly but significantly different expressive effects. In considering stylistic variations of the same message, we were able to isolate the stylistic values of the original and, perhaps, explain why one form worked more pleasingly than another. This skill is, surely, of great value to the creative writer. It is worth considering what Rob Pope (1994) terms **textual**

intervention in one's own work (changing it, rewriting it, in structured ways; for example, changing the point of view from third- to first-person, or removing all adjectives), either as part of the creative process itself or afterwards during the revising of the work.

2.4 Practice

(1) Here are more examples of the potential potency of minute stylistics choices, in this case from fictional prose:

They made tapes and mailed them back and forth. (compare: 'They made tapes and mailed them to each other')

This blind man, an old friend of my wife's, he was on his way to spend the night (compare 'A blind man who was an old friend of my wife's was on his way to spend the night') [both from Raymond Carver's short story, 'Cathedral', 1998].

Someone must have been telling lies about Joseph K., for without having done anything wrong he was arrested one fine morning (compare '... the authorities arrested him one fine morning') [from Franz Kafka, *The Trial*].

I'm finding out that a lot of what I thought had been bonfired, Oxfam-ed, used for landfill, has in fact been tided away (compare '... what I thought had been burnt, given away or thrown away')

Select individual sentences from your own work and try reworking them at a similar level of detail. What changes? What stays the same? Which version do you prefer? Why?

(2) Look at these examples from poems.

The windows were open and the morning air was, by the smell of lilac and some darker flowering shrub, filled with the brown and chirping trills of birds. As they are if you could have nothing but quiet and shouting. Arts, also, are links. I picture an idea at the moment I come to it, our collision. [Lyn Hejinian]

age of earth and us all chattering

a sentence or character
suddenly

steps out to seek for truth fails
falls

> into a stream of ink Sequence
> trails off
>
> must go on [Susan Howe]

What happens to these poems if you rewrite them, 'normalising' their syntax? And what do we mean by 'normalising their syntax'?

(3) Rewrite the poem 'Jabberwocky' using 'real' language instead of Carroll's nonsense originals (neologism). What changes in terms of the way the poem works? Does it still come to 'mean' in the same way?

3 Building Blocks II: Narrative and Structure (Story Narratology)

3.1 Overview

To study narrative is to study everything. That may seem like a bold statement (and this book is full of them), but narrative is a huge subject. It lies at the core of (almost?) all literary texts, be they fiction or poetry. It surrounds us in our daily lives, and is not just confined to literature. Narratives lie right at the heart of media discourse, for example, and so shape the way that we understand the world beyond our immediate experience. Media texts present versions of the world through the 'packaging' of events and characters into stories. These narratives may then be extended and developed, as in film dramas or documentary programmes which often purport to tell if not the whole 'story' then at least its most interesting or scandalous aspects. Narratives can also be continuous or serial, and, indeed, very long and complex indeed, such as the best TV dramas (think of the great HBO TV series such as *The Sopranos*, *The Wire* or *A Game of Thrones*) or even soap operas. They may also be mini-narratives, or narrative 'snapshots', limited or single-narrative events which leave the viewer to complete the narrative, a technique which is used in many magazine or television advertisements. News stories in particular are shaped and mediated by the wider 'meta-narratives' into which they are situated (think 'national decline', 'economic catastrophe', 'social breakdown', 'environmental collapse'); thus it is, in many ways, the medium which shapes the message. The story is mediated to fit the context in which it is assumed to belong. To put it as succinctly as possible: we cannot avoid *storying* our lives. It is what human beings do in order to make sense of a highly complex and confusing world.

Narratives also determine the way we perceive our immediate experience. We construct narratives every time we tell someone what we have done with our day. We construct narratives when we remember our pasts and we envisage our futures (these are often as fictional, if not

more so, than literary texts, showing once again how many of the conclusions we draw about language through stylistics are applicable in
many different contexts, not just the literary). Narratives both capture
and shape our world. Indeed, it could be argued that they are the tools
we use to make coherent that which is essentially chaotic. They are a
way of capturing and preserving evanescent, mutable experience, and
have been since humankind first learned to construct them. Indeed,
just as Chomsky argues for humans as being 'hard-wired' for language,
so, it could be argued, are we hard-wired for narrative.

The academic study of narrative has become correspondingly large
and multifaceted; the subject as a whole is often referred to as **narratology** (as we saw in the introduction, a discipline closely related in aims
and scope to stylistics, in that it aims to provide a rigorous account of
particular functions of – often – linguistic representation[1]).

It is interesting to speculate as to where we find the first instances of
narratives – the first instance of humankind striving to make sense of
the world, to somehow 'capture' facets of evanescent reality for poster-
ity. In European terms, perhaps we could look to the prehistoric cave
paintings at Lascaux in France, dated as being between 17, 000 and
12, 000 years old. These depict hunts and the chasing down of the
quarry. It is possible that they fulfilled some sort of pedagogical purpose: to pass on the skills of hunting to younger members of the group.
Or perhaps they are simply frozen moments in time: the first attempt
that we know of in 'the West' to pin down experience in a manner external to the mind. Following this, of course, comes the oral and musical
folk tradition (think of the songs and ballads of the English, Scottish
and Irish traditions, for example, which nearly always involve strong –
and often tragic – narratives), religious narratives, the epic and heroic
poetry of the classical period and on into the present age.

Poems too are often full of narrative: the *Lyrical Ballads* (1798) of
Wordsworth and Coleridge, some of Keats's odes, formal poems, especially sonnets (which often advance a particular argument through
a narrative structure), the epics of Homer, Virgil and Byron and, of
course, the poem cycle. Narrative can also be construed in the unifying
principle of a body of poetic work (see, for example, Nancy Gaffield's
poem sequence *Tokaido Road* (2011), which bases itself on an imaginative journey along this ancient route from Kyoto to Tokyo).

Narrative, it would appear, is a fundamental aspect of what it is to be
human, and a fundamental means of communication. Hence, its study
should be of great importance to anyone with an interest in language,
creative writing – and culture in general.

We can begin by thinking about the importance of the concept of narration, and some of the ways in which it works. A list of possible types of narratives might include the following: personal histories, news stories, fairy tales, jokes, dreams, thrillers, ghost stories, comics, movies, video games, digital fiction, a cricket match, a diary entry, a Facebook status update, a Tweet... (The contents of this list may have become steadily more surprising as it went on; and it is nothing like exhaustive.) Through this we become aware of the fact that each of these has certain common elements, but have different characteristics, they might be told in different ways, styles, or from different points of view. In this way also we become aware of the blurred boundary that exists between 'fact' and 'fiction': both are 'narrated', told, ordered, selected and shaped – **mediated** – for an audience, and present – however hard they try not to – subjective views of the world.

3.2   Definitions: the act of narration

In any 'tale' there are two basic components: the tale and the teller (as, arguably, there is in any speech event). What makes narrative different is that *the teller is particularly noticeable*. Take this example from Coleridge's 'The Rime of the Ancient Mariner':

> IT is an ancient Mariner,
> And he stoppeth one of three.
> 'By thy long grey beard and glittering eye,
> Now wherefore stopp'st thou me?
>
> 'The Bridegroom's doors are opened wide,
> And I am next of kin;
> The guests are met, the feast is set:
> May'st hear the merry din.'
>
> He holds him with his skinny hand,
> 'There was a ship,' quoth he.
> 'Hold off! unhand me, grey-beard loon!'
> Eftsoons his hand dropt he.
>
> He holds him with his glittering eye –
> The Wedding-Guest stood still,
> And listens like a three years' child:
> The Mariner hath his will.

The Mariner accosts the wedding guest and begins to tell him a story. The wedding guest is held rapt almost in spite of himself by the power of the Mariner's story. This is, in effect, a narration within a narration. There is the poet's voice, which sets the scene, and then the voice of the Mariner, who recounts the story itself. We will examine the distinction between these agents in more detail in Chapter 4. Note how in a narrative the attention of the reader (or, indeed, listener or viewer) is divided between teller and tale. This is always true of any narrative; however, the degree to which you focus on teller versus tale fluctuates from one narrative to another and, indeed, is an important source of creative energy for the writer. It is an aspect of narrative that you should always be conscious of. In Coleridge's poem, I would argue, our focus is very much on the second teller, the Mariner, and not the original (the poet). Even when watching a film or TV drama, you are conscious of the ways in which the story is being told to you: via camera angles, cutting of scenes, lighting, the effect of music, sound and so on. You are less conscious of the teller here than you are in the poem, though. So, every narrative has a tale and a teller. Intervening between the two, and providing the material through or via which the narrative is **mediated**, comes the **discourse**.

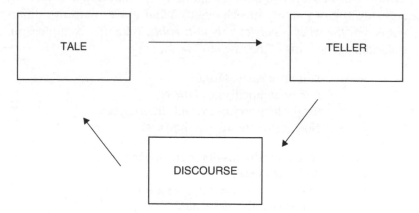

As the diagram above should illustrate, all three aspects of narrative (tale, teller and discourse) are fundamentally interrelated. In linguistic terms, narrative discourse is *a way of matching up patterns of language to a connected series of events* (Simpson 2004: 19), just as we saw with syntax in the previous chapter. So, the most basic form of narrative discourse will contain two clauses which are chronologically ordered. Paul Simpson (2004: 19) uses the following simple example to illustrate this:

John dropped the plates and Janet laughed.

Note how the syntax itself mimics or reflects the action being described. In 'the tale', first comes the dropping of the plates, and then comes Janet's reaction. So it is with the discourse. Thus, the syntax itself has a mimetic function. Swapping the syntactic position of the clauses creates a different tale; a different chain of events leads to a different chain of syntax (or is it the other way around?[2])

Janet laughed and John dropped the plates.

This may seem like an obvious point, but it is one we often forget. It illustrates a fundamental truth about narrative: the discourse must, in some way or other, mediate the tale rather than obscure or cloak it (although, of course, there may be times when you want to obscure or cloak the tale deliberately), and it has many different options when it comes to doing this. In fact, in linguistic terms, we can treat narrative discourse as **signifier** and the tale itself as **signified** (just as the word 'tree', say, signifies in and of itself a concept of 'treeness'). Saussure (1916/1995) argued that it was impossible to separate signifier from signified. They are, he says, like two sides of a sheet of paper. Arguably, the same is true of narrative discourse and the tale or story it mediates. We will return to this issue shortly.

Most narratives are, of course, more complex than the Janet and John example, and require exposition, development, complication, sometimes resolution, and always *change* or *transformation* of some kind of another (we will also return to this point). It is also often possible to discern a 'stylistic fingerprint' (Simpson 2004: 14), which signals the presence of a (hopefully) interesting and beguiling individual authorial voice. If no such voice is present, the story will feel flat and dull. The teller is not worth listening to; Coleridge's wedding guest would have turned his back on the Ancient Mariner and headed for the bar (as it turns out, that would have been his best course of action).

So, has any of this discussion brought us any closer to a rigorous definition of narrative? Is it simply the same thing as a story, that is, a sequence of events with a beginning, middle and end? Is it enough to say that a narrative is a form of communication which presents a sequence of events caused and experienced by characters? What about the narrator, though? Is the 'narrator' the same thing as the 'author'? What *is* a story? Narratologists have been discussing these issues since the time of Aristotle, and, indeed, some might argue (although of course I would not agree) that not much has changed in terms of our basic understanding of narrative since Aristotle wrote his *Poetics*. However, perhaps we can begin to explore this fascinating topic with the following assertion: that all narratives are *representations* of a world[3] (be they primarily linguistic, or visual, or abstract) which is somehow recognisable to the 'receiver' of the narrative – for our purposes, the reader. If the representation distances itself too far from the kinds of reality we know, then it will be incomprehensible to us. This would violate what Ryan (1980) terms 'the principle of minimum departure'; whenever we encounter a narrative presenting an alternate world, we reconstruct this world as being the closest possible to the reality we know.

In order for a narrative to perform its function of representing the world, it needs a medium in/through which to do this. Claude Bremond (1964) suggests a distinction between story and medium which corresponds to the distinction between tale and discourse already mentioned. The result of distinguishing between the two implies an important concept: *stories can be transposed from one medium to another without losing their essential properties*. So, 'Cinderella' exists independently as a story (or narrative) which can be mediated, or told, in an (almost-infinite) number of ways: in a sanitised Disney version, in the full horror of the Brothers Grimm version (in which The Ugly Sisters cut off their toes to try and squeeze their feet into the glass slipper) or in a postmodern contemporary re-telling (the family lives in social housing and the Fairy Godmother delivers cheques on behalf of the National Lottery, say). This idea is important in terms of our search for a definition of narrative. Narratives need to be told, and they can be told (or mediated) in many different ways. Roland Barthes (1977) argued, for example, that narrative is present in written literature, oral conversation, drama, film, painting, dance and mime. So the term 'medium' is a broad one, and embraces all of the following and more besides: text, spoken language, simulated language on a stage, moving images, static images, stylised and patterned movement, movement alone without speech.

Ryan (2003) proposes two definitions of *medium* which should be of interest to creative writers. She terms the first the **transmissive** definition, and the second the **semiotic** definition. Transmissive media include TV, radio, the Internet, CDs, phones (technology, in other words) as well as so-called cultural channels such as books and newspapers (cultural channels now cross over with technological ones, of course, in the form of e-books and online editions of journals and newspapers). Semiotic media include language, sound, image, or more narrowly, paper, clay, the human body. In transmissive media, the message is encoded and sent via a channel before being decoded at the other end of what Ryan refers to as the 'pipeline'. But somebody still has to paint the painting before it can be transmitted. Someone has to play the guitar before the signal can be encoded and transmitted as an MP3. The problem with this definition is that it overlooks the influence of the pipeline. The shape and size of the pipeline 'imposes conditions on what kind of stories can be transmitted' (2003).

Until the development of digital technology and the rise of what we now refer to as **multimodality**,[4] the idea of medium was fairly straight-forward: the medium of a work was both the substance out of which the work was fashioned by the artist, and the material support, or body, under which it was meant to be apprehended by the audience. Now, it has become much more complicated, and the ways in which medium and message interact have multiplied accordingly. Just look at the pro-fusion of transmissive media available for dissemination of the 'semi-otic product' today: Kindles, iPads, the Internet in general, hypertext, video games, online fiction, audiobooks... The list could, of course, go on, and need not detain us unduly. The two significant points to rec-ognise are, first, that in narrative the medium and message are closely intertwined, if not inseparable, and that, second, the range of media now available to the creative writer has never been wider or more excit-ing. The two points are related, of course, in that the way you write for specific media will, presumably, be affected in some way by the trans-missive nature of the medium you are aiming towards. It is beyond the scope of this book to discuss this issue in the detail it deserves, but it would not be doing its job if it did not at least allude to it.

So, it could be argued that narrative (in the widest sense of the term, not only in its literary sense) is first and foremost a method of commu-nication between two agencies – a way of making a chaotic and confus-ing world manageable and coherent. Even if we take the example of the everyday refashioning of experience – the repackaging of our everyday lives into narrative-sized 'chunks' – that goes on inside our own heads, then this is still, I would argue, a form of communication between two agencies: you articulate these stories to yourself, as it were.

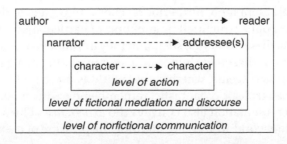

The diagram above (adapted from Jahn 2002) illustrates this stand-ard structure of fictional narrative communication. Communicative contact takes place at various levels: (1) between implied author and implied reader[5] (Booth 1983: 71); (2) between narrator and audience or addressee(s) on the level of fictional mediation; and (3) between characters on the level of action. We can term the first level 'extratex-tual' (at the level of the act of communication, say, hearing a story in a pub or reading this book) and the second and third 'intratextual' (taking place in the 'possible world' – or fictional world, if you prefer – of the narrative).[6] Being aware of these different levels of communica-tion is helpful to the creative writer in that it can show when and where discourse is straying across the different boundaries, and which voice within the narrative belongs to which agency. Also, keeping an eye on narrative levels can create interesting 'epistemological gaps' in your narrative. What might the reader be told that a character is unaware of? Conversely, what might characters know that the reader will not?

Finally, I want to re-emphasise that the idea of mediation and, if you prefer, 'spin', is common across narrative in all genres, not just the fic-tional or creative. You only need to glance at the headlines in a left-leaning (or liberal) newspaper versus those in a conservative one on the day a significant story breaks to see this in practice. Ostensibly, both newspapers are mediating the same 'facts', but the aspects of the story that they choose to emphasise will be very different in each case, and influenced by ideology.[7]

So: where does all this leave us in terms of our search for a defini-tion of narrative? David Herman (2009) has come up with the following detailed model to describe the 'prototypical' narrative, which covers all of the possible incarnations of narrative referred to in our discussion so far and acts as a very useful summary of this wide-ranging topic:

A prototypical narrative can be characterised as follows:

(i)   A representation that is situated in – must be interpreted in light of – a specific discourse context or occasion for telling.
(ii) The representation, furthermore, cues interpreters to draw infer-ences about a structured time-course of particularised events.
(iii) In turn, these events are such that they introduce some sort of dis-ruption or disequilibrium into a storyworld involving human or human-like agents, whether that world is presented as actual or fictional, realistic or fantastic, remembered or dreamed, etc.
(iv) The representation also conveys the *experience* of living through this storyworld-in-flux, highlighting the pressure of events on real

or imagined consciousnesses affected by the occurrences at issue. Thus – with one important proviso – it can be argued that narrative is centrally concerned with *qualia*, a term used by philosophers of mind to refer to the sense of 'what it is like' for someone or something to have a particular experience. The proviso is that recent research on narrative bears importantly on debates concerning the nature of consciousness itself. (2009: xvi)

Herman abbreviates each of these features of narrative as follows; the subsequent brief elaborations are my own.

(i) Situatedness (what is the context of the act of telling?).
(ii) Event sequencing (things happen, usually one after another).
(iii) Worldmaking/world disruption (a world is built through narrative, and then the initial stability of that world is somehow disturbed).
(iv) What it's like (a central point: we **empathise** in some way or other with the narrative; if not reliving it, then experiencing it by proxy; good writing exploits this crucial human capacity: the ability to experience the world from someone else's point of view).

In fact, as Monika Fludernik points out in tribute to the universality of narrative, it is certainly possible to ask 'What is **not** some kind of narrative?' (2009: 2). She offers the following definition as a way of distinguishing narrative discourse from other kinds of discourse:

A narrative is a representation of a possible world in a linguistic and/ or visual medium, at whose centre there are one or several protagonists of anthropomorphic nature who are existentially anchored in a temporal and spatial sense and who (mostly) perform goal-directed actions (action and plot structure). It is the experience of these protagonists that narratives focus on, allowing readers to immerse themselves in a different world and in the life of the protagonists. In verbal narratives of a traditional cast, the narrator functions as the mediator in the verbal medium of the representation. Not all narratives have a foregrounded narrator figure, however. The narrator or narrative discourse shape the narrated world creatively and individualistically at the level of the text, and this happens particularly through the choice of perspective (point of view, focalisation). Texts that are read as narratives (or 'experienced' in the case of drama or film) thereby instantiate their narrativity.

(Fludernik 2009: 6)

Notice how Fludernik's definition intersects with Herman's in several ways, homing in on the idea of **representation** and **world creation**, on the essential relationship to our condition as human beings, and on the level of **empathy** that narratives induce (Herman refers to qualia, Fludernik to immersion and instantiation) in the reader/listener/viewer.

This book may well, in places, and to some, seem unduly proscriptive in its approach to creative practice. As pointed out already, the ideas which I have drawn from stylistics and narratology are not rules but just that: ideas. They are concepts to play with, experiment with, use or discard as you see fit in the context of your own creative work. However, this is the sternest of all the 'ideas' in this book (if it is possible for an idea to be 'stern'; ask Chomsky), and one that I am prepared to defend. I see a piece of writing's capacity to inspire (or simulate, or induce, or whatever) **empathy** as a signal of the level of quality of that writing. To restate the position: if empathy – the ability to see the world as others see it – is a fundamental human attribute, then the fact that creative writing exploits this attribute is what makes it, also, a unique and fundamental tool with which to make sense of the world. And the best writing is that which does this the most effectively. To put it as simply as possible: it makes you see the world in a different way. It releases you from the prison of your own perspective. As writers, we should be ready and willing to shape and craft our work in the best way possible in order to take greatest advantage of this miraculous facet of what it is to be human.

It will be useful, finally, to look at an example. Here is a very short story:

> She decides to make a list of the things that make her happy.
> She writes 'plum-blossom' at the top of a piece of paper.
> Then she stares at the paper, unable to think of anything else.
> Eventually it begins to get dark.[8]

Here, we find all of the elements alluded to in the definitions and model above:

- A character (a protagonist, a human-like agent) referred to simply as 'she'.
- A representation of a situation, in this case, in the linguistic medium through which you just 'read' the story); the situation is *mediated* for us through language (discourse). This is level 2 in the diagram.
- A situation (or context) for that representation: that the story appears in this book, as you read it, for purposes of exemplification

in answer to the question 'what is a narrative?'; of course, the narrative could find purpose in many other contexts, most obviously in that of being read for pleasure in the collection of stories from which it comes. This is level 1 in Jahn's diagram.

- A world; here, the fictional world – a 'possible world', other than the actual world – in which this character makes her list.[9]
- A narrator, the entity who tells us the story; in this story, the narrator is not foregrounded, and not conspicuous (we will discuss narrators and their voices in more detail in Chapter 4).
- We are aware of an author too, but he (in this case) is an implied author (see note 6 in this chapter); we treat his voice and the voice of the narrator as more or less interchangeable (of course, this is not the case with all narratives, as we will see).
- The situation undergoes *change* or *transformation*; at the beginning of the story, 'she' decides to make a list; she fails to make more than one entry on it, and gradually it gets dark. This is the 'literal' summary of what happens. The events of the narrative also have a figurative resonance, of course (it is hard to avoid reading the 'getting dark' as an external echoing of the character's internal state of mind).

Note that, unusually for a narrative fiction, there is very little presentation of other discourse (i.e. characters' voices and thoughts) in this story, only of a short fragment of the protagonist's writing: 'plumblossom'. There is no character–character communication (Jahn's level 3), unless you count the list that the protagonist is writing for herself. Consider the following extract, though, from a set of 'vignettes' by Leonard Michaels entitled 'Eating Out' (2007: 110):

> I said, 'Ma, do you know what happened?'
> She said, 'Oh, my God.'

All of the elements mentioned above are still present, but there is much less diegesis and, arguably, far more mimesis (less telling, more showing).[10] The narrative is simply a representation of the speech of two characters, presumably mother and child (son? Grown up? Why do we assume these things? Is it the way they talk?). In terms of 'message', this is all there is. However, hidden between these two lines the reader will be able to find an enormous amount of information. What happened? Of course, the reader won't know. But he or she will be able to guess, and will fill in the gaps with an almost-infinite number of possibilities. The 'what happened' could easily be something good, or something bad. It is never related within the narrative discourse itself. Indeed,

Ma's instant reaction ('Oh my God') would appear to precede the narration of the event itself. Perhaps terrible things are always happening to her son, so she gets her reaction in early, as it were, out of habit. Or perhaps the reaction is there in the story world but left out in the discourse itself. Imagine a complete separation between the words on the page and the fictional events described (between what we will term **discourse** and **fabula** in the next section). There is no reason why the two should correspond; nor can they, as we shall see. This useful separation between story events and the language used to mediate them will be discussed in more detail in the next section.

If you are reading this book in the vicinity of someone else, ask them to read the story too and then see what they think happened. The answer is very unlikely to be the same as your own. Perhaps it doesn't matter what happened. The ellipsis[11] points the way to infinite possibility, and that is a story in itself. This very terse story illustrates three fundamental points about narrative which will be/have been expanded upon in section 3.2, in Chapter 1 and in Chapter 6:

(1) It is creatively enervating to leave 'space' for the reader's imagination to interact with the text (while being mindful of **the principle of minimum departure**[12]). Resist the temptation to rely overly on diegesis – to tell too much, or to give too much away.

(2) Each reading is a performance in itself, and no two readings are ever likely to be the same (hence, writingandreading). Creative writing should fully exploit its performative nature.

(3) Narrative discourse and the world of the story are inextricably linked; however, it can be useful for the purposes of creative practice to consider them separately.

To attempt a summary: all narratives are mediated representations of a world[13] involving a 'tale', a 'teller' and a form of discourse (although multimodality complicates these distinctions somewhat). The reader will interpret this narrative world through the lens of their own experience and understanding of reality. Narrative theory has attempted to identify other key elements which all narratives have in common, each of which will be foregrounded to a greater or lesser degree depending on the particular narrative in question (indeed, the foregrounding of one or more of the elements below is a key indicator of genre; structure may well be foregrounded in certain types of experimental poetry, for example, and, very, very broadly speaking, it could be argued that nineteenth-century novels foreground character). We will now look at some of these key elements in a little more detail, and expand upon two of the most significant from the creative writer's perspective in later sections of this chapter: story/medium and narrative structure.

3.3 Discourse versus fabula

To build on the distinction made in point 3 above, it will now be useful to look at what narrative theory has to say on the subject of 'the act of narration' versus 'the story itself', and to see how its observations might be useful for the creative writer. We have already mentioned the basic conceptual distinction that is revealed here between story and narration, or between 'tale' and 'telling'; that is, between the story itself that is told, the order in which its events are related, and the point of view from which this information is mediated for the reader. The exact same series of events, of story, containing exactly the same characters, will produce contrasting complete narratives depending upon whether the story is mediated according to the conventions and codes of, say, a joke, a news bulletin, a lyric poem or a nineteenth-century novel. (My sincere apologies in advance for what follows.)

(1) This guy walks into a pub, right, and he asks the landlord for a pint.

(2) A man in his mid- to late-30s was spotted this evening walking into a pub on Harbour Street, Whitstable. Witnesses already in the pub when he entered report that he ordered a pint of beer from the owner of the establishment.

(3) A man was wandr'ing through the town
In hope of buying something brown.
He spied a hostel, warm, aglow
And straight inside the man did go.

(4) The snow was falling evenly onto the cracked pavements and settling like a cloak on the abutments and roofs of the shuttered shops that lined the street. Will Barlow picked his way through the puddles and slush toward the enticing orange-lined door of The Duke of Cumberland. As he pushed it open and stepped inside, Bob Stallard the Landlord looked up from polishing a glass.
'What will you have, Will?'
They both smiled. They knew the question needed no answering.

Narratology has come up with a wealth of different terminology to describe the difference between the tale and the telling, which we need to simplify slightly for our purposes. As we have seen already in section 3.1, the act of narration requires some key elements: a narrator, a character (or characters), a represented situation, a situation of representation, a medium of representation (in our case, language) and a listener or audience. We can now alter – and, arguably, simplify – this list slightly, and make it more relevant to the writer, by substituting the terms **discourse** for 'medium of representation' and **fabula** for 'represented situation' or, simply, *story*. These distinctions were first made by the Russian Formalists (notably, Skjlovsky (1917) and Propp (1928) but have remained relevant within modern narratology too.

In each of the short examples above, the fabula is (more or less) the same. It is just that it is mediated in very different ways, and differing areas of focus and differing amounts of narrative detail are added in each case. Of course, the reader will interact with each 'act of mediation', with each discourse, in different ways, but it could be argued that the underlying actions, the fabula, are the same: a man walks a short way through a town, and then goes into a pub. These examples simultaneously demonstrate the interconnectedness of discourse and fabula; as we have pointed out, it is certainly possible to argue that the two are in fact inseparable. A final point here: the first, second and, more arguably, the third could all be envisaged as oral narratives (even if the second would, presumably, be read aloud from a text or autocue), highlighting once again the fact that narrative is a fundamental aspect of all communication, and not just the literary.

It is the *manner* of the telling, then (the deft manipulation of the discourse) that will contribute to the success or failure of the narrative. Example 1 would need to have an amusing or surprising ending, a punch line, and be told wittily, with suspense, and with good timing and delivery. Example 2 would need to have some importance for or bearing on the community to which it was being reported if it were not to seem irrelevant. Example 3 draws attention to its use of language, and so would need to use that language in interesting and/or aesthetically pleasing ways – and so on.

William Labov (1972) provides us with a simple example of an oral narrative to demonstrate the truth of this fact (quoted in Simpson 2004: 19). Labov is a sociolinguist who has done a great deal of research into oral narratives among African–American communities in North America, and has found striking parallels between the way narratives are structured in natural speech and the way they are ordered in literary discourse.

> well this person had a little too much to drink
> and he attacked me

and the friend came in
and she stopped it

The listener will ask questions in response to this. When? Who? Whose friend was the friend? Is that the end? What else happened? In other words, this narrative lacks closure, lacks context and lacks dramatic or rhetorical embellishment (Simpson 2004: 19). The response of an interlocutor would probably be 'so what?' The narrator here seems uncomfortable, reticent, constrained. The fabula is there, but the discourse does not do a good job of mediating it. It is essential, then, to find the type of discourse that is most appropriate to the fabula you wish to mediate, given the contexts and conditions of the project you are working on. As an exercise, think about you might mediate the fabula quoted by Labov above, were you to write it as a piece of narrative fiction or poetry. Try writing it and, if possible, compare it to someone else's response to the same exercise. The choice is a crucial one, and there are, as you would expect, quite a few variables. We will attempt to simplify these and discuss discourse narratology in more detail in the next chapter.

3.4 Structure

Prototypical narratives begin with the presentation of an initial stable situation (Cinderella lives with her evil stepmother and her two sisters, working as a servant in the kitchen) which is in some way disturbed, disordered or upset due to a particular obstacle or problem. This is often set up by a particular desire or wish that a character will have (Cinderella wants to escape and 'find fulfilment') and an obstacle that stands in the way of the character achieving that goal (Cinderella's imprisonment in the home). The particular nature of the obstacle and how it is overcome (or not) is, as already mentioned, a key feature of genre: finding the killer, solving the mystery, giving the villain his just desserts or obtaining the sought-after thing or person. As you should now expect, this universal narrative form is by no means unique to literature; it can also be found in the ways in which newspapers and the media in general present the news (who is to blame for this problem which has disrupted our lives? How will it be resolved? What explains the situation?). The same structure may be found in TV quiz shows (who will win the cash prize?) or in sport (who will win the match, or the league?). Even advertisements make use of this fundamental structure. This is the problem you have (less-than-white teeth), or this thing is lacking in your life (a sexual partner). Here is how you solve the problem (whitening toothpaste), or fill the gap (perhaps the same product).

The achievement (or otherwise) of this goal is what brings about some sort of **change** or **transformation** in the initial situation. This is fundamental, I would argue. Narratives, in short, have to be about change, disturbance and/or disorder. (Cinderella marries Prince charming, Manchester City are league champions,[14] your teeth are white and now you have a partner.)

Burroway (2003: 32) models this basic structure as being made up of **conflict** (between characters, between a character and her inner self, between a character and something he desires or wishes to possess), **crisis** (the situation comes to a head in some way, and the tension peaks) and **resolution** (the crisis is resolved, as is the conflict). Baldwin (1986) describes a similar approach in his guide to writing short stories, terming it the 'angel cake'[15] approach to fiction. He prefers the terms **exposition**, followed by **complication** and ending in **resolution**. Other models add a fourth stage, **climax**, which comes in between the complication and the resolution:

(1) **Exposition**: the part of the story which sets the scene and introduces the character.
(2) **Complication**: the part of the story where the lives of the character(s) are complicated in some way.
(3) **Climax**: the point where suspense is highest and matters are at their most threatening.
(4) **Resolution**: a solution to the complication is introduced (it need not be a happy one).

According to structuralist versions of narratology, *all* narratives have these essential tripartite or four-part structures (some models are more complex but advance the same kinds of arguments). The structure is universal, and can be found in texts ranging from the Christian Bible to the Medieval Mystery Plays, from the Koran to *The Lord of the Rings*, from *EastEnders* to *The Arabian Nights*. If structuralist approaches to narratology are correct, then narrative has a grammar or syntax of its own, just like the language of which it is (often) made up, and that structure is universal: it applies across cultures and in all situations. Just as a sentence will have a subject and a verb, and perhaps an object (no matter how these are represented orthographically or phonologically), so narrative, which, like the sentence, is an attempt to mediate between us and the world, has a beginning, a middle and an end.

Let us return to Labov (1972) to examine his model of how *oral* narratives are structured (from Toolan 1998: 137–8). Labov identifies six aspects of narrative, not all of which will always be present; also, they need not occur in the order presented here. Toolan has added questions which usefully summarise the supposed content of each segment.

ABSTRACT	What is this about?
ORIENTATION	Who? When? Where? What?
COMPLICATING ACTION	Then what happened?
EVALUATION	So what?
RESOLUTION	What finally happened?
CODA	How does this relate to us here and now? This section also acts as a bridge back to the 'real world'.

We find many of the same stages in most literary narratives, if not all of them. Remember too that short stories, novels and, indeed, poems can contain many narratives, not just one (although there may well be a central, dominant narrative). To draw an analogy with video games: these often involve a 'main quest' which the character must complete to finish the game, but from this main quest will spring many 'side quests', like tributaries of a river, which the player does not *have* to follow or complete, but doing so will greatly enrich and augment the player's experience and enjoyment of the game. All of these will contain most if not all of the Labovian elements identified above.

So, from Labov's naturally occurring narratives (of everyday speech) to novel trilogies like *The Lord of the Rings* to the highly crafted and intricate narratives of modern video games, the same essential pattern can be discerned. All involve the transformation and mediation of experience via the syntax of narrative syntax, no matter whether they are presented orally, via text or via a screen.

3.4.1   Tension and momentum

Of course, it is not enough simply to present the elements of your narrative and hope for the best. The trick to successful mediation of your fabula comes through the use of tension and momentum. The reader must want to read on, or hear more. You should aim to have the reader asking questions internally, just like in the example from Labov above. What happened next? Why did it happen this way?

This rising and falling of tension in a narrative is often presented like this, using an inverted tick shape.

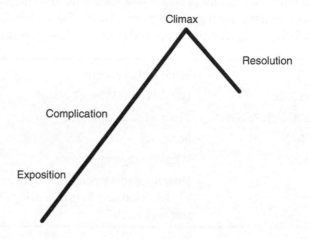

So, the plot begins with the exposition, moves up a slope where suspense and tension gradually increase in response to the complication (or series of complications), reaches a point of climax, and then quickly descends and ends in the resolution. This pattern of suspense need not, of course, be as neat as the tick diagram would suggest. In a novel or longer piece of writing, it may well resemble a staircase up until the point of the climax, with tension rising and falling at different stages of the story.

3.5   Narrative chronology

3.5.1   Complex structure

Following on from the idea of tension through structure above: it is crucial to grasp that the relentless progression of the fabula **need not be matched by the ordering of the discourse**. This is why I suggested that the creative writer should try to picture them separately (even though they are in many ways inseparable). The discourse can mediate the fabula in any order that you wish it to, including by starting at the beginning and simply following it through to the end. It would equally be possible, of course, to begin with the climax, move to the beginning, and then come back to the end. You could also start at the end.

Genette (1980) called this aspect of narrative **order**, and it concerns structure at the level of story. For example, imagine the structure of a murder mystery. First, the clues of a murder are discovered by a private investigator (call this Event A). Then, what actually happened – the circumstances of the murder – is revealed (Event B). Finally, the private investigator identifies the murderer and brings him or her to justice (Event C). Now, we can give each of these events a number corresponding to the *order* in which they are actually presented to the reader (or viewer, or listener) during the act of narration (or representation). Say the story is to be narrated chronologically (in the order that the events 'happened' in the story world). We could notate this as follows: B1, A2, C3. First comes the murder, then its discovery, then the revelation of the murder's identity. However, in the 'text' as described above, the order is as follows: A2 (discovery), B1 (flashback), C3 (resolution). The disjunction between story (what happened) and discourse (how it is represented) is full of creative potential, heightening suspense, causing the reader to ask questions and to want to read on. It is helpful to the creative writer, then, to envisage a separation between narrative discourse itself and the story (or fabula) being mediated by that discourse and to remember that order can play a crucial role in how the story works. It can even function as a crucial actor in the story itself. It can act as a kind of 'plot' in its own right, running alongside the plot of your fabula. The points of interest occur in the way in which (when and how) the details of the fabula are revealed to your reader. Just as tension and momentum should get your reader to ask questions, so can innovative use of order (or structure): 'What is happening here, and why is it happening in this order?'

Imagine that the exposition of a narrative is 1, the complication 2 and so on. The structure of Book Two of J.R.R. Tolkien's *The Lord of the Rings* ('The Two Towers') would look something like this: A1, B1, A2, B2, A3, B3. We simply alternate between the two narrative threads. What about a film like Quentin Tarantino's *Pulp Fiction*, though? Here, the structure is highly complex. Let us say there are three principal narrative threads (for the sake of illustration; there are more, in fact): A (the story of the hitmen), B (the story of the boxer) and C (the story of the two robbers holding up the diner). The structure goes something like this, say (an approximation): C1, B2, A1, A2, A3, B1, B3, C3. This is complex, but very effective. The viewer is constantly asking questions, being surprised, and works quite hard in putting the various narrative strands back together from their broken-down sections. At one point, a character appears in the film who has already been killed *in the world of the fabula*. In the narrative discourse, though, he is alive and well (but is lent a tragic air by the fact that we know what will happen to him). An example from fiction: in Martin Amis's novel *Time's Arrow* (2003) the discourse runs backwards, from the protagonist's death to his birth. Characters walk backwards, speak backwards and eat backwards. There are interesting ideological reasons for this, connected to the book's exploration of a horrendous subject: The Holocaust. The fabula runs forwards, of course. How could it not?[16]

If you elect to use complex structure like this, it is a good idea to be very sure of why you are doing it. If you simply do it because it seems clever or sophisticated, then perhaps you are not doing it for the right reasons. If the complex structure helps mediate the plot in interesting ways, makes the reader more imaginatively engaged and allows the characters to develop then it is working well. As you work out plots (if you do this) and as you work, try to be aware of the various ways your fabula could be mediated. It is often the case that a story which seems unpromising or uninteresting can be transformed simply through a redraft that makes use of a new structure.

3.5.2 Analepsis and prolepsis

In syntax, analepsis and prolepsis refer to the ways in which elements of a sentence can refer back or forwards to other elements. The easiest example is of the pronoun which refers back: 'This is the guy **who** installed our new kitchen' (where 'who' refers back to 'the guy'). Just like sentence syntax, narrative syntax can also flashforward and flashback. Narratology terms flashback **analepsis** and flashforward **prolepsis**. They are moments when the discourse moves either back or forward in fabula time before returning to the main narrative thread. There is an argument for saying that we should be suspicious of both devices, and that (as the many films that use the device would attest) their use can be clichéd. They interrupt the flow and pace of the narrative too. As if that were not enough, they interrupt the principle of favouring mimesis over diegesis. If you can mimetically represent the emotional scars (through dialogue, through behaviour, through artefacts in the character's possession – a photo or two – or through foibles – a fear of glass?) that your protagonist still bears from a former disastrous and abusive relationship rather than diegetically introducing it via analepsis, then do so.

Flashbacks have their moments, of course (no pun intended). The ways in which Kazuo Ishiguro's narrator in *The Remains of the Day* (1989) relives his past are nothing short of masterful, and play an important role in building up his complex character. Analepsis and prolepsis can also fulfil a role in terms of foreshadowing. A character who will eventually fall to her death from a window spends an early part of the story looking out from behind one. A candle burns continually in a particular room where a long-lost brother and sister will eventually meet. Even if the reader fails to notice the shadowing (and it is often wise to keep it subtle) this technique can both resonate between and glue together the components of a fragmented structure.

3.5.3 Duration

Finally on the subject of narrative and time, we should mention Genette's (1980) concept of **duration**. As we have seen, there is a discourse time and a story (or fabula) time. Genette called the relationship between these two times **duration** (1980: 86). 'Twenty years passed' is a long time in story terms, but is a short piece of discourse which takes only a second to write or read. Conversely, James Joyce's *Ulysses* is set in a relatively short story period of one day; however, it takes a great deal longer than that to read… In short, it has a long discourse time. Again, duration can be exploited by writers to great effect in terms of creating suspense, ironic distance, and in summarising lengthy information which is important in plot terms but need not be represented in detail by the discourse. *Time's Arrow* also exploits this facet of narrative discourse and the tension that is created between discourse and fabula in terms of compression and reversal. The discourse time and the story time are running in opposition to one another.

3.6 Practice

Much of the information in this chapter has been of a highly technical nature. Nevertheless, I think it has numerous applications to creative practice, as I hope the following series of exercises will demonstrate. As Brian Evenson (2010) writes, these techniques can replace (or at least complement) the slightly slippery notion of expressivism and intuition, even if they are only brought to bear at the editorial stage of the work:

> Elements and techniques are better understood not in relation to intuitive expressivist standards but in relation to their function in bringing about certain effects in the work as a whole. Intuition is not an end point but an initial response to be tested with the tools of narrative theory and the idea of means-ends relations between

techniques and effects – so that we can offer clearer reasons for our intuitions or come to a new evaluation. (2010: 72)

(1) *The sun was out.*
    Is this a narrative? Why? Why not?
    The sun was out but then it started raining.
    Is this a narrative? Why? Why not?

(2) If you have access to a group of like-minded individuals, try telling the story of Cinderella aloud to each other. Almost certainly, you will notice particular linguistic features about the way you tell the story:
    - Present tense
    - Oral speech
    - Fillers
    - Phatic language
    - Hedging and uncertainty.

    If the version you hear doesn't match this pattern, why not? Was the speaker using the past tense, for example? Did they start the 'telling' with 'Once upon a time' and end with 'And they all live happily ever after'?

    Oral features of narrative differ from written ones, then. The mediation of the fabula is carried out in a different manner. The same basic building blocks of the story are there, but the 'telling', the 'mediation', the **discourse** is different. This use of discourse will be the focus of the next chapter.

(3) Try writing a narrative poem (this exercise is adapted from 'The Short Narrative Poem' by Roland Flint, in Behn and Twitchell (1992)). Write a short poem (11 to 15 lines long). Make sure it tells a story of some kind.
    - Your poem must involve an incident that *really happened*, at a specific time and in a specific place, either to you or someone you know; or, if not, it should be an incident you know enough about to imagine the rest.
    - The lines may vary from nine to ten syllables, but must not all be nine or all ten or all eleven. You are not allowed to include any rhymes.
    - Not an absolute requirement, but try not to have more than one line in four or five ending in a full stop (or period); that is, you are to vary the structure and length of sentences and, obviously, the relation of sentence endings to line breaks. One mark of beginners writing poetry is that many of the lines end exactly where the sentence does, the worst case being that every sentence is only one line.

- Obviously it is useful to ask yourself if this is an incident worth telling about, worthy of a poem, of possible interest to others. But don't tell, in the poem, why it is interesting or what it meant; use all your space to tell what happened. The poem's 'meaning beyond itself' (the theme?), your attitude, your feelings, your ideas about it – these must all be implied, not stated. Don't worry too much about this at first, though; just tell the reader what happened, exactly as you remember (or imagine) it, and all of your most important feelings, prejudices, biases, convictions, will be implied – which is to say that the careful reader will be able to infer them.

- Why not start, after you have decided on the incident to relate, by writing it out as prose, with no concern for length or syllable counting. Do this to make clear to yourself what details exactly are essential for telling this story. When you have it as nearly complete in this form as you can make it, then cast it into lines in the required number that make the best reading sense and come as close as possible to the variable nine-, ten-, or eleven-syllable count model. If what you have written is much too long, then you must consider again what is essential to telling the story, revise accordingly; then go to work on the form. In other words, this should be a continual process of reduction and distillation (an excellent skill as it happens, to writers of fiction as well as poetry). It may be easier than you expect; you may find that only a little tinkering will bring it into compliance with the simple technical demands of the assignment. And if you tinker, with attention to keeping the language and the story clear, you will probably also improve the piece as narration.

- It is important to remember when revising that you want it to be as plain and direct as you can make it: as ever, remember that you should not aim to be deliberately 'poetic' in any obvious way; if you use figures of speech, metaphors or similes, then only use those that come naturally to the story. At the same time, *avoid all clichés* of both lexis (word choice) and metaphor.

(4) Plot out a story in detail. Focus on the exposition, complication, climax, resolution. Know exactly what will happen when, to whom and how. When you have finished, write each scene out on a piece of paper and cut them out individually.[17] Try rearranging the scenes into a different order to create a non-linear narrative or complex structure. It might not work for all stories but if it does, has it revealed anything new about the plot, theme or characters?

4 Through the Looking Glass: Who Sees? Who Tells? (Discourse Narratology)

4.1 Overview

In this chapter we will be focussing on one of the most essential methodological choices that any creative writer makes in the act of sitting down to begin a new project: who tells, and who sees? This may or may not be the same thing, as we will see when we start to discuss the differences between them in section 4.2. It is important to point out straight away that, while this topic sounds like something connected mainly to narrative fiction (focussing as it does on the notion of 'telling' a story and 'perceiving' the events within that story world), there will also be much here of relevance to the writer of poetry. Both poetry and fiction, then, will (almost always?) entail a teller and a seer, who, once again, need not be one and the same. Think back to the Cinderella exercise in Chapter 3. If you took up the challenge, then presumably you 'told' the story in your own voice. You said something like:

> Once upon a time, there was a young girl called Cinderella who lived with her stepmother and her three ugly sisters.

Or

> Right. Cinderalla lives with her stepmother. And her father. Or is he her stepfather? He might be dead. I can't remember. Anyway, it doesn't matter.

Indeed, it doesn't matter. In both cases, we have the 'teller', or **narrator**. He or she has no obvious identity at this point (as far as we can tell from the textual cues here on the page), other than that of the agency responsible for mediating the fabula for our benefit via discourse (spoken language, in this case). Perhaps, later on in the act of telling, you said something like:

> Cinderella noticed a very handsome man in the corner of the ballroom. Suddenly, she realised that the man was walking towards her with a smile on his face. He stretched out his hand towards hers...

Here, you are adopting Cinderella's point of view (quite literally), and *seeing* the events in her stead, and the reader's behalf. As we discussed in Chapter 3, there is a process of **empathetic identification** taking place, and it is this that helps the reader experience and interact with your story world (more on this later).

Too often, the term 'point of view' is used as a catch-all phrase that attempts to embrace both 'who tells' and 'who sees'. We might describe a book as being 'in the third-person', when all this really does is make a grammatical distinction between a narrator who says 'Cinderella noticed a very handsome man' and one who says 'I noticed a very handsome man'. The more rigorous taxonomy which we will introduce and discuss in this chapter will be of great benefit to the creative writer because it redefines this purely grammatical distinction in ontological/ epistemological terms. In other words, it allows us to capture precisely our narrator's relationship with the world he or she describes, whether he or she exists within or without that world, what kind of information he or she will be privy to (and, even more importantly, the things that he or she *won't* know), and also allows us to establish the same details in terms of our characters. You may of course want this information to be imprecise, by the way, for various creative reasons; but even then, I would argue that these categorisations will allow you to envisage the ways in which this imprecision may work in practice, and why it works. As briefly as possible: it is beneficial to the creative writer to be able to identify that who *sees* what is happening in a scene need or need not be the same as who *tells* the reader what is happening; stylistics and narratology can help to make this distinction clear.

A brief explanatory point: in Chapter 3, we referred to the subject of narratology in terms of its relevance to story shape and structure. Here, we turn to the other 'side' of narratology and draw on its insights into **discourse**.[1] As we have emphasised throughout, the two facets of the act of narration are intertwined, but it is useful for the writer – as a kind of thought experiment[2] – to be able to contemplate them separately sometimes.

4.2   Seeing versus telling

We have talked a great deal about the processes of seeing through language. The narrator is the agency that gives us the language through which to see, and that agency, as we will see, can help us in the process or, indeed, obfuscate us (deliberately).

We will use an example from a Raymond Carver short story, 'Are these Actual Miles?' to illustrate this difference between telling and seeing in narrative fiction.

> Fact is the car needs to be sold in a hurry, and Leo sends Toni out to do it. Toni is smart and has personality. She used to sell children's encyclopedias door to door. She signed him up, even though he didn't have kids. Afterward, Leo asked her for a date, and the date led to this. This deal has to be cash, and it has to be done tonight. Tomorrow somebody they owe might slap a lien on the car. Monday they'll be in court, home free – but word on them went out yesterday, when their lawyer mailed the letters of intention. The hearing on Monday is nothing to worry about, the lawyer has said. They'll be asked some questions, and they'll sign some papers, and that's it. But sell the convertible, he said – today, *tonight*. They can hold onto the little car, Leo's car, no problem. But they go into court with that big convertible, the court will take it, and that's that.
>
> (Carver 1998: 103)

Who tells here? What is the linguistic evidence that shows how marked the narrator's point of view is in the text? Let us return to Mick Short's (1996: 286) checksheet of linguistic indicators of point of view; we can find almost all of the features he mentions in the excerpt above:

(1) *Is there evidence of schema-oriented language? Which details are observed, 'facts' presented?*
     Very little account of the reader's 'need to know' is taken here. 'Fact is…' says the narrator. Certain 'facts' are presented, such as the circumstances of how Leo and Toni met, as well as the 'fact' that they need to sell the car. Much is left unexplained for now, though.
(2) *What value-laden or ideologically slanted expressions are used?*
     We see lots of descriptive language here. Toni is described as 'smart' and as having 'personality'; these are subjective judgements. Also,

the last sentence is a prediction from the narrator about what will happen if they don't sell the car.

(3) *What role is played by Given vs New information?*
This is the beginning of the story. Everything here is new to the reader, and yet the narrator assumes a level of familiarity. It is as if we are coming (*in media res*) into a monologue that has already begun.

(4) *Are there any deictic expressions related to place? Time? Social deixis?*
Tomorrow. Monday. Tonight. The use of first names.

(5) *Are there any indicators of the presentation of a character's thoughts or perceptions?*
No. Only of the narrator's, not another character's. The narrator presents another character's *speech* ('But sell the convertible, he said.'). This is further evidence of the subjectivity of this narrative voice. It is 'monocular', and told from one single perspective.

(6) *Is there any coding within or across sentences?*
Afterward, Leo asked her for a date, and the date led to this.

A narrator is very clearly in evidence (i.e. the narrator is **overt**; see section 4.4). In other words, the world of the fabula is being mediated conspicuously via the discourse on our behalf. A story emerges, but blurred almost by the narrator's ways of telling. He (it is a he, isn't it? How do you know?) clearly knows the characters well, and has a lot of information about circumstances surrounding their lives which should surely be private. How does he have access to all this information? This and the everyday tone (due in large part to the effect of *in media res* combined with the oral register of the voice) create a sinister effect. To modern ears, it sounds like the narrator of a Martin Scorsese gangster film (think Robert De Niro or Joe Pesci).

Who sees, then? This is also clear. The narrative voice is so subjective, so 'monocular', that it is the narrator himself who also sees. The narrative situation in the Carver story is relatively uncomplicated, then: we have a single, identifiable (overt) narrator who is our only witness to the events of the fabula. It is he and he only, and his viewpoint and that viewpoint alone, which mediate the fabula. For the beginning writer of prose fiction, or for those who have trouble finding, developing and maintaining an authentic and interesting narrative voice, this is often the easiest kind of narrative situation to adopt. The voice will come more naturally if you can identify it as belonging to a particular figure in the story, as here – even if the exact identity of that figure remains mysterious. The term 'first-person point of view' does not begin to capture this level of detail.

From here on in, then, we will attempt to ignore or bypass the terms 'point of view' or 'perspective', which, as I hope I have shown, are too general to be of much use in the kind of critical approach to creative writing adopted here. Instead, we will refer to the issues combined via the term **narrative situation** (from Stanzel 1986), and within that umbrella term refer to **narrative voice** (who tells/speaks) and **focalisation** (who sees).

To flesh this out in more detail: **narrative situation** is an aspect of discourse, and refers to *how* a narrative is told (rather than the fabula being mediated, which is the focus of story narratology and the previous chapter). Coming to **narrative voice** first: it is characteristic of narrative fiction and poetry that it is always told by someone, that is, it is always mediated in some way through a 'voice'. Compare this to the situation in drama or film, where characters speak 'directly' while the audience listens and watches. When we focus on narrative voice, we want to know who tells the story or speaks the poem. This question is asked of the narrative as a whole, remember; a narrator can, of course, report on other characters' words and thoughts.

Second, when it comes to **focalisation**: the narrator will sometimes tell the events from a position outside the story or poem, adopting what you may have learned to call an 'omniscient point of view'; this agency somehow (it often doesn't matter how) knows everything about what is going on and can enter into any of the characters' minds at will. However, it is also possible for the narrator to adopt the limited point of view of one character or another in the story and in consequence to remain ignorant (or pretend to be ignorant) of what happens outside this character's range of perception. Crucially, this choice of 'perspective' has nothing to do with the question of whether or not the narrator is a character in the story (as will become clear below). To express the distinction between narrative voice (who speaks?) and perspective (who sees or perceives?), Genette has introduced the term **focalisation** (Genette 1980: 189–94). Genette's terms have been modified subsequently by Rimmon-Kenan (1989) upon whose definitions this chapter is largely based.

4.3   Narrative voices

We have been using the term *diegesis* throughout this book to represent the processes of telling. The world that is created by this telling, the world of the fabula, could be represented diagrammatically like this.

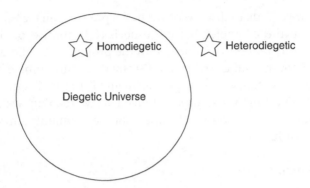

Notice the position of the two different types of narrator in relation to it. Using this concept of a diegesis or story world, we can now deploy terminology drawn from Genette[3] (and Rimmon-Kenan 1989) to distinguish between differing types of narrative voice in terms of their relationship to that story world: within it or without it.

4.3.1   Heterodiegetic

A **heterodiegetic narrator** takes no active part in the action being narrated, and is not a part of the story world (fabula) being created/represented by the discourse. Consider the etymology of the word itself for an insight into the relationship it represents: the prefix *hetero-* (from the Greek ἕτερος, meaning 'of another kind' or 'different'; think of heterogeneous or heterosexual) and *diegetic* (as we know, from *diegesis*, or διήγησις in Greek, meaning 'the act of narration' or, sometimes, 'the *product* of narration'). He or she (or it?) is therefore not a character in the story being told – if you like, not 'of the same material' as the fabula. Sometimes (very often, in fact) a heterodiegetic narrator is omniscient, all-seeing, all-knowing, and able to occupy characters' minds and perspectives at will. A heterodiegetic narrator will also have insight into characters' thoughts and feelings.

> Emma Woodhouse, handsome, clever, and rich, with a comfortable home and happy disposition, seemed to unite some of the best blessings of existence; and had lived nearly twenty-one years in the world with very little to distress or vex her. (7)

The narrator of Jane Austen's *Emma* (1815) is heterodiegetic, then, but seems, even from this short extract, to be very 'close' to the perspective of her protagonist. The narrator sees the world simultaneously through

Emma's eyes ('little to distress or vex her', a phrase which could almost come from the character herself, especially in its use of the word 'vex' – a word very much in tune with the protagonist's idiolect as we come to know it) and from beyond ('seemed to unite some of the best blessings of existence'). Perhaps this 'seemed', though, is more internalised than it might first appear. Indeed, as we read on, we discover that behind Emma's outward appearance of contentment hides a different truth.[4]

4.3.2   Homodiegetic

The definition of a homodiegetic narrator should be reasonably predictable, given the description of heterodiegetic narration in section 4.3.1. The prefix *homo-* (from the Greek ὅμο-), means 'the same' or 'of the same kind'. Thus, the homodiegetic narrator *is* part of the diegetic universe, or story world, and is often a character in the story. Dickens's *David Copperfield* (1850) and J.D. Salinger's *The Catcher in the Rye* (1951) are excellent examples of homodiegetic narration.

What about second-person narration? This is an intriguing type of narrative voice, and quite rare. The voice can be both homodiegetic (the narrator is talking to the reader or narrates from within the story world), or heterodiegetic (the narrator speaks to a character in the story world from outside; this technique can create quite a sinister effect[5]).

4.3.3   Intradiegetic and extradiegetic

These two categories of narrator go together, and work as a binary opposition: you cannot have one without the presence of the other. Rather than attempting to define them separately, it will be easier to grasp the concept if we go straight ahead with an example. Consider Geoffrey Chaucer's epic poem cycle *The Canterbury Tales*. Here, we have the poet figure (Chaucer himself) who describes the journey from London to Canterbury and what happens along the way. Within this wider narrative scheme, we also have the pilgrims who step forward to tell their stories in their own voices. The pilgrims are intradiegetic narrators (inside the universe), while Chaucer is extradiegetic (outside the universe within a universe) in relation to the story worlds of the pilgrims. Another good example is found in the novel *Heart of Darkness* (1895) by Joseph Conrad. Here, a fictionalised version of Conrad himself, a sailor aboard the yawl *Nellie*, introduces the setting as the crew await the turn of the tide in the Thames Estuary. After several pages describing the scene, the sailor Marlow pipes up: 'And this too has been one of the dark places of the Earth.' The rest of the novel is related almost entirely via Marlow's speech. Thus, Marlow is an intradiegetic narrator, and the Conrad figure extradiegetic. *Both* are homodiegetic.

4.4   Overtness and covertness

To reiterate the discussion in section 4.3 before continuing: it is very useful for the creative writer to envisage their narrator in relation to the diegetic universe, story world or text-world (depending on the extent to which you wish to 'zoom in' on what you are doing): within it or without it, integral to the story or removed from it and so on, and thus be alert to the epistemological status of that narrator. Briefly, this will impact upon the kinds of knowledge he or she will or will not (or should or should not) have access to or possess and, crucially, the kinds of *language* that he or she will or will not have access to. A case in point might be where a homodiegetic narrator who is a child that has an idiolect suspiciously similar to that of a writer in their mid-40s...

An important concept flows from this last point, and relates to the degree to which your narrator is *ostensible* in the narrative (or, indeed the poem). In a homodiegetic narration, the matter is (usually) fairly clear: the narrator will be obvious and his or her act of mediation highly ostensible by virtue of the very fact that he or she exists within the story world or text-world and is its source. The homodiegetic narrator both creates the story world and acts as its centre. However, this need not always be the case. Again, it should be a source of creative energy for you to speculate on the kind of writing that might emerge were this *not* to be the case. Is it possible to envisage a form of homodiegetic narration where the influence of the narrator and his or her perspective on events is negligible; in other words, there is a striving towards some kind of objectivity?

Stylistics and narratology have evolved terms to discuss this concept, and a rigorous set of linguistic indictors to help us examine it.[6] Rimmon-Kenan[7] (1989: 96) refers to this as a narrator's 'degree of perceptibility' (discussed in terms of **overt** forms of narration versus **covert** ones).

You can evaluate a narrator's visibility by looking for certain linguistic features which indicate intrusiveness, or what we should call **overtness**. As you go along the scale from one to six, the narrator becomes

increasingly overt and discernible. At the start, the narrator's presence
is **covert**.

(1) *Description of settings*

> The mountains on the other side of the valley were tall and grey.
> On this side of the valley there were no trees. The house stood at
> the end of a road with no boundaries.

The signs of a narrator's presence and influence here are minimal.
In the terms of Chapter 1, there is little or no evaluative language.
Note that there is still, there must be, a narrator. The scene is still
being mediated for us, in this instance through language. In narrative, there is no escaping some form of mediation. However, it is
reasonable to say that here the narrator is as covert as it is possible
to be (think too of the minimal descriptions of official reports of
incidents by the Police, say: 'The vehicle was proceeding in a west-
erly direction at 17 miles per hour...').

(2) *Identification of characters*

> The woman who lived alone in the house had something of the
> wolf about her. She prowled around the garden, pawing at the
> gate, simultaneously watching the road for someone to come,
> and willing them not to.

Here, the narrator shows prior knowledge (Rimmon-Kenan 1989: 97)
of the character and, importantly, makes the assumption that the narratee (or implied reader) does not have access to this information. This
encapsulates the narrator's role (in any communicative situation): to
communicate to others what they do not already know (ibid.).

(3) *Temporal summaries*

> It had been many years since she had last seen another human
> being. People had come, bringing food, sometimes post, but she
> always hid behind the kitchen blind until they left again.

By their very nature, temporal summaries of this kind draw attention to the presence of a narrator. The narrator summarises events
that have taken place for the benefit of the reader. They indicate
the presence of a narrator because they are evidence of a judgement: the narrator has decided, consciously, what information
needs to be imparted, and in how much detail.

(4) *Definition of characters*

> The woman's thoughts were intangible. Her life had never begun,
> yet sometimes it felt to her like it would never end. Inasmuch as
> she ever contemplated her situation, it was as if it belonged to
> someone else. She was at the same time in complete control of
> her actions, yet helpless to influence their course.

Identification of character gives the reader the narrator's prior
knowledge of the character; definition of character is more abstract,
often involving a generalisation or summary which aims to be
authoritative. As Rimmon-Kenan points out (98), these definitions
tend to be more authoritative when presented by an extradiegetic
narrator rather than an intradiegetic one (e.g. characters will often
make these kinds of statements about other characters).

(5) *Reports of what characters did not think or say*

> If she had had any sense of herself, she would surely have won-
> dered about how she got there, how she came to be alone, and
> why it was she simultaneously embraced her situation and yet
> longed to escape it. But she never thought like this. She simply
> waited behind the windows.

Of course, a narrator who can report on thoughts and speech which
the characters themselves never have or make is highly overt. The
narrator acts as a source of information which is completely independent of the character.

(6) *Commentary – interpretation, judgement, generalisation*

A narrator's commentary will either be on the narration, or on the
story itself (in the terms of Chapter 3, on the discourse or the fabula). *Interpretation* could, for example, take the form of a direct
explanation of a character's actions, words or thoughts.

> Sometimes, at night, she talked to herself, as if this had any
> chance of keeping the wolf at bay.

Judgement implies some kind of moral or ethical perspective on
the character or situation, and is thus connected directly to expressions of ideology:

> It is clear that the woman was guilty of self-absorption, and a
> tendency towards self-pity.

Generalisation moves the narrator's perspective outwards from the 'matter' of the fabula. He or she extracts general, often abstract, truths from the story and comments on them to the reader.

> Perhaps People who live alone are prone to these failings. Perhaps they bring them upon themselves.

There may also be Commentary on the discourse itself rather than the fabula, often, for example, on the problems the narrator is having in adequately representing or mediating that fabula.

> It is very hard, in fact, to capture the essence of this woman, and to get to grips with the depths of her character. She is, at one and the same time, unknowable and yet so recognisable.

This model can be connected to the observations made in Chapter 1 on seeing through language, and to the discussions there of mimesis and diegesis. As we move along the cline from 1 to 6, from covertness to overtness, from subtlety to explicitness, so the orientation and function of the narrative voice moves from mimesis ('showing') towards diegesis ('telling'); in the case of generalisation, highly ostensible telling. Movement back and forth along this cline has expressive potential, of course. You should consider carefully the extent to which you wish your narrator to be overt or covert in terms of the extent that you want the reader to be focussing on the fabula or the discourse. Narrative which spends most of its time at points 4 through 6 will involve a highly overt narrator, whose 'ways of telling' are of as much interest to the reader, if not more, than the fabula being mediated, or the tale being told. The narrator of discourse that situates itself between 1 and 3 will be covert; the narrative will have an air of objectivity and detachment, and the reader's interest will focus predominantly instead on the fabula. It is, of course, absolutely possible to fluctuate back and forth along the cline at various points in your narrative (see John Fowles's novel *The French Lieutenant's Woman* (1969) for an example of a narrator who does just that – to extremes, in fact).

To generalise for a moment (arguably, to advance a position that is in fact untenable; let us call it another thought experiment), consider the following proposition: the narrators of fiction which will be categorised as 'literary' (within the academy, the literary media and so on), the kind of fiction that wins prestigious prizes, will often be located between 4 and 6 on the scale (i.e. it will foreground diegesis). So-called popular fiction tends to narrate at a degree of overtness from 1 to 3. Can you find of exceptions to this generalisation? Of course you can, and if you cannot then you are not looking hard enough. But I think it is an interesting model to measure narrative fiction with, one that can provoke worthwhile debate, and can indicate a certain resurgence of the dominance of diegesis in contemporary fiction (see Lodge 1990, particularly Chapter 1, for more discussion of this idea).

Once you have finished the draft of a story or a chapter from a novel, then, or even the opening of one, or, indeed, a piece of poetry that relies to some or other extent on narration, try applying this model to your work as you re-read and re-write it (you could even highlight instances of overt and covert narration in contrasting colours). The process will often reveal very interesting aspects of your technique which you may have overlooked, and which you can hone to greater effect in sub-sequent rewrites. Once again: remember the importance of leaving space for your reader's imagination to work (we will discuss why this is important in more detail in Chapter 6).

Finally, look at this example (a very short story said to have been written by Ernest Hemingway, which he allegedly occasionally referred to as the best work he ever did):

> For sale: baby shoes, never worn.

Apply the perceptibility model to this example. Where does it come on the scale? I would argue that it proves the need for a new grade on the scale: 0. There is no perceivable narrator here. The discourse is a pres-entation of an advertisement in whatever form (thus, writing presenta-tion; for some reason I imagine it tacked to a noticeboard in the corner of a run-down shop) with no identifiable narrative voice or focaliser. What does it tell you about the way this story works? There is not much discourse here, but an enormous amount of fabula...

4.6 Focalisation

If narrative voice concerns who tells, then the other important aspect of the act of narration is *who sees*. Narratology and stylistics use the term **focalisation**[8] to describe this aspect of narrative. We can define focalisation as the point from which the diegetic universe, or story world or text-world (again, depending on the level of detail into which you wish to go) is perceived at any given moment of the narrative; this may or may not be the same as the perspective of the narrative voice, and may or may not vary over the course of the narrative.

There is a problem to address first, though. A great deal has been written about this topic by stylisticians and narratologists, with the result that there are conflicting terms and theories to sift through.

I have tried here, then, to present a reasonably straightforward distillation of the concept with a view to making it as relevant as possible to creative writers, and will demonstrate the different types of focalisation through example. Because of the variety of narrative styles and forms, as well as the complex stratification of the kinds of 'entities' who populate narratives as well as the different levels of mediation (abstract author, narrator, characters), most narrative texts (and I include poems here) make use of a complex array of dimensions and modes of perspective. It benefits the creative writer to be aware of these, of how they work, and of the ways they can be exploited for expressive effect.

There are three types of focalisation to concern us here, then:

4.6.1   Fixed focalisation

In fixed focalisation, the facts and events of the narrative are presented from a consistent and unvarying perspective (which is often that of the narrator, especially if that narrator is homodiegetic, as in the Carver excerpt above). There is only one **focaliser**, then. The presentation of narrative facts and events is from the constant point of view of a single entity. A very well-known example of a novel written entirely through fixed focalisation is Joyce's *The Portrait of the Artist as a Young Man* (1916) in which the protagonist, a fictionalised version of Joyce himself named Stephen Dedalus, is the focal point of everything that happens, and 'witnesses' everything that happens (even though the narrative voice itself is hereodiegetic, i.e. external to the story world).

4.6.2   Variable focalisation

As you can probably deduce for yourselves, variable focalisation involves the presentation of different episodes of the narrative as seen from the perspective of different focalizers. Virginia Woolf is a master of this kind of technique, and in her novel *To the Lighthouse* (1927) presents the events of the novel, at various points, from the perspective of all of the characters involved. This technique is also fairly common, especially in heterodiegetic narration where the narrator is able to 'access all areas', and inhabit the minds of all of the characters in turn.

4.6.3   Multiple focalisation

This technique is rarer, and involves presenting the same episode again, often repeatedly, but from the perspective of a different focaliser in each repetition. The point here is to demonstrate 'narratively' the ineluctable fact that different people will interpret or perceive the same event in different ways – often in *very* different ways. Modernist writing in particular was characterised by a desire to represent the world of the mind; under the burgeoning influence of Freud and Jung's work on the nature and influence of the unconscious, writers and artists were becoming more and more aware of the importance of subjectivity in determining and characterising world view, and it was important that literature could do justice to this through its narrative methodology (hence also the rise in so-called 'stream-of-consciousness' writing – see Chapter 5 on representing thought). This technique demonstrates the fact that different people tend to perceive or interpret the same event in radically different fashions. See Patrick White's novel *The Solid Mandala* (1966) for an interesting example of multiple focalisation.

4.6.4   Extended example

To illustrate how a writer can manipulate focalisation to great expressive effect, I would like to follow Paul Simpson's lead and use an excellent example from Iain Banks's (1993) novel *The Crow Road* (in Simpson 2004: 27):

> He rested his arms on the top of the wall and looked down the fifty feet or so to the tumbling white waters. Just upstream, the river Loran piled down from the forest in a compactly furious cataract. The spray was a taste. Beneath, the river surged round the piers of the viaduct that carried the railway on towards Lochgilpead and Gallanach.
>
> A grey shape flitted silently across the view, from falls to bridge, then zoomed, turned in the air and swept into the cutting on the far bank of the river, as though it was a soft fragment of the train's steam that had momentarily lost its way and was not hurrying to catch up. He waited a moment, and the owl hooted once, from inside the dark constituency of the forest. He smiled, took a deep breath that tasted of steam and the sweet sharpness of pine resin, and then turned away, and went back to pick up his bags.
>
> (Banks 1993: 33)

A good way to understand how focalisation works is to imagine a film camera. If you were going to film the scene in question as a director, where would you position it? What would the best 'angle' be to capture the scene most effectively, and would you want that angle to be constant or to change? This is a very useful way to picture your scene as you write. From whose perspective are events being viewed? In existing writing (or your own text in draft, say), there will be clear textual clues which should help answer this question; we will examine these shortly. The first point to notice, though, is the way in which this passage illustrates a clear distinction between *who tells* and *who sees*. A detached heterodiegetic narrator tells the story, but it is the particular character who sees what unfolds and, crucially, **the reader is limited to the same perspective**. We call this character (or entity) the **reflector**.

What happens if we rewrite this excerpt as if the narrator were homodiegetic, that is, as if the narrator were the character (called McHoan) himself?

> **I** rested my arms on the top of the wall ... and **I** waited a moment ...
> **I** smiled and took a deep breath ... and went back to pick up **my** bags.

The answer to that question is, as Simpson makes clear, very little (2004: 28). The fact that nothing really changes (apart from a grammatical shift to the first person) shows how strongly McHoan is the focaliser in Bank's original. However, remember that homodiegetic narration is very different from heterodiegetic; in the former, we are closer to the narrator/character in psychological terms and thus lose much of the 'distance' (which can often be exploited ironically) that can be placed between the narrator and a character.

In terms of the particular linguistic features of focalisation: **deictic** language is particularly important here as it situates the narrating voice in a physical context. The reflector of the fiction constitutes a deictic centre, or **origo**, around which objects are positioned relative to their proximity or distance from/to that origo. For example, certain verbs in the extract express movement *towards* the speaking source:

> [A grey shape] zoomed...

On the other hand, movement *away* is signalled when he 'went back' (not *came* back) to pick up his bags. This deictic anchoring at the origo is further signalled by groups of prepositions which indicate spatial locations and relationships (Simpson 2004: 29):

> [Looked] down
> Just upstream
> [Piled] down
> Beneath
> Across the view
> From falls to bridge

> Into the cutting
> On the far bank of the river
> From inside the dark constituency of the forest

Lastly: notice how McHoan's perspective is limited temporarily (or **attenuated**); he cannot see objects on the other side of the river clearly, and Banks represents that fact in the extract using attenuated focalisation:

> A grey shape flitted silently across the view...

McHoan can't make out what it is that flits; however, this is soon resolved: in this case (interestingly) the resolution comes about through something he hears rather than sees ('the owl hooted'). Thus, McHoan has realised that the grey shape was an owl.

The lessons for the creative writer here are manifold: focalisation works by restricting the reader to the perceptions of the focaliser. In other words, it represents mimetically the way the scene would be perceived in real life. We experience the owl flitting across the scene in the same way as the character does: at first, unable to discern it, then realising (thought its hoot) what it is. This is an excellent example of the increased effectiveness of mimesis in comparison to diegesis. A simple textual intervention exercise will demonstrate this. Look what happens if we change 'shape' to 'owl': 'A grey owl flitted silently...' Now, the events are being 'told' to us rather than 'shown'. Note also the use of the definite article ('**the** owl hooted'); what happens if we change 'the' to 'an'? Again, the effect is lost. In short, the deft manipulation of focalisation in this excerpt invites us into the text. We are experiencing the events of the narrative on the same plane as the character. We enter the story world. We experience *empathy*.

4.7   The poetic monologue

I hope that we have demonstrated that both narrative voice and focalisation are integral facets of the act of narrative; discourse that involved neither would be non-narrative. There must always be someone who tells and someone who sees, even if they are the same entity. This aspect of narrativity is by no means the preserve of narrative fiction. As mentioned, we find it widely in media discourse and also, of course, in poetry.

The question of whether *all* poetry also involves narrative voice and focalisation is an interesting one. I suspect that the answer is that it does not. It is possible to conceive of poetic writing that pours itself almost entirely into the concrete, into non-narrative, in a similar manner to Hemingway's tragic six-word short story. This story is pure mimesis because it presents discourse, and thus a world (which the reader imagines in response to the fragment of discourse) without narratorial intervention. Poetry can attempt something similar; look at the work of William Carlos Williams and the Objectivist poets, who tried to expunge any sense of 'subjectivity' from their writing and to focus on *things* rather than abstract ideas ('Say it, no ideas but in things', said Williams famously in his long autobiographical poem *Paterson* (1963)).

Having said all this, the poetic or dramatic monologue form is an excellent example of poetry that makes explicit use of narrative form (see Chapter 3), and also of point of view and focalisation. A fine example of this form can be seen in Carol Ann Duffy's series of linked poems *The World's Wife* (1999). In this collection (or is it rather a single extended narrative poem?) the poet adopts different personas, with accompanying point of view and focalisation features. Look also at Coleridge's 'The Rime of the Ancient Mariner', which we discussed in the previous chapter. Here, we begin with a heterodiegetic narrator (the poet), who hands over to an intradiegetic one (the Mariner) who proceeds to tell the story of the poem (rather like Marlow in *Heart of Darkness*). The Mariner is the focaliser throughout this nested narrative.

'The house of fiction has ... only one or two windows,' then. Perhaps the next-door neighbour, poetry, has managed to install a few more, with a beneficial effect on the way the light shines in.

4.8   Practice

Exercise:

(1) 'Never trust the teller, trust the tale.' (D.H. Lawrence)
     The exercises for this chapter are based on textual intervention. Choose a short extract from a novel or a poem, depending on your interest. It must have a clear homodiegetic narrator, though. I would suggest using either Kazuo Ishiguro's *The Remains of the Day* (1989) or Carol Ann Duffy's poem sequence *The World's Wife* (1999) if you are stuck for ideas. The narrator of *The Remains of the Day*, Stevens, is a notoriously **unreliable narrator**. In this respect

he is typical of homodiegetic narrators, including David Copper-field, Nick Carroway (*The Great Gatsby*) and Holden Caulfield (*The Catcher in the Rye*). Select an appropriate passage from *Remains of the Day* or *The World's Wife* (or your own choice) and analyse focalisation and point of view, highlighting in particular locative expressions (deictic features and adjuncts) and any examples of limited focalisation. Now, re-write a section of the novel of about 500 words or one of the poems from a heterodiegetic perspective.

Consider the following stylistic questions, which should high-light the interrelationships between style and mimetic process.

- What grammatical and syntactical changes are necessitated?
- What is lost (in expressive terms, in terms of world creation, and in terms of the reader's experience of the narrative) and what is gained?
- Is it possible to transform a character idiolect (an individual way of using language) into an exterior narrative voice? What happens in expressive terms when you do this (if you can)?
- Can you carry out this intervention as easily as with Paul Simp-son's chosen extract from Iain Banks above? Why not?

(2) Rewrite *either* the famous 'brown stocking' scene (as discussed by Auerbach 2003) from Virginia Woolf's novel *To the Lighthouse* (1927) from Mr Ramsay's point of view only, either in homodiegetic of heterodiegetic form, *or* Susan Howe's poem 'The Liberties', which makes use of different focalisations and points of view, from one unified perspective. Consider the same questions, with a view to contrasting the expressive potentialities of limited perspective versus 'omniscient' ways of seeing, with reference, again, to how we can explore the tension between mimesis and diegesis.

(3) Apply the same kinds of analysis to a piece of work in progress. Examine a particular key section of the text for its use of point of view and focalisation, and attempt a rewrite of that section which involves significant changes of one or both of these. Then consider the results as per exercise 2.

(4) Write a short story or poem from one of the following prompts:
- A wheelchair-bound woman spends her day behind the same window.
- Three different people witness an assassination in a restaurant from three different locations in the room.
- On the first day of school, a child spots another child that he or she wants to make friends with. Write from both children's perspectives.

- Recall an argument you once had with someone. Write about it from the other person's perspective. The purpose of this exercise is, of course, to practice empathy with perspectives that you find irritating or unacceptable.

  As you will have noticed, each prompt suggests different approaches to point of view and focalisation. Which did you choose, and why? (You could, of course, have aimed to eschew narrative... Again: if so, why? And how?)

(5) Plot out a story, using the advice on structure and story narratology in Chapter 3 to help you. If you can, use the structure you plotted out in response to exercise 4 in that chapter. Write the opening of this story from three different points of view. This could be first-person, second-person, third-person, or from the point of view of the protagonist, then another character, then an omniscient author... or any other points of view that you can envisage. Be imaginative. Which one is most effective? Why? Continue the story.

5 Writing Voices: Presenting Speech and Thought

5.1 Overview

In Chapter 4, we drew a distinction between the entity 'who tells' and the entity 'who sees', labelling the former as the narrator and the latter as the focaliser (they may or may not be one and the same). We also discussed the separation between the agencies of author and narrator, and the ways in which the space between them and the tension which arises within that space can be exploited for creative effect. This chapter will build on those observations by focussing on the next link in the chain of communication between creative writer and reader: the relationship between narrative voice(s) and character voice(s). The narrator, 'the one who tells', will, more often than not, be called upon to represent these voices, and can do so with varying degrees of mediation; that is, with more of the character's 'real' voice (as it is heard in the text-world), or *less* of it, and, correspondingly, *more* of the narrator's voice. To reiterate: the creative writer can exploit the space and tension between character voices and narrative voices to great creative effect. So, a further question arises which we should consider: who *speaks*, rather than *tells*?[1]

I intend the verb *speak* to apply in the broadest possible form here, referring to any utterance, or, more broadly, any part of the text in which the character *speaks aloud* or *'speaks' internally* as thought (although the relationship between actual words on the page and thoughts inside the mind is a complex and troubling one, as we shall see). Stylistics has established a detailed taxonomy (see Short 1996; Leech and Short 2007; Toolan 1998, 2001; Short 2007) for distinguishing in linguistic terms between the different strategies which writers have available to them to present narrator and character voices, as well as the blending of the two. Like so many of the insights into textual mechanics gained from stylistics, these strategies can also be seen at work in everyday language, not just literary language.

Imagine you are telling an anecdote to a group of friends about an encounter you had had the previous day. Let us say that your anecdote tells of an occasion when you found yourself gaining unwanted attention from a member of the opposite sex, perhaps in a pub or café. You would, almost automatically, use various linguistic strategies in order to make your story, your *narrative*, more vital, more engaging, more alive – and all of these would make it more *mediated*, more impregnated with the perspective of its narrator.[2] You were sitting at the bar on a stool, enjoying a drink, when this unappreciated intervention in your day occurred. The stranger complimented you on your haircut. You have various (in fact, very many) options available to you for conveying your particular reaction 'in the text-world' to this compliment to your assembled listeners.

(1) I told him to go away and carried on sipping my drink.
(2) I wanted him to go away, and I carried on sipping my drink.
(3) I ignored him and carried on sipping my drink.
(4) I didn't say anything but I was thinking 'Oh my god!'
(5) I said, 'Thank you. Now go away, please.'
(6) 'Thank you. Now go away, please.'
(7) I waved my hands in a 'go away' gesture.

It seems to me that all of these reactions are possible, and credible, but range in intent and effect from the first two, which are the most mediated (or *told*), and summarising what you said or what you thought, to the last, which is the most enacted (or *shown*). The first one contains the narrator's rendition of what you said. The second one contains no direct discourse at all, but *does* contain a simple summary of what you were thinking ('I wanted him to go away'). The third is descriptive of your actions. The fourth contains a direct presentation of your thought, including its 'contents' (bearing in mind the previously mentioned complexities involved in presenting thought as language). The fifth one contains direct speech, but also a brief intervention by the narrator to indicate who is speaking. In the sixth example, this interjection has disappeared and we are left only with the content of the utterance itself. Finally, in example 7, there is only gesture.

This basic but essential dichotomy – between *telling* and *showing* – lies also at the heart of this chapter, building on the distinction set out in the introductory section of the book: between **mimesis** and **diegesis**, or, if you prefer, levels of mediation. In the first example, the narrative function is in the ascendency; it is predominantly diegetic. We the listeners 'hear' only the words of the narrator, and a summary of what was uttered aloud. In the last, the teller of the tale has become a character in that tale; the discourse is mimetic in orientation, aiming at a precise representation of what actually happened. Notice also the way in which thought is presented in example 4. There is no essential difference in formal terms between this presentation of thought and the example of speech presentation in 5 except that 'I was thinking' has been replaced by 'I said'.

Which of the various strategies is most appropriate to mediating the particular situation? This is a technical question that the creative writer asks (unconsciously or otherwise[3]), then answers, in the writing of each sentence which contains a character's voice – to whatever degree – and it is, crucially, an expressive one. To provide you with the necessary appreciation of the topic to explore the many answers to that question for yourselves, and to appreciate the expressive capital which can be gained from artful manipulation of these strategies is, the central purpose of this chapter.

5.2 Taxonomy

We can represent the different forms of speech and thought presentation available to the writer diagrammatically, and stylistics has evolved a useful taxonomy with which to distinguish between them.[4] I am using the term 'discourse' in this taxonomy to apply to both speech and thought; for example, IS stands for Indirect Speech, IT for Indirect Thought. We will discuss the differences between the presentation of the two in the second half of the chapter.

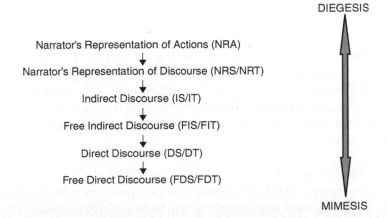

Let us now examine these categories in a little more detail, look at some examples, and discuss the implications of these methods for the practising writer. We will not be dealing with these in the order presented in the diagram, for reasons that will become apparent later. Firstly, we will look at NRA[5] (as, most of the time, this form has little to do with representing the character's own discourse). Secondly, we will explore speech presentation, and then thought presentation. Following that, we will move to the middle of the cline to examine in detail the intriguing method which sits at the mid-point between mimesis and diegesis: free indirect discourse (often combining free indirect speech and free indirect thought).

Notice throughout how different methods of representing character discourse shade into one another along the cline between mimesis and diegesis. We start with the Narrator's Representation of Action (or Pure Narration), purely diegetic, and focussed on *telling* the reader what is happening in the text-world – a process of stage management, as it were. Gradually, as we move closer to the mimetic end of the scale, the character's discourse begins to leech, at first almost imperceptibly, then explicitly, into the discourse of the narrator, as a drop of ink diffuses into water. At the most mimetic end of the scale, Free Direct Speech, we read as though privy to exactly what the character says in the text-world without any interference on the part of the narrator. As we move from there up the scale towards NRA (see section 5.3), we face a blend of the voices of character and narrator; the character's discourse becomes increasingly more mediated. When we finally reach NRA, the character's voice has disappeared, and the narrator is in full command.

5.3   Narrator's Representation of Action (NRA), or pure narration

This category is located firmly at the diegetic end of the cline, and is used to refer to sentences which are concerned with physical description. Character discourse is not represented at all.[6] The kinds of text-world components which would be represented through NRA are listed below (see Short 1997: 296), with examples from Raymond Carver's short story 'Errand' (1988):

(1) *Character action*
     The young man entered the room carrying a silver ice bucket with the champagne in it and a silver tray with three cut-crystal glasses. (118)

(2) *Events (caused by inanimate agents who are not usually characters)*
It was at this moment that the cork popped out of the champagne bottle; foam spilled down onto the table. (120)

(3) *Descriptions of states*
It was three o'clock in the morning and still sultry in the room. (119)

(4) *Character perceptions of 1–3*
... suddenly, the young man saw the door open. (122)

As we saw in Chapter 4, NRA is perceived by the reader (conventionally) as transparent, that is, like a clear window through which we view the contents of the text-world. The glass can be (almost) clear, or it can be frosted. In other words, be mindful of the ways in which the 'transparency' of the narrative voice can be manipulated by the writer for creative effect, from the (arguably) objective, perspicuous narrative voices of Hemingway and Carver to the playful subjectivity of Joyce and Sterne. We will return to this topic briefly in section 5.5.

5.4 Representing speech

5.4.1 Real speech and fictional speech?

Another question which sits at the heart of this chapter could be phrased as follows: can written language represent 'authentic' speech? This is in issue that should exercise the creative writer greatly, and I would suggest that careful consideration of it can lead towards a better command of dialogue, and a better ear for the rhythms and cadences of discourse as represented in narrative fiction. Mick Short describes the situation as follows:

> [In fictional speech] the events being described as part of the mock reality are themselves linguistic, and so language is used to simulate, rather than simply to report, what is going on in the fictional world.
> (Short 1997: 128–9)

The word *simulate* is crucial here. Your writing should aim to *simulate* the speech (and, as we shall see, the thought) of your characters with what Short calls 'a special kind of authenticity' (129), not attempt to represent it with absolutely fidelity – were such a thing even possible. Some writers have strained towards this fidelity, though, with good results. Look at the way David Mamet attempts to represent what linguists call **normal non-fluency** in the script of *Oleanna* (1993), admittedly a type of text destined for oral performance as opposed to the 'silent performance' typical of narrative fiction, but nevertheless an example of an attempt to render spoken discourse faithfully in textual form:

> CAROL: I'm just, I'm just trying to …
> JOHN: … no, it will not do.
> CAROL: … what? What will …?
> JOHN: No. I see, I see what you, it … (*He gestures to the papers.*) but your work …
> CAROL: I'm just: I sit in class I … (*She holds up her notebook.*) I take notes …
> JOHN (*simultaneously with* 'notes'): Yes. I understand. What I am trying to *Tell* you is that some, some basic …
> CAROL: … I …
>
> (Mamet, 1993: 5–6)

Real spoken language includes many such features which interrupt the normal fluency of speech:

- *false starts* (unnecessary repletion and reformulation of previous utterances in an ungrammatical manner); e.g. 'I'm just, I'm just trying to' and 'No, I see, I see what you';
- *syntactical anomalies* (sentence formulation that would be deemed unacceptable in written language); e.g. 'I'm just: I sit in class I';
- *interruptions* (numerous in the example above, and notated by ellipses);
- *hesitation pauses and fillers* such as 'um', 'ah' (even Mamet shies away from these, leaving the actors to inject them during performance).

All of these features would be present in most everyday conversations (listen carefully next time you are privy to one). For the creative writer, it would be a reasonably simple task to capture a real conversation using some sort of recording device, and then transcribe the language using particular types of notation (including phonetic spellings, or even symbols), and markers for stress, intonation and so on. It should even be possible, as Mamet has done, to devise a notation that could indicate where interruptions take place, where characters talk over one another and so on (or simply to write: Charles interrupted her, saying '…'). Of course, representing discourse in this way is eminently feasible in drama, as Mamet has demonstrated, but is a different matter in narrative fiction. Indeed, reading Mamet's highly naturalistic dialogue is hard work, and, as you would expect, the voices only really come alive in performance. So, should the writer be aiming for greater and greater authenticity in his or her presentations of speech (and thought) – in other words, reaching towards pure mimesis? Is that particular game worth the candle? Rimmon-Kenan has argued that it is not, in accordance with the premise underlying the overall approach of this book:[7]

> No text of narrative fiction can show or imitate the action it conveys, since all texts are made of language, and language signifies without imitating. Language can only imitate language, which is why the representation of speech comes closest to pure mimesis, but even here ... there is a narrator who 'quotes' the characters' speech, thus reducing the directness of 'showing'. All that a narrative can do is create an illusion, an effect, a semblance of mimesis, but it does so through diegesis.
>
> (Rimmon-Kenan 1989: 108)

Some degree of mediation is inevitable, then (indeed, as we have seen, desirable, otherwise what is the text's status: verbal art or pure documentary?), and it is the writer's job to exploit this with the greatest possible expressive effect. Literary mimesis, as the term is applied throughout this book (see note 7), relies for its success upon the establishment of a convention between writer and reader, agreeing upon the essential artifice of the illusion. The overly fastidious pursuit of 'authentic' speech (and thought) may lead the writer up a blind alley.[8]

5.4.2   Accents, dialects, idiolects

What about when a writer wishes to represent accents and dialects, then? Dialects can be defined as varieties of language which are linguistically marked off from other varieties and aligned with various sections of society in accordance with geographical location, class and so on. According to Leech and Short (2007: 134), 'a dialect is thus the particular set of linguistic features which a defined subset of the speech community shares'[9]. Crystal (1991: 102) defines it as follows:

> A regionally or socially distinctive variety of language, identified by a particular set of words and grammatical structures. Spoken

dialects are usually also associated with a distinctive pronunciation, or accent. Any language with a reasonably large number of speakers will develop dialects, especially if there are geographical barriers separating groups of people from each other, or if there are divisions of social class.

Having concluded already that pure mimesis in fictional discourse is a chimerical goal, that is, that all fictional representations of discourse, no matter how 'realistic' they aspire to be, are mediated simulations, and that the thoughtful writer should take account of this fact, how does a writer best represent these types of speech, particularly those aspects of it such as the 'distinctive pronunciation' which are non-standard and, usually, not represented orthographically? More interestingly, should she or he even try? Much has been written elsewhere on this subject,[10] but it is worth pausing briefly to consider some of the issues. See, for instance, the following example of what Leech and Short (2007: 135) term *eye-dialect*, where the impression of dialectical speech is given by using non-standard, phonetic orthography from James Kelman's (1995) short story 'Nice to be nice' (which we discussed briefly in chapter 2):

> Ay kin they no, says Moira. The coarpiration kin dae whit they like Stan. (34)

And

> Right Stan it's aw right, he says, A'll see ye the morra – dont worry aboot it. (35)

Kelman uses a combination of phonetic orthography (*coarpiration* for *corporation, dae* for *do*), dialect words (*ay* and *kin*, or *aye* for 'yes' and *ken* for 'know'), and non-standard punctuation (a lack of quotation marks, no apostrophe in *dont*) to represent Glaswegian speech textually. There are ideological as well as artistic reasons for this,[11] and these will be discussed briefly below. Perhaps more famously, Irvine Welsh tries a similar device in his novel *Trainspotting* (1994).

Consider also the following piece of dialogue from Alan Sillitoe's *Saturday Night, Sunday Morning* (1958):

> 'I said I was as good as anybody else in the world, din't I?' Arthur demanded. 'And I mean it. Do you think if I won the football pools I'd gi' yo' a penny on it? Or gi' anybody else owt? Not likely. I'd keep it all mysen, except for seeing my family right. I'd buy 'em a house and set 'em up for

life, but anybody else could whistle for it. I've 'eard that blokes as win football pools get thousands o' beggin' letters, but yer know what I'd do if I got 'em? I'll tell yer what I'd do: I'd mek a bonfire on 'em. ...'

(Sillitoe 1958: 28)

Here, the representation is less linguistically deviant, but the same ideological assertion is evident: that dialects[12] have the right to appear textually in narrative fiction, and that standard English is not the only language suitable for literature.[13] In both cases, though, it could be argued that a person unfamiliar with the 'target' dialects here (Glasgow or Midlands English) might well have problems in reconstructing the sound of the voice from these representations; this problem is compounded by the fact that English is a notoriously *un*phonetic language. The ambition to represent authentic kinds of speech on the page is a fascinating artistic project, but can lead to banality, unintelligibility and even, arguably, a degree of condescension if taken too far, leading to stereotypical representations of character based simply on whether or not they drop their aitches. The character becomes defined by their 'non-standard' voice (of course, it needs to be emphasised that the very notion of a 'standard' language can be contentious), rather than by their deeper ipseity (or, if you like, 'true self').

Another important, and complex, issue arising from this might be phrased as follows: there is a distancing effect which is created by the use of non-standard, deviant forms of language. By their very nature, these deviant forms imply a norm, a binary opposite, which is standard English, and/or the author's own standard language. This implication of difference can also (too often) imply superiority, even chauvinism. Furthermore, it could be argued that highly deviant forms of spelling detract from the reader's experience by drawing undue attention to themselves; to return to the metaphor used in section 5.3, the reader is looking *at* the window rather than through it into the text-world (granted, this may sometimes be artistically desirable, but surely not often). This is not to say that writers such as Kelman and Sillitoe do not have an admirable ear for the rhythms, cadences and inflections of demotic voices – they do. Also, as already mentioned: by using the dialect in heterodiegetic narration (as the narrative voice itself, and not just imprisoned within inverted commas) they make a crucial ideological point through narrative method: that these authentic voices have as much right to be the principal medium of fictional narration as so-called standard English. However, at the risk of glossing over the issue, it should be sufficient for the purposes of this book to propose as follows: that the creative writer interested in reproducing dialect and other forms of the vernacular in their narrative fiction would do well to keep dialect markers in direct discourse to a flavouring minimum, unless they are very confident of their technique.

5.4.3   Direct Speech and Free Direct Speech (DS/FDS)

We will jump now to the other end of the cline presented in section 5.3: from the 'pure' diegesis of NRA to the 'pure' mimesis (as far, as we have seen, as such as such a thing is possible). In direct speech, characters speak directly for themselves (or, to be strictly correct, are represented as doing so), and the mode of presentation is, arguably, as close to 'pure' mimesis as is possible in narrative fiction. The words on the page correspond more or less directly to the actual words spoken by the character in the world of the fiction. There is little or no intervention on the part of the narrator.

> 'Thank you,' she said. 'Now go away, please.'

Only two words here belong to the narrator (*she said*) while the rest issue directly from the character. Note also the punctuation: inverted commas (or quotation marks), double or single, with a comma before the last quotation mark in the first clause, heralding the return to diegetic NRA, and a full stop before the last quotation mark in the second. It is possible, of course, to remove even this minimal intervention:

> 'Thank you. Now go away, please.'

This is **Free Direct Speech (FDS)**. FDS, as you can see from the diagram in section 5.2, is the most mimetic of all the discourse presentation strategies (bearing in mind Rimon-Kennan's objections as discussed previously), free of any diegetic NRA. It centres completely on processes of *showing* rather than *telling*. Notice how Dickens makes use of it in the following extract from *Nicholas Nickleby*:

> 'This is the first class in English spelling and philosophy, Nickleby. We'll get up a Latin one, and hand that over to you. Now, then, where's the first boy?'
> 'Please, sir, he's cleaning the back parlour window,' said the temporary head of the philosophical class.
> 'So he is, to be sure. We go upon the practical mode of teaching, Nickleby; the regular education system. C-L-E-A-N, clean, verb active, to make bright to scour. W-I-N, win, D-E-R, winder, a

casement. When the boys knows this out of book, he goes and does it. Where's the second boy?'

'Please, sir, he's weeding the garden.'

'To be sure. So he is. B-O-T, bot, T-I-N, bottin, N-E-Y, bottiney, noun substantive, a knowledge of plants. When he has learned that bottiney means a knowledge of plants, he goes out and knows 'em. That's our method, Nickleby. Third boy, what's a horse?'

'A beast, sir.'

'So it is. Ain't it, Nickleby?'

'I believe there is no doubt of that, sir.'

'Of course there ain't. A horse is a quadruped, and quadruped's Latin for beast. As you're perfect in that, boy, go and look after *my* horse, and rub him down well, or I'll rub you down.'

There is little or no narrative comment or interpretation (only to mark the speech of the boy in turn 2). The ignorance of Squeers the Headmaster is put across to the reader without any need for explanation on the part of the narrator, and the reader is like a witness to the scene, left – to an extent – to make their own judgements. Notice also the subtle renderings of Squeers's individual habit of speech (his idiolect) and his dialect[14] and the ways in which it contrasts with the formal standard English' of Nicholas Nickleby himself. It is clear who is speaking at any given moment (regardless of the ordering of the conversational turns), and so there is no need for continual diegetic intervention. The dialogue flows. As we saw in Chapter 3, allowing a text world to be set up in this way (relying on the reader's existing schema and resisting the temptation to spell things out in too much detail) can lead to a richer and more satisfying reading experience.

The same effect is discernible in the following extract from 'The Greening of Mrs Donaldson' (2010) by Alan Bennett, which contains similar ironic, humorous undertones:

'I gather you're my wife,' said the man in the waiting room. 'I don't think I've had the pleasure. Might one know your name?'

Middle-aged and scrawny he was bare-legged and underneath his shortie dressing-gown Mrs Donaldson thought he might be bare altogether.

'Donaldson.'

'Right. Mine's Terry. I've been away.'

He put out his hand and as she shook it briefly the dressing-gown fell open to reveal a pair of tangerine Y-fronts with, tucked into the waistband, a mobile phone.

'Trouble in the back passage,' he said cheerfully.

'No,' said Mrs Donaldson. 'I don't think so.'

'Mine not yours, dear,' said Terry. 'You're just my wife.'

'I was given to understand,' said Mrs Donaldson, 'that it was your waterworks.'

'No fear.' Terry hitched up his Y-fronts. 'No way.'

'Frequency,' said Mrs Donaldson. 'Waking up at night.'

'Absolutely not. I go before I come to bed and then first thing in a morning. Well, you know that,' and he sniggered. 'You're my wife.'

(Bennett 2010: 9)

Once the characters are established (notice, through direct speech, not through narration; through mimetic discourse rather than diegetic), the narrator withdraws. NRA gives way to direct speech, with only a single adjective, *cheerfully*, to lend colour to the scene. We as readers learn a great deal through this dialogue, and our minds at the same time fill with questions. Why is this man in hospital? Why doesn't he recognise his wife? Why doesn't he know the history of his own condition? ('I've been away' offers a big clue, of course). Why does she introduce herself with a surname, and speak and act so formally? Why doesn't she show any sort of affection? There is a lot for the creative writer to learn from Bennett's technique about how direct speech can be used to drive the narrative along as well as do a great deal of expositional work without the need for overt diegetic intervention on the part of the narrator. Notice also, as with the extract from Dickens, the way in which Mrs Donaldson's more formal idiolect contrasts with the more informal register of Terry, making their conversational turns easy to distinguish from one another.

In the final example, from Pat Barker's *Regeneration* (1991), a similar 'terseness' of narrative voice is used, with direct speech doing most of the expressive work. This time, a tremendous amount of emotion and tension lies, just buried, beneath the characters' speech.

'Your father's dead too, isn't he? How old were you when he died?'

'Eight. But I hadn't seen much of him for some time before that. He left home when I was five.'

'Do you remember him?'

'A bit. I remember I used to like being kissed by him because his moustache tickled. My brothers went to the funeral. I didn't – apparently I was too upset. Probably just as well, because they came back terrified. It was a Jewish funeral, you see, and they couldn't understand what was going on. My elder brother said it was two old men in funny hats walking up and down saying jabber-jabber-jabber.'

'You must've felt you'd lost him twice.'

'Yes. We did lose him twice.'

Rivers gazed out of the window. 'What difference would it have made, do you think, if your father had lived?'

A long silence. 'Better education.'

'But you went to Marlborough?'

'Yes, but I was a year behind everybody else. Mother had this theory we were delicate and our brains shouldn't be taxed. I don't think I ever really caught up. I left Cambridge without taking my degree.'

'And then?'

Sassoon shook his head. 'Nothing much. Hunting, cricket. Writing poems. Not very good poems.'

'Didn't you find it all... rather unsatisfying?'

'Yes, but I couldn't seem to see a way out. It was like being three different people, and they all wanted to go different ways.' A slight smile. 'The result was I went nowhere.'

Rivers waited.

'I mean, there was the riding, hunting, cricketing me, and then there was the ... the other side ... that was interested in poetry and music, and things like that. And I didn't seem able to ...' He laced his fingers. 'Knot them together.'

'And the third?'

'I'm sorry?'

'You said three.'

'Did I? I meant two.'

'Ah. And then the war. You joined up on the first day?'

'Yes. In the ranks. I couldn't wait to get in.'

'Your superior officers wrote glowing reports for the Board. Did you know that?'

A flush of pleasure. 'I think the army's probably the only place I've ever really belonged.'

'And you've cut yourself off from it.'

'Yes, because...'

'I'm not interested in the reasons at the moment. I'm more interested in the result. The effect on you.'

'Isolation, I suppose. I can't talk to anybody.'

'You talk to me. Or at least, I think you do.'

'You don't say stupid things.'

Rivers turned his head away. 'I'm pleased about that.'

(Barker 1991: 35–6)

Note in particular how the narrator at times interrupts the FDS turns with NRA descriptions of small gestures ('He laced his fingers together', 'Rivers turned his head away'), in the first case reinforcing the content of the character's utterances, while in the second beautifully expressing Rivers's embarrassment and quiet pleasure at Sassoon's comment. This highly controlled blend of FDS and NRA services to reinforce the tension (erotic? Something else?) between the two men. It is also worth noting how the FDS can obfuscate as well as reveal; Sassoon says that he is going to describe how it was to feel like three different people. He goes on to list only two, an omission which Rivers, as a psychologist, is of course quick to pick up on. Sassoon says that he had only in fact intended to talk about two. Why the omission? It seems unlikely that Sassoon has simply forgotten the third. The third 'person' is someone he would rather not talk about, surely. Again, all of this expositional information, essential in the process of building our knowledge of the characters, is implicit, unstated and inferred. It is not necessary for the narrator to struggle through lengthy descriptions of which character felt what and why; it is all there (or not) in the dialogue.

Hemingway formulated what has become known as the 'Iceberg Principle of Prose' (in his non-fiction work *Death in the Afternoon*, 1932), which in part helps, I think, to account for the effectiveness of Barker's technique here;

> If a writer of prose knows enough about what he is writing about he may omit things that he knows and the reader, if the writer is writing truly enough, will have a feeling of those things as strongly as though the writer had stated them.
>
> (Hemingway 1932: 12–13)

Eight-tenths of an iceberg is beneath the surface of the sea, just as eight-tenths of the emotional force of a piece of prose will hide beneath its discourse. Applying this notion to the presentation of speech in these three examples, we might summarise the main point as follows: it is almost always better to allow the reader as much imaginative space as follows. Avoid the temptation to continually use DS as opposed to FDS (imagine the example from Barker above re-written with 'said Rivers' and 'said Sassoon' after each conversational turn), and, especially, avoid using verbs such as 'shouted', 'ejected' or 'murmured' and modifiers such as 'loudly', 'brusquely' and 'seductively'. These, I would argue, are almost always surplus to requirements if the FDS *itself* suggests or shows the way in which the utterance is being made in the text-world. To return to the exchange mentioned above:

> 'And the third?'
> 'I'm sorry?'

'You said three.'
'Did I? I meant two.'

There is no need here for the narrator to interject with something like 'Sassoon was clearly confused' or 'Sassoon was thinking aloud, unsure of his ground' or 'Sassoon was hiding something, that much was obvious'. It's all there in the FDS, and implied much more effectively as a result. This assertion chimes precisely with the central theme of this book: aim towards what we have defined as mimesis rather than diegesis wherever possible, towards text-worlds which build without overt and unnecessary narratorial intervention. To be glib for a moment, let the speech do the talking...

When your narrator does take it upon him or herself to intervene, remember, too, the potential of understated NRA in conveying subtle emotion. Of course, it goes without saying (to be unintentionally glib once again) that we do not always communicate with words. Language and communication are so often gestural rather than purely rooted in speech. Coming back once again to the simple but exquisite way in which the narrator conveys Rivers's pleasure and embarrassment at Sassoon's compliment ('Rivers turned his head away'), and the way in which Sassoon uses a subtle hand gesture (the lacing together of his fingers) to emphasise the point he is struggling to make: in both cases, the reader empathises with the discomfort, frustration and uncertainty. The characters shake their heads, look out of the window, wait, smile. Barker achieves here a very effective marrying of NRA and DS/DFS, using the former only to narrate essential character action – action which enhances the content of the dialogue – and to inject a variation of pace.

5.4.4   Indirect Speech (IS)

There is one essential difference between DS and IS: DS uses (as far as possible) the exact words which were spoken in the text-world by the person concerned, whereas IS reports these words second-hand, expressed in the words of the narrator. There is, in essence, a greater degree of mediation, and, accordingly, IS is positioned closer to the diegetic end of our cline in section 5.2. The easiest way to understand how IS is constructed is to take an example of DS and convert it into IS, observing what happens during the process.

'I'll come here tomorrow,' she promised.

The above is a standard example of DS, containing the exact words spoken and representing the character's manner of speech. (Notice also that I've broken one of the 'rules' mentioned in section 5.4.3 by using 'promised' instead of 'said'; this, as will be seen, is for purposes of exemplification, and hence forgivable...).

Converting DS into IS requires a series of grammatical transformations as follows (see Short 1997: 304, and Simpson 2004: 31):

> She promised that she would be there the next day.

(1) The punctuation marks associated with DS and IS (e.g. quotation marks and associated commas) are removed: I'll come here tomorrow, she promised.[15]

(2) The reported clause (I'll come here tomorrow) becomes subordinated to the reporting clause (she promised). This subordination is made clear by the conjunction, *that*.

(3) In IS, it is perfectly acceptable to place the reporting clause before the reported clause (She promised that she would be there tomorrow). In DS, the reverse is generally true (She promised, 'I'll be there tomorrow' would be unusual).

(4) Pronouns are shifted so that first- and second-person pronouns ('I', 'you', 'we') become third-person ('he', 'she', 'they' or 'it').

(5) Deictic words are shifted from their proximal form ('here') to their distal form ('there').

(6) Tenses shift one step 'backwards' in time; that is, if the principal tense of the sentence is present simple ('come'), the IS version will use past simple ('came'). In the same way, a modal verb such as 'will' becomes 'would'. If the primary tense were already in the past simple, it would become past perfect (i.e. 'came' to 'had come').

(7) Deictic expressions of time must also be attended to. 'Tomorrow' may well be tomorrow in terms of the speaker's/text's deictic centre or origo (see Chapter 4), but when the discourse shifts from the character's sphere of influence (i.e. from the text-world which the speaking character inhabits) to that of the narrator, 'tomorrow' is no longer the same tomorrow... It is changed in this example to 'the next day'.

All this should demonstrate that IS is more mediated than DS, and two steps closer to diegesis. It is a good tactic to vary the use of DS and IS, especially when – as is sometimes the case – it is the **content** of the character's utterance which will be of interest to the reader, rather than its specific **form** (i.e. the particular pattern of language that is used).[16] Notice the patterns of speech presentation which Joyce uses in this extract from the short story 'The Dead' (in *Dubliners*):

> – Miss Kate, here's Mrs Conroy.[17]
> Kate and Julia came toddling down the dark stairs at once. Both of them kissed Gabriel's wife, said that she must be perished alive and asked was Gabriel with her.
> – Here I am as right as the mail, Aunt Kate! Go on up. I'll follow, called out Gabriel from the dark. (177)

FDS is followed by NRA, then IS, and finally DS. This patterning of different speech presentation strategies lends the narrative a pleasing texture by virtue of variation.

IS is also an economical device, and a method by which the writer can keep control of narrative pace. Compare the DS of:

> 'Oh, to tell you the truth, I'm sick of my own country, sick of it!'

With the briefer, more succinct

> He said that he was sick of his own country. [IS]

In IS the colloquial features and emotional force of the actual speech are lost – but the discourse is more economical, more terse, and might be more effective as a result for the particular job in hand. Once again, the decision about which form to use depends to a large extent on context; in short: fitness for purpose. IS provides variation, as we have seen, but can also be used to increase tension by leaving out certain details relating to the exact form of the utterance. These details can be irrelevant, or they can be omitted to inject suspense. By virtue of the fact that it is intrinsically more *mediated* than DS, IS also allows an ironic distance between narrator and character to evidence itself in which intrinsic commentary can be made. An exercise at the end of the chapter will explore this concept in more detail.

5.5   Representing thought

5.5.1   Real thought and fictional thought?

In section 5.4 we discussed the fact that fictionalised speech is ineluctably a simulation or representation, and that it will benefit the writer to bear this fact in mind. The same stricture can be applied – indeed, much more strongly – to attempts to render consciousness in fiction; the more and more internalised a voice becomes (or the closer and closer the creative writer attempts to get towards a 'true' representation of consciousness), so its status as composition, as an attempt to *communicate* something, or as an essentially mediated work of narrative fiction, becomes doubtful. The question arises: 'What *is* this text's intended status?' Perhaps we can assume that a record of external (or internal, if such a thing were ever possible) reality is facile in terms of the act of creative writing: it is not creative as such (there is, supposedly, no mediation), and therefore anti-fiction and anti-artistic. Once again, as we have seen: the process of mediation is integral to the text's status as narrative art.

When it comes to representing thought in narrative discourse, the problems are, arguably, even more acute than when attempting to represent speech. Despite this, the categories proposed by stylistics for representing speech and thought (see section 5.2) are formally similar:

Direct speech	'I think she might like me,' he said.
Direct thought	'I think she might like me,' he thought.
Indirect speech	He said that she might like him.
Indirect thought	He thought that she might like him.

However, they are different conceptually. Speech can, quite literally, be overheard, whereas thought (as far as we know) cannot. For the creative writer to attempt to represent 'real' thought, with its blend of words, images and the even murkier machinations of the subconscious, is a completely different aspiration than to represent the spoken word in all its raw glory (as Mamet tries to do). As we move through the world, surely, we will often be thinking coherently in words, but just as often will not, thinking instead in terms of image, sensation, memory, in ways that are (arguably) not articulable through the medium of language. How should a writer represent all this, and, just as we saw with 'authentic' patterns of speech, including normal non-fluency, should they even aspire to? It is tempting to conclude once again that the ambition is chimerical, as writers who have taken techniques such as the so-called stream of consciousness to their limits have found out. This example from the final chapter of James Joyce's *Ulysses* is a case in point:

> I wish hed sleep in some bed by himself with his cold feet on me give us room even to let a fart God or do the least things better yes hold him like that a bit on my side piano quietly sweeeee theres that train far away pianissimo eeee one more tsong

that was a relief wherever you be let your wind go free who knows
if that pork chop I took with my cup of tea after was quite good with
the heat I couldnt smell anything off it

(Joyce 1986: 628)

Joyce's approach removes all punctuation, including the apostrophes
from *hed* and *theres*, and all commas and full stops between sentences
and clauses, and phonetically represents certain utterances: *sweeeee* and
tsong, for example. All formal devices of cohesion (attributes that link different parts of a text together) are also absent, and the discourse meanders
along like the stream which it is attempting to mimic. Again, the reader
may well have difficulty engaging with writing of this kind, just as with the
more extreme examples of eye-dialect in section 5.4.2.

Presentations of thought, then, like presentations of speech, will
always be a simulation – but even more so than is the case for representing speech. Once again, the same rule of thumb applies: it is the
task of the writer to find the best linguistic form for this simulation, and
that which is most appropriate to character and context, but (unless
very confident of the approach) to shy away from techniques which are
overly alienating to the reader.

5.5.2   Direct Thought (DT) and Free Direct Thought (FDT)

As we have seen, in formal terms these two categories of discourse
presentation are similar to those for speech, and thus relatively simple
to explain and illustrate. DT includes the reporting clause:

Please go away and leave me alone, she thought.[18]

Whereas FDT contains only the words 'thought':

Please go away and leave me alone.

However, the situation is more complicated than that, and different
approaches to the task of representing a character's interior discourse are
available to the writer. As discussed in section 5.5.1, writers have evolved
various strategies for the presentation of thought; literary criticism has
tended to refer to the most mimetic (in intent, at least) of these either as
'stream of consciousness' or 'internal monologue', often using the terms
interchangeably. Stylistics, in general terms, tends to elide these two
different forms into one: direct thought (with stream of consciousness
writing sometimes also manifesting itself as free direct thought, one of
the most common forms of thought representation – see section 5.4.7[19]).
However, we will try to distinguish between the two terms below.

The term 'stream of consciousness' was originally used by William James (brother of novelist Henry) in *The Principles of Psychology* (1890), and was initially applied by literary critics to the work of French writers such as Edouard Dujardin and Paul Bourget, and later to that of Virginia Woolf, Dorothy Richardson and James Joyce. Laurence E. Bowling defines the technique as follows:

> The stream of consciousness technique may be defined as that narrative method by which the author attempts to give *a direct quotation of the mind* – not merely of the language area but of the whole consciousness. ... The only criterion is that it introduce us directly into the interior life of the character, without any intervention by way of comment or explanation on the part of the author.
>
> (quoted in Steinberg 1958: 248, emphasis in the original)

Linguistically, as we saw in section 5.5.1, it is common to find elliptical, deviant sentence structures with grammatical words removed, and a lack of cohesion overall, especially, in pragmatic terms, when it comes to the Gricean Maxims of Quantity and Manner (Grice 1975; Short 1997: 317). Look at the following example from William Faulkner's *The Sound and the Fury* (1989):

> *What did you let him for kiss kiss*
> *I didn't let him I made him watching me getting mad What do you think of that? Red Print of my hand coming up through her face like turning a light on under your hand her eyes going bright*
> *It's not for kissing I slapped you. Girl's elbows at fifteen Father said you swallow like you had a fishbone in your throat what's the matter with you and Caddy across the table not to look at me. It's for letting it be some darn town squirt I slapped you you will will you now I guess you say calf rope. My red hand coming up out of her face. What do you think of that scouring her head into the. Grass sticks criss-crossed into the flesh tingling scouring her head. Say calf rope say it*
> *I didn't kiss a dirty girl like Natalie anyway* (115)

As with Joyce's version of this representation strategy, punctuation is missing (although not all), and there is a lack of cohesion, with a diegetic statement ('Caddy across the table not to look at me') blending with the more mimetic 'what's the matter with you'. These diegetic elements attempt to represent images rather than words (see also 'Grass sticks criss-crossed into the flesh tingling scouring her head'), and must blend with those linguistic areas of the stream which are meant to correspond with more 'articulated' thought: 'I didn't let him I made him watching me getting mad'.

Where thought is almost entirely articulated, we tend to refer to it as interior monologue. This is defined by Steinberg as occurring

> [W]hen a character speaks silently to himself, in his own mind; the character can hear himself in his mind's ear, but no one else can hear him or need even be aware that he is thinking.
>
> (1973: 254)

The character is more conscious of his or her own thoughts, and is, as it were, thinking about/conscious of what he or she is thinking. Stylistically, the syntax tends to be less deviant, grammatically correct, and cohesive in terms of topic, theme and so on. Here's an example from Graham Swift's *Last Orders* (1996):

> Well they must be there by now, they must have done it. Tipped him in, chucked him. For all I know, they're halfway back again or they're making a day of it, they're on a spree, donkey-rides all round, now the job's done, down there in Margate.
>
> But I still think this is where I should be. My own journey to make. The living come first, even the living who were as good as dead to him, so it'd be all one now, all the same, in his book. And I'd already said goodbye to him for the last time, if not the first. Goodbye Jack, Jack old love. (228)

The sense of inner articulation is evident in the coherence of the language, which is oriented to the diegetic, to a telling of a story, almost entirely, apart from the last line, with its farewell to the character's dead husband.

To summarise: stream of consciousness writing tends to concentrate more on thought sensations, on emotions, on perceptions of the external and so on, whereas internal monologue is inherently verbal in nature, springing from interconnected internal memories and recollections. Some form of inner articulation is taking place, rather than an uncontrolled outpouring of thought and sensation. It should be pointed out that instances of 'genuine' stream of consciousness writing are rare; indeed, it is perfectly possible to argue that the extreme examples quoted here and in section 5.5.1 are in fact closer to interior monologue in that, barring the deviant punctuation (or lack of), there are discernible clauses and sentences and a traceable narrative.

Does the creative writer need to be aware of all of this in order to include convincing representations of thought in his or her work?

Almost certainly not. I would argue, though, that an awareness of the different techniques which stylistics and literary criticism in general have identified in the approach of other writers to this task will lend, at the least, a more sophisticated and nuanced appreciation of the process of literary simulation and, at best, the ability to apply lessons gleaned from these methods to one's own work with an appreciation of their *limitations* as well as their potential.

While bearing these distinctions – between articulated, 'verbalised' thought and an unmediated outpouring of the contents of a conscious-ness – in mind, the term **Free Direct Thought** will be used to refer to 'simulations' of consciousness *or* internal monologue throughout the rest of this book – essentially, those which aspire to be free of mediation on the part of the narrator.

5.5.3   Indirect Thought (IT)

This category need not detain us for long, as it is straightforward; for-mally the same as IS and, since it is more mediated than the direct ver-sions, it does the same job for a writer: it allows the semantic content of thoughts to take precedence over their actual syntactical form. The rea-sons why this might be desirable have been discussed in section 5.4.4. Like IS, IT is more mediated by the narrator than DT or FDT, and thus closer to the diegetic end of our cline. To intervene in the example from *Last Orders* in the last section:

> 'For all I know, they're halfway back again or they're making a day of it,' she thought. (DT)

Becomes more mediated as:

> She thought that, for all she knew, they were halfway back again or they were making a day of it. (IT)

5.6   Narrator's Representation of Speech (NRS) and Narrator's Representation of Thought (NRT)

There is one more category of speech and thought presentation which requires brief explanation, and that is the one situated closest to the diegetic end of our cline, one step away from the purely diegetic NRA, and at the point where the character's voice disappears. This is Nar-rator's Representation of Speech (or Thought), and occurs when the narrator intervenes between the actual content of the character's speech or thought and its reception by the reader. Crucially, there is no indication of the actual words used. In a reversal of the situation present in DS or DT, the narrator presents a summary of the content of the speech or thought act without any attention to its linguistic form. For example:

> She told him of her hopes and fears for the long journey ahead, and of her need for company.

Likewise:

> She pondered on the true nature of her feelings for him.

Compare these two approaches to:

> 'I'm worried that the plane might be late, or that my luggage might get lost, or that the food won't be up to scratch. I'm also worried whether I'll get bored, or whether this extended stretch of time in each other's company will prove too long. I'm hoping all will be well, though, and I think – I *think* – I'm glad that you're coming with me.'

In short, NRA and NRT are useful ways of condensing important information, and also come into play when the content is much more important to the development of the narrative rather than the way in which it was communicated in the story world. These modes can also be used to summarise long pieces of speech or thought, and, of course, incline towards the diegetic mode of discourse presentation rather than the mimetic. They explicitly 'tell' rather than attempt to 'show'.

Just as described in section 5.4.4 in relation to indirect speech, NRS/NRT can also have the effect of changing the pace of the narrative and of varying its texture. It can also be used to inject an element of suspense, as here in an example from Dan Brown's thriller *The Lost Symbol* (2010):

> The two men stood in silence for a long while at the foot of the monument.
> When Langdon finally spoke, his tone was serious. 'I need to ask you a favor, Peter … as a friend.'
> 'Of course. Anything.'
> **Langdon made his request … firmly.**
> Solomon nodded, knowing he was right. 'I will.'
>
> (650 – my emphasis)

The nature of Robert Langdon's request is not revealed until several pages later. The narrator knows what it was. So does the character in the story world, Peter Solomon. But the reader does not, and pushes onwards through the narrative in order to find out. NRS and NRT place even more distance between the reader and the character, but this can lend narrative momentum, allowing the author to control tension.

5.7   Free Indirect Discourse (FID)

We will now move back to the middle of our cline, to a point of equilibrium between mimesis and diegesis, between showing and telling, to what is, arguably, one of the most fascinating and flexible methods of representing character discourse. It also allows for a very successful and enabling resolution of the eternal tug of war between mimesis and diegesis, between character and narrator, as discussed and illustrated so far in this chapter.

I have deliberately amalgamated Free Indirect Speech (FIS) and Free Indirect Thought (FIT) into one category here (FID) as very often (although not always, of course) it is difficult to say with any certainty whether the discourse is being spoken aloud or simply thought – and herein lies the device's attraction to the writer. It constitutes an enabling flexibility, and gives the reader an impression of both a character and narrator speaking simultaneously, in what Simpson calls 'a dual voice' (2004: 81–2).

In its simplest form, the strategy consists simply of removing the reporting clause from IS or IT (in the same way as we would remove the reporting clause to change DS to FDS). So, to take an example from earlier:

> She promised she would be there the next day.

becomes, after the removal of the reporting clause 'She promised':

> She would be there the next day.

Similarly (adapted from *Last Orders*, see section 5.5.2):

> She thought that, for all she knew, they were halfway back again or they were making a day of it.

becomes:

> For all she knew, they were halfway back again or they were making
> a day of it.

The device becomes especially interesting, though, when the character's
own idiolect – their particular, often demotic, way of speaking – survives
the transition into what at first glance appears to be a narrator's third-
person discourse. This happens to an extent in the example above with
the preservation of 'for all she knew' (transferred from the colloquial
'for all I know'). For example:

'I'll be here tomorrow and that's a promise.'	FDS – pure mimesis??
'I'll be here tomorrow and that's a promise' she said.	DS
She promised she would be there the next day.	IS; typically the second clause of the original DS would be elided for the sake of summary
She would be there the next day and that was a promise.	FID

Notice how smoothly FID gives the impression of combining both
character and narrator voices, keeping the character's habit of speech
while maintaining the diegetic flexibility offered by the heterodiegetic
(see Chapter 4) narrative point of view. Notice too how it is closer to
the mimetic effect of FDS than the IS version, which is more mediated,
more explicitly *reported*.

In the examples above, the discourse is (more or less) obviously
spoken by the 'she' character. However, as I have already mentioned,
sometimes the situation is much less clear. In Chapter 2 of *A Portrait of
the Artist as a Young Man*, Joyce's narrator describes a character's morning routines as follows:

> Every morning, therefore, Uncle Charles repaired to his outhouse but
> not before he had greased and brushed scrupulously his back hair
> and brushed and put on his tall hat.
>
> (1916: 61)

A contemporary critic, Wyndham Lewis, singled out Joyce's use of the
word 'repaired', seeing it as inappropriate and out of place: 'People
repair to places in works of fiction of the humblest order', he opined,

spectacularly missing the point. In fact, as Hugh Kenner (1978: 14) makes clear, it was Joyce's intention, not mistake, to use the word 'repaired', and it should be read as wearing invisible quotation marks, a punctuation mark which, as we've already mentioned, Joyce reviled (see note 6). Perhaps that is why they are invisible. In any case, to put it as starkly as possible: 'repaired' *is the word which that character would have used had he been given the opportunity to narrate his own story* (very like Emma's use of the word 'vex' as discussed in Chapter 4). Uncle Charles smokes a particular noxious form of dark tobacco, and thus has been advised by his nephew Simon that he should enjoy his morning pipe in the toilet at the end of the garden. Imagine the sentence written in the first person, as a form of DS.

> 'Every morning, therefore,' said Uncle Charles, 'I repair to my outhouse.'

What happens when we report the utterance using IS?

> Uncle Charles said that every morning he would repair to his outhouse.

The word 'repair' seems to be crying out for those invisible quotation marks to become visible, signalling that it belongs to another's voice. What happens if we render the fragment in NRS?

> Uncle Charles explained that this was why he always went to the outhouse to smoke in the mornings.

Now, the word 'repair' has disappeared altogether, along with the character's habit of speech. The discourse has moved back to the diegetic end of the scale; with FID, it manages to hover at the midpoint. Joyce's ostensibly heterodiegetic narrative voice is continually subject to the influence of the voices of the characters it narrates, just as a beam of light is subject to the gravitational pull of the stars and planets it passes.

Peter Cobley (2001) defines FID as follows:

> [Free Indirect Discourse is a] term which refers to an extension of the mixed mode of mimesis and the poet's or narrator's voice. In free indirect discourse, the voice of the character becomes embedded in the voice of the narrator; thus, the character's habit of speech is present, *but direct imitation* and quotation marks are not. (85)

A defining difference between FID and NRA interspersed with direct discourse (character speech or thought) is that FID allows *continuity* to be preserved, and an enabling flexibility. Rimmon-Kenan (1998) describes the effect this way:

> On the one hand, the presence of a narrator as distinct from the character may create an ironic distancing. On the other hand, the tinting of the narrator's speech with the character's language or mode of experience may promote an *empathetic* identification on the part of the reader.
>
> (103; my emphasis)

The following example is also taken from Joyce's *A Portrait of the Artist as a Young Man* (1916):

> He knelt in the silent gloom and raised his eyes to the white crucifix. God would see that he was sorry. He would tell all his sins. His confession would be long, long. Everybody in the chapel would know then what a sinner he had been. Let them know. It was true. But God had promised to forgive him if he was sorry. He was sorry. He clasped his hands and raised them toward the white form...

The first sentence is pure NRA, but the subsequent ones 'segue' into the character's point of view and take on his habit of speech while maintaining the characteristics of heterodiegetic narration: for example, past tense, third-person verbs. Imagine what would happen if you were to change the above to a first-person voice, re-writing it as free direct thought:

> God will see that I am sorry. I will tell all my sins. My confession will be long, long. Everybody in the chapel will know then what a sinner I have been. Let them know. It is true. But God has promised to forgive me if I am sorry. I am sorry.

The give-away occurs in the repetition of 'long'; this is, categorically, a character's voice, and the ease with which it can be transposed to FDT demonstrates this.

The point is that, by orienting itself towards the discourse of character, Free Indirect Discourse may create a satisfactory illusion (it is an illusion, of course) of a rescinding of authorial control. Mikhail Bakhtin characterises Dostoevsky's writing as having this quality:

> [In Dostoevsky] a character's word about himself and his world is just as fully weighted as the author's word usually is; it is not subordinated to the character's objectified image as merely one of his characteristics, nor does it serve as a mouthpiece of the author's

voice. It possesses extraordinary independence in the structure of the work; it sounds, as it were, *alongside* the author's word and in a special way combines both with it and with the full and equally valid voices of other characters.

(1984: 7)

The discourses of character and narrator coexist simultaneously. Once again: FID grants the narrative discourse an enlivening *flexibility* in that the character is allowed to 'own' the words at times, while the limitations of homodiegetic perspective (see Chapter 4) combined with a form of thought presentation are avoided. Crucially, the reader can engage with the text-world via both the narrator's *and* the character's discourse. As we arrive at the mid-point of our diagram, at the position of free indirect discourse, mimesis and diegesis, rather than being separate, become intertwined and part of a cline of influence between narrator and character, with the discourse of one combining and merging with the discourse of the other.

This solves, to my mind at least, a particular problem arising when one attempts to anatomise diegesis properly and account rigorously for what it means. It has always been slightly troubling to me that mimesis and diegesis become difficult to disentangle at times (in support of this, see the quote from Rimon-Kennan in section 5.4.1). When does 'showing' becoming 'telling' and vice versa? Isn't all diegetic action in a narrative (i.e. NRA) also part of the process of mimesis? In narrative fiction rooted irrevocably in language, how can there be any showing without telling? Thinking about discourse presentation in the way described here, along with the assertion that mimesis occurs *through* diegesis, goes some way towards resolving this. It illustrates how mimesis and diegesis shade, barely perceptibly, along a cline, merging, arguably, in the middle in Free Indirect Discourse. The thoughtful writer can move their narrative discourse backwards and forwards along this cline to create particular expressive effects. We will look at how one writer has taken advantage of this opportunity in the next section.

5.8   Creative potentialities

We will conclude this discussion of discourse presentation from a stylistics perspective with an example from James Kelman's novel *How Late It Was, How Late* (1994). Look at the way in which the opening of the novel involves a range of discourse presentation strategies, and also

combines (or blends) homodiegetic and heterodiegetic narrative perspectives (see Chapter 4):

> Ye wake in a corner and stay there hoping yer body will disappear, the
> thoughts smothering ye; these thoughts; but ye want to remember
> and face up to things, just something keeps ye from doing it, why can
> ye no do it; the words filling yer head: then the other words; there's
> something wrong; there's something far wrong; ye're no a good man,
> ye're just no a good man. Edging back into awareness of where ye are:
> here, slumped in this corner, with these thoughts filling ye. And oh
> christ his back was sore; stiff, and the head pounding. He shivered
> and hunched up his shoulders, shut his eyes, rubbed into the corners
> with his fingertips; seeing all kinds of spots and lights. Where in the
> name of fuck ... (3)

Firstly, and most obviously, there is an attempt to represent an authentic Glaswegian voice, notated using orthographic representation with
words such as 'ye' and 'yer', and in the lower-case 'c' of 'christ'). We can
also notice a deviant syntax in the convoluted and flowing sentence
structure associated with FDT (especially stream of consciousness).
These parts adopt the present tense, also signalling FDT ('there's something wrong; there's something far wrong; ye're no a good man, ye're
just no a good man'). All of these serve mimetic functions. However,
we can also identify some NRA which is diegetic in intent ('He shivered
and hunched up his shoulders, shut his eyes, rubbed into the corners
with his fingertips; seeing all kinds of spots and lights'), which uses the
past tense in 'traditional' narrative style. These two perspectives then
combine in a form of FID: a blend of mimetic FDT (for example, 'Where
in the name of fuck...') with diegetic NRA characteristic of a heterodiegetic narrator, yet still using the demotic Glaswegian. This is seen
at work in the following: 'And oh christ his back was sore; stiff, and the
head pounding.' The implied present tense of the DT is transformed
into the past tense and third-person typical of NRA, yet remaining
within the scope of the character's demotic idiolect. Then, we come
back to DT: 'Where in the name of fuck...'.

Who is the narrator here? Is it the character? Is he telling his own
story, yet from a third-person perspective? And what about the use
of the second-person voice ('*Ye* wake in a corner and stay there hoping *yer* body will disappear...')? This seems to imply an external presence of some kind, or is it simply an aspect of the character himself?
Kelman employs a fascinating narrative technique here, which seems
to blend the perspectives of narrator and character within the same

demotic voice (an effect aided by the double-voicedness of FID), so that the distinction between mimesis and diegesis, between showing and telling, is elided. Speech/thought and narration occur on the same plane. Kelman, as we mentioned earlier, challenges the notion here that standard English is the only register capable of heterodiegetic narration, and that the character's 'true' voice must always be imprisoned within inverted commas.

This example and the stylistic reading of it should give us as creative writers a sense of the possibilities inherent in discourse presentation strategies, and the creative potential and expressive capital that can be gained from thoughtful exploitation of them. The exercises in section 5.10 will help you being the process of exploring these possibilities further.

5.9   Distillation

- Character speech or thought can be used to move the narrative along, and to do a lot of diegetic work. It can show rather than tell.
- Be frugal with verbs of speech and thought; 'he said' or 'she said' will suffice in most cases. If it is clear who is speaking or thinking, then FDS or FDT will probably be the most effective method.
- Avoid unnecessary descriptive language, such as adverbs and adjectives, when indicating the providence of speech or thought.
- Vary the different types of discourse presentation that you use in order to lend 'texture' to your prose, and to vary its pace. Beware also of the potential for heightening suspense or quickening the momentum of the narrative.
- Where the content of the speech is paramount, try using IS/IT.
- Where the information contained within the character's discourse is complex, or lengthy, or both, trying using NRS/NRT.
- Where the *form* of the discourse is paramount, try using DS/DT.
- Avoid stereotypes of speech or thought, including clichés.
- Match dialogue to character to create an idiolect.
- Use dialect sparingly.
- Remember the enabling flexibility offered by FID.

5.10   Practice

(1) Use the excerpt from Kelman's *How Late It Was, How Late* in section 5.8 as a basis for this exercise. We are going to try out some

textual intervention to explore the effects of different discourse presentation strategies. In each case, after you have carried out the intervention, consider what changes in terms of the passage's effect on the reader.

(a) Rewrite the text using standard English as far as possible.

(b) Rewrite the text as pure FDT.

(c) Rewrite it as NRA.

(d) Finally, try rendering the whole passage as FID, using the results from (b) and (c) to help you. You should notice that you are blending the language of (b) and (c) together.

(e) Which of all these, including the original, do you prefer? Why?

(2) In this exercise you will produce two descriptions of the same text-world instant moment (based on the abstract of the Hemingway story 'Hills Like White Elephants' in Chapter 1).

(a) First, try using free direct discourse, either speech or thought, spoken or internalised monologue, to represent the scene.

(b) Now write it again using narrator's representation of action (NRA).

(c) Next, combine the two pieces using free indirect discourse. Consider the relative strengths weaknesses of each technique, with close attention to particular linguistic features and their effects.

(d) Finally, try a mix of approaches, focussing on as many different discourse presentation strategies as possible. Notice how the reader's experience of the characters speech of thought is subtly altered depending on the strategy used.

(3) This exercise will focus on writing dialogue. Converted the following examples from IS to FDS, paying attention to the way in which the latter version should seek to *show* the features of speech and articulation which are 'told' in the original:

(a) The driver addressed me abruptly, asking if I was from Kent.

(b) David queried the meaning of the word 'discourse'.

(c) As he opened the door, he told her to move over.

(d) Roughly, Carl said she should stop being so stupid.

Now try converting following direct speech to indirect speech.

(a) 'So he says,' Mrs. Peters gossiped, '"Annie wouldn't have done that,"' he says, so I says, "Blast, and she would." And so she would.'

(b) He insisted on putting the car into the barn for me, so I got out and directed him into the narrow space.

Which method works best in each case? Why?

(4) If you have access to the technology (and, crucially, the permission of the participants...), try recording a conversation between two friends or colleagues. Then, write it out in a fictionalised form. What changes have you made between the 'original' version and the fictionalised one? Why have you made those changes? Think in terms of narrative as well as discourse presentation. Think about this in terms of our discussions of mediation thus far. Now try writing it out as a poem. What changes? Why?

(5) Use the excerpt from Swift in section 5.5.2 as a model, write a short scene entirely as an internal monologue. The character (like Swift's) is on public transport, and on their way to visit someone very important to them. They are also very nervous about the visit for some reason. Try and express these details indirectly, through FDT. When you have finished, analyse the results linguistically, looking for the following features, highlighting them in the text if you find them:

- Lack of cohesion
- Elliptical sentence structure
- Elision (including of grammar words)
- Solipsism
- Violation of the Gricean Maxims of Quantity and Manner
- Non-standard syntax or spelling

If possible, show the results to someone else. How effective do they find your attempts to represent the mind, and how easy to read? Think about why this might be, in relation to the linguistic features mentioned above.

(6) Write a two-page scene using *only* FDS. There should be *no* interventions on the part of the narrator, not even to indicate who is speaking. Have one character trying to get something from the other (for example, a daughter begging her father for a new pair of shoes) but create a clear sub-text (e.g. the daughter is really seeking attention). How does using only FDS help you put this sub-text across?

(7) Two friends are in love with the same person. One describes his or her feelings in detail, with honesty, and articulately. The other is unwilling to do so, but betrays these feelings through appearance and action. Write the scene. What kinds of discourse presentation strategies have you used, and why?

(8) Write a scene in which two people who live together or who work closely together have had an argument and are not communicating with one another. What strategies have you used to put this across to the reader, and why?

(9) Do you speak with a variety of English that might be considered non-standard? If so, what grounds are there for it being considered so? Try writing a dialogue between someone who speaks this particular variety of English and someone who speaks another. How successful do you find the results? Think about the methods you have used to represent the dialect. Try and account for the success or failure of the experiment in stylistic terms, with reference to schema theory as explored in Chapter 3. (We will discuss the issue of standard language in more detail in Chapter 7).

(10) Here are two poems that involve presentation of speech; notice that in both, only one side of the conversation is presented.

My Last Duchess
That's my last Duchess painted on the wall,
Looking as if she were alive. I call
That piece a wonder, now: Fra Pandolf's hands
Worked busily a day, and there she stands.
Will't please you sit and look at her? I said
'Fra Pandolf' by design, for never read
Strangers like you that pictured countenance,
The depth and passion of its earnest glance,
But to myself they turned (since none puts by
The curtain I have drawn for you, but I)
And seemed as they would ask me, if they durst,
How such a glance came there; so, not the first
Are you to turn and ask thus. Sir, 'twas not
Her husband's presence only, called that spot
Of joy into the Duchess' cheek: perhaps
Fra Pandolf chanced to say 'Her mantle laps
Over my lady's wrist too much,' or 'Paint
Must never hope to reproduce the faint
Half-flush that dies along her throat': such stuff
Was courtesy, she thought, and cause enough
For calling up that spot of joy. She had
A heart – how shall I say? – too soon made glad,
Too easily impressed; she liked whate'er
She looked on, and her looks went everywhere.
Sir, 'twas all one! My favour at her breast,
The dropping of the daylight in the West,
The bough of cherries some officious fool
Broke in the orchard for her, the white mule
She rode with round the terrace – all and each
Would draw from her alike the approving speech,

Or blush, at least. She thanked men, – good! but thanked
Somehow – I know not how – as if she ranked
My gift of a nine-hundred-years-old name
With anybody's gift. Who'd stoop to blame
This sort of trifling? Even had you skill
In speech – (which I have not) – to make your will
Quite clear to such an one, and say, 'Just this
Or that in you disgusts me; here you miss,
Or there exceed the mark' – and if she let
Herself be lessoned so, nor plainly set
Her wits to yours, forsooth, and made excuse,
– E'en then would be some stooping; and I choose
Never to stoop. Oh sir, she smiled, no doubt,
Whene'er I passed her; but who passed without
Much the same smile? This grew; I gave commands;
Then all smiles stopped together. There she stands
As if alive. Will't please you rise? We'll meet
The company below, then. I repeat,
The Count your master's known munificence
Is ample warrant that no just pretence
Of mine for dowry will be disallowed;
Though his fair daughter's self, as I avowed
At starting, is my object. Nay, we'll go
Together down, sir. Notice Neptune, though,
Taming a sea-horse, thought a rarity,
Which Claus of Innsbruck cast in bronze for me!

Robert Browning (1842)

Dover Beach
The sea is calm to-night.
The tide is full, the moon lies fair
Upon the straits; – on the French coast the light
Gleams and is gone; the cliffs of England stand, Glimmering
and vast, out in the tranquil bay.
Come to the window, sweet is the night-air!
Only, from the long line of spray
Where the sea meets the moon blanch'd land,
Listen! you hear the grating roar
Of pebbles which the waves draw back, and fling,
At their return, up the high strand,
Begin, and cease, and then again begin,
With tremulous cadence slow, and bring
The eternal note of sadness in.

Sophocles long ago
Heard it on the Aegaean, and it brought
Into his mind the turbid ebb and flow
Of human misery; we
Find also in the sound a thought,
Hearing it by this distant northern sea.

The Sea of Faith
Was once, too, at the full, and round earth's shore
Lay like the folds of a bright girdle furl'd.
But now I only hear
Its melancholy, long, withdrawing roar,
Retreating, to the breath
Of the night-wind, down the vast edges drear
And naked shingles of the world.

Ah, love, let us be true
To one another! for the world, which seems
To lie before us like a land of dreams,
So various, so beautiful, so new,
Hath really neither joy, nor love, nor light,
Nor certitude, nor peace, nor help for pain;
And we are here as on a darkling plain
Swept with confused alarms of struggle and flight,
Where ignorant armies clash by night.

                                  Matthew Arnold (1851)

(A) 'My Last Duchess' is based on a real person, Alfonso, a six-
     teenth-century Duke of Ferrara. The Duke is the narrator of
     the poem; its narratee (or hearer) is a messenger who has
     come to negotiate the marriage of the recently widowed Duke
     to the daughter of another noble family. As he shows the visitor
     through his palace, he stops before a portrait of his late wife,
     the Duchess, apparently a beautiful young girl, and begins
     reminiscing about the portrait sessions, and then about the
     Duchess herself. What transpires is open to interpretation …
     Rewrite the poem from the messenger's perspective. How does
     he react to the Duke's unwitting revelations? Try to present
     both the speech and the thought of the messenger. You could
     also include the Duke's words from the original in places if you
     like. Can you mediate the events underpinning the poem as
     subtly as Browning does? Reflect on how presentation of char-
     acter discourse can also be a narrative-advancing device.

(B) 'Dover Beach' also implies a narratee ('Ah, love, let us be true to one another!). Write a poem detailing the lover's response to the narrator's ardour using presentation of speech. Notice the spiritual malaise he articulates in the final stanza. How might the lover respond? Try, if possible, to stick to the form of the original (we will discuss poetic form in more detail in Chapter 9).

(11) T.S. Eliot said that 'Every revolution in poetry is apt to be ... a return to common speech' (1942: 16). If possible, and providing you have the participants' permission, record ten minutes or so of a conversation between friends or colleagues. Turn snatches of it (or even all of it!) into a poem. Of course, you will need to edit it. Remove sentences, phrases or words that don't fit your scheme. **But don't add anything**.

6 Creating a World: Text-world Theory and Cognitive Poetics

6.1 Overview

This chapter will introduce you to the rich and burgeoning field of cognitive poetics, a relatively new sub-field of stylistics which builds on the principles of cognitive psychology and linguistics to draw conclusions about the processes involved in the interpretation of literary texts, or, more broadly, in reading. It has been argued that in its focus on how readers process the language of literature, cognitive poetics is in some sense a return to the pre-Romantic roots of literary criticism that can be found in classical rhetoric (i.e. in its focus on texts, readers and the art of communication rather than on sociocultural histories of authors, genres and periods). However, it is at the same time a very modern approach to understanding literary mechanics due to its connection with the latest advances in cognitive linguistics.[1] Here are just a few of the many topics which cognitive poetics explores:

- Deixis
- Schema theory
- Script theory
- Reader attention
- Conceptual metaphor
- Foregrounding
- Genre
- Text-worlds
- Possible Worlds.

It is, of course, beyond the scope of this book to consider all of these aspects of cognitive poetics in detail, and the reader is referred to the list of suggested further reading at the end of this book.[2] We will focus here on a central sub-field of cognitive poetics – **text-world theory** – and also look at what the field in general has to say about the linguistic feature of **foregrounding**, and, of course, at how the creative writer can put knowledge and understanding of these two theoretical concepts to service in practice.

6.2   A literary analogy

While researching and writing this book, although not directly in connection with the project, I happened to re-read the well-known short story by Jorge Luis Borges, 'Tlön, Uqbar, Orbis Tertius' (2000). The parallels between the ideas presented there and some of the aims and assumptions of cognitive poetics, particularly text-world theory, forcibly struck me. This discussion of the story will serve as a useful introduction to the field. The by-line to Wikipedia's useful précis of the story is instructive given the subject matter of this chapter:

> In the following summary, statements refer to the world within the story, not to the real world. Consequently, historical personages may have actions attributed to them that they did not take in the real world. Their real-world aspects are discussed in the following section.

This is an exploration of the nature of *truth* in fiction. Different worlds – story worlds, actual worlds, past worlds – coexist, it would seem, and blend. Some are, supposedly, real, and some imaginary. Some *were* real, but have now passed into history and continue to recede. They influence each other, though, in fascinating and often perplexing ways. Borges's story is an exploration of this interplay of worlds, and cognitive poetics shows us as creative writers how language is used to create (or re-create) them as well as understand the myriad ways in which they interact.

Borges's narrator (who sounds like a fictional alter-ego of the writer himself) tells of the discovery of a strange entry in the *Anglo-American Cyclopedia*, present in some editions and not in others, which dwells on a country called Uqbar, and its mythological creation Tlön, in which the legends of Uqbar literature take place.[3] Uqbar turns out to be the creation of a conspiracy of 'intellectuals' who aim to create a complete 'fictional' world within our own 'real' world (these terms 'fictional' and 'real' soon become problematic, if they were not already so). As the story moves forward, the narrator comes across various objects from the supposedly mythical Tlön which become progressively more real, or 'concrete', until, by the end of the story, our own planet, Earth, is in the process of becoming Tlön. While the fictional Borges and his academic colleagues pursue their obsessive speculations about the epistemology, language and literature of Tlön, the rest of the world gradually learns about the project and begins to adopt the Tlönic culture – an extreme examples of abstract ideas invading reality and becoming concrete.

The story contains much discussion of the languages, philosophy and epistemology of Tlön. If you are familiar with it you will know that, as well as being a playful exploration of the blurring borderlines between fiction and fact, it is also to some extent a parable of Bishop Berkeley's particular version of **idealism**: the philosophy of perception, where our experience of the external world is seen as nothing more than bundles of sense data. What would normally be called 'the external world' is created by the mind. According to Berkeley, a material object consists of nothing but ideas, whether in the mind of god or of the conscious agents that he has created.[4] In philosophical terms, this concept is closely connected to phenomenalism: the view that physical objects, properties, events, etc. are reducible to mental objects, properties, events, etc.; that is, that there is an irrefutable link between our experience and the world of physical objects. Put simply, our thoughts don't just shape our world; they *are* our world.[5]

This concept can be viewed as analogous to the ways in which we create worlds from language, and the ways in which these worlds take on a powerful and resonant existence in the imagination. They also raise various, albeit slightly tired, philosophical questions such as: are literary worlds any less 'real' than actual worlds? Like Tlön, do these worlds take on a very 'real' existence of their own? (An intuitive answer to this question would surely be 'yes', as anyone who has had the experience of being truly gripped, moved, heartened or upset by a poem or story will know.)

The connections between the central conceits of Borges's story and a field such as cognitive poetics, which attempts to make sense of how texts and minds interact to create new 'realities', should be obvious. However, it will be useful to list a few of these here and to keep them in mind as we move on to discuss text-world theory in more detail.

6.2.1 'Concrete' versus 'abstract'

Cognitive poetics combines two apparently contradictory approaches to the act of writingandreading: **autonomous** and **heteronomous**. The former describes something which exists independently of perception, while the latter term refers to that which is in some sense 'abstract'. Creative writing as an artefact, as typed/printed words on a page or screen, is autonomous. It has a physical presence as we turn its pages or, perhaps, scroll through it with a mouse or fingertip. The ideas that it plants in our minds, the worlds that it creates there, the things that we imagine in response to its language – these things are, at least intuitively, heteronomous. They exist only in our heads.

Or do they?

In Borges's story, the two categories merge. Tlön, formally an abstract (heteronomous) concept in the mind of a group of intellectuals, becomes concretised, autonomous (and remember that Tlön, in its turn, is a mythical adjunct to an equally abstract world, Uqbar; think of Russian dolls, each encasing a smaller version of itself). To put it more simply: Tlön takes on a life of its own. Cognitive poetics also aims to examine how the heteronomous and the autonomous can blend, merge and interchange, and to understand how the heteronomous and autonomous facets of the text come together in the acts of creative writingandreading.[6] Arguably, then, cognitive poetics gives us a partial resolution to the problem of idealism: the proposition that the external world is created solely by the mind. In Borges's story, Tlön, an invented world within another invented world (Uqbar), with a complete, equally invented, history and culture, takes on its own, very concrete, very real existence as it seeps into the consciousness of the world, just as the discourse of creative writing becomes a world in the mind of the reader – something with its own definable sense of reality. Jostein Gaarder's award-winning novel *Sophie's World* (1994) explores the same ideas. In that story too, a world which was previously assumed to be fictional also becomes real (or real inside the fictional world of the novel, which is of course itself fiction. We continue to pick our way through the labyrinth...[7]). We are left with the following fascinating question, which has bearing on our previous discussions of the importance of creative writing and empathy: what, then, truly separates the world of the creative writing text from the world outside it? How best can we make the worlds built from our words have a genuine, concrete and vital existence in the imaginations of our readers? The exercises at the end of this chapter will explore these ideas in more detail.

6.2.2   Linguistic relativity: language and thought

The relationship between language and thought[8] is of course key to the assumptions of text-world theory. There are many languages and dialects thereof spoken in Tlön, including a language without nouns. Borges's narrator provides us with an example, using the following sentence:

The moon rose above the water.

The sentence contains a subject (*moon*), a verb in the past tense (*rose*), a deictic preposition (*above*), denoting position, and an object (*water*). From these basic grammatical building blocks, interacting with pre-existing schema[9] stored in his or her mind, the reader creates a mental image, a text-world, consisting of the moon rising above water. The sentence is rendered by Borges's narrator in a language of Tlön as follows, (apparently) without nouns:

Hlör u fang axaxaxas mlö. (ibid.)

In English (translated yet again from the original Spanish; the nest of Russian dolls continues) this can best be represented as:

Upward behind the onstreaming it mooned.

This sentence has two prepositions (*upward* and *behind*), an article, a verb-as-noun (*onstreaming*; is it a gerund?) and a past-tense verb (*it mooned*); remember, this is an attempted rendering into English, so the verb-as-noun 'onstreaming' is a translation of the untranslatable. In keeping with the premises of text-world theory, this syntactical pattern has a 'real world' (or fictional world) effect. In a linguistic world which contains no nouns – or where nouns are composites of other parts of speech, created and discarded according to a whim – and thus no things, most of European or Western thought and philosophy becomes impossible. Without nouns about which to state propositions ('*I* think, therefore *I* am', 'To be or not to be, that is the *question*', 'Which came first, the *chicken* or the *egg*?'), there can be no a priori deductive reasoning from first principles. Thus, in a sophisticated and, indeed, playful reworking of the (in)famous Sapir–Whorf Hypothesis[10] and the principles of linguistic relativity in general, the story posits language as integral, and anterior, to thought. From language comes thought. From thought comes the world.

You can view this with equal relevance from the perspective of creative writer or reader (or creative writerandreader). Your words on the
page are the building blocks of the world your reader imagines as he
or she reads. Refer back to Chapter 2 for more discussion of how the
syntax of your clauses and sentences directly affects the way in which
your reader forms (inhabits?) a text-world in response. What kind of
text-world does the sentence 'Upward behind the onstreaming it
mooned' create for you? What do you see? Reflect upon the complex
relationships between language and thought, thought and the world,
and language and the world. Try to make awareness of these issues part
of your creative practice.

6.2.3   Compatibility: language and the 'real' world

A central tenet of cognitive poetics concerns the extent to which discourse can be related or tied to real-world objects. 'To call a spade
a spade' is to state that which is true and verifiable in its own terms
(those of the world in which it is uttered, i.e. the actual world). To
call a spade a badger raises certain questions about the relationship
between signifier and signified in this sentence; the **truth conditions**[11]
of the sentence are to some extent called into question. A spade is
not a badger.[12] To call a spade an *axaxaxas* creates a situation where
the world of the discourse and our own world are not compatible.[13]
The sentence, in effect, is meaningless. As you might expect, Borges's
story engages with this idea too. At one point in the narrative, some
objects connected with Tlön are described called *hrönir. Hrönir* are
objects or things that arise when two people find the same 'lost' object
in different places – a fantastical notion, of course. Imagine losing a
mobile phone, which you find in one place at the same time as someone else finds your phone in a different place. This episode would create a *hrönir*. And ... it simultaneously creates a new world. Now we
have two phones in two worlds. In one, you find your phone under
the passenger seat of your car. In another, somebody else finds your
phone in a luggage locker at the central station in Dubrovnik.[14] You
might argue: but how can both situations be 'true'? Cognitive poetics
would respond that one world is 'actual' while another is, obviously,
'fictional' – but, arguably, none the less coherent, solid or tangible for
being so.[15] This other world allows statements that are not true in this
world to be deemed as true by creating another in which they are. As
I have implied throughout, language really does create worlds (even
the world?).

Unsurprisingly enough, the idea of the *hrönir* is omitted from later drafts of the encyclopaedic narrative of Tlön. Borges's narrator writes:

> It is reasonable to suppose that these erasures were in keeping with the plan of projecting a world which would not be too *incompatible with the real world.*
>
> (Borges 2000: 32–3, my italics)

Incompatible with the real world... This is the fascinating issue here, which has a lot to teach us about the process of creative writing, especially when it comes to consideration of the role of the reader (the key premise of this chapter). The lessons for the creative writer, the fabricator, are twofold.

First: we should be wary of that 'moment of arrest', that point at which the world of the story or poem becomes, in some way, too incompatible, too at odds with, the reader's understanding of that which operates in the real world. I am not talking about the creation of fantasy or science fiction worlds and so on (of course, these possible worlds have a viable reality all of their own, even if it is very different from the actual world). Rather, I'm referring to character actions, dialogue, imagery, narrative registers or situations which, as far as the reader is concerned, do not follow from the premises of the fictional/poetic world which you have created. A character does something which does not accord with our understanding of her from the rest of the story (of course, actions can surprise, but should not stretch credulity). A narrator uses language that does not match our understanding of his sensibility. A metaphor is drawn from somewhere outside the coherent world of the poem. A narrator leaves gaps in his or her mediation of the fabula that are too large to be filled by the reader, with the result that the reader loses patience with the story. When this happens, the process of world-building is interrupted and the vital contract between creative writer and reader (what you might call 'the will to suspension of disbelief') is broken.[16]

To attempt a summary of this idea, I would like to make use of Marie-Laure Ryan's phrase **'the principle of minimal departure'** (in Semino 1997). This principle proposes that when readers construct fictional worlds, they naturally fill in the gaps in the text by assuming a similarity between the fictional world and their own experiential reality. This response can only be overruled by the text itself; so, if a poem mentions a green fox, the reader will imagine an animal that resembles his or her perception of foxes (his or her 'fox schema') in every aspect apart from its colour. The statement 'foxes have four legs and a tail' will, of course, remain true of this fictional world, but the statement 'foxes have white wings and a single horn made of gold' will be false, unless it is specified by the text. Readers will default to their understanding of the actual world, in short; they will only depart from this understanding if made to do so by the writer.

Second: language, inescapably, creates other worlds when its **truth conditions**[17] are not matched in the actual world. A famous example comes from the statement: 'The present King of France is bald.' Of course, there *is* no present King of France. So that statement can only meet truth conditions if we set up another (possible, or fictional) world in which there *is* a King of France, and he is bald. This very simple example shows us, in essence, exactly how creative writing works. In Borges's terms, a *hrönir* is created; an artefact is brought into existence from the interaction of two co-existing worlds. We draw on our knowledge (schema; see 6.4 below) of Kings and French history and culture from the actual world (where there is no present King of France) to create a possible, fictional world in which such an entity *does* exist. We treat the possible world as fictional by virtue of its difference from the actual world. Nonetheless, it has an integrity and coherence of its own by virtue of its resemblance to that actual world and its exploitation of our schema. It is up to you as a creative writer to act as a guide through your world, however small, however complex, keeping your reader in mind at all times.

Tlön, then, is a world of Berkeleian idealism with one critical omission: it lacks the omnipresent, perceiving deity on whom Bishop Berkeley insisted. God, for Berkeley (1710), provided a point of view that demanded and helped shape an internally consistent world.

> The ideas imprinted on the senses by the author of nature are called real things. ... The ideas of sense are allowed to have more reality in them, that is, to be more strong, orderly and coherent than the creatures of the mind. ... They are also less dependent on the spirit or thinking substance which perceives them, in that they are excited by the will of another and more powerful spirit. ...
>
> (*The Principles of Human Knowledge*, §33)

To paraphrase, creation needs both a creator and a perceiver in order to exist. So creative writing needs both a writer and a reader. For our terms, it helps to think of Berkeley's omnipresent, perceiving deity as the **implied reader** of the text, the one who imposes order and form on the worlds of the narrative, and judges it accordingly a success or a failure. Herein lies the fundamental relevance of cognitive poetics and text-world theory to the creative practitioner: it is in the appeal to the reader that a piece of writing stands or falls.

6.3   Figures and grounds

Look at this image. What do you see? An old woman in a headscarf? Or a young woman wearing a feathered hat? You can only see one or the other at the same time. It is possible to 'flip' perception between two interpretations of this image, but it is very difficult (impossible?) not to emphasise one over the other. For me, it is the old woman (I have no idea why). In short, we see one as figure and the other as ground. Our brains are hard-wired to do this, and it is impossible for us to interact with objects in any other way. Before I typed this sentence, I looked out of my office window. It was not possible for my mind to take in everything that I saw outside, so it settled on foregrounded objects: a man walking across the view looking at his phone (our minds like to latch on to movement), two street lamps that had just switched themselves on (their lights stood out against the sky, which was getting darker), and the waving branches of a tree in the middle distance (again, movement). There were countless other things I could have focussed on (cars in the car park, grass on the verges, the shades of colour in the hedge on the other side of the road), but our minds do not work like that. They have to focus on something. Something will always function as foreground, and something else will always function as background.

Drawn from Gestalt psychology (see Köhler 1992), the notion of **fig-ure** and **ground** constitutes a central plank of cognitive stylistic analysis. In short, we foreground certain patterns in language against the background of the language as a whole; typically, this foregrounding comes about because the piece of language in question **deviates** in some way from the norm. Deviations from the actual world in Borges's story are foregrounded; hence, they stand out. There is a set of encyclopaedias, only one of which contains any mention of Uqbar. The entry does not appear in any other editions of the book. This is foregrounded against the 'background' of our understanding of how books are produced. The description of a green fox above would be foregrounded against our understanding of what foxes look like in this world. In terms of discourse, the sentence 'Upward behind the onstreaming it mooned' is foregrounded against the background of English language norms. To use a slightly crude example, one word is foregrounded against the background of the following list: 'Cooker, toaster, washing machine, blender, monkey, fridge'. The term refers to any break in an established pattern that will grab your reader's attention. We will return to this concept in more detail in Chapter 7, but it is important to grasp fully the idea of figure and ground at this stage.

6.4   Text-world theory[18]

As you will have gathered from the discussion so far, text-world theory (and cognitive poetics in general) aims to explain how we construct mental representations based on and around linguistic prompts. In stylistics and cognitive linguistics, these mental representations have acquired various names which, again, we have referred to already, such as *scripts*, *schemata*, *frames*, *mental spaces* and, most relevantly here, *worlds*. According to schema theory (see note 5), human cognition is organised around *scripts*. Scripts are familiar situations, places or events (a family meal, a pub, Christmas) and by activating a stereotypical script (a meal with your family in a local pub on Christmas Eve) we can better understand unfamiliar events and situations (a feast to celebrate the coronation of a Mogul prince in seventeenth-century India).

These examples are, of course, extreme in their diversity, but the central point to be put across is that there is a mysterious and often remarkable facility in the mind of the reader which enables him or her to be transported imaginatively to fictional worlds which bear only slight relation to his or her 'real' world: from modern Sheffield to modern Bangkok (and in the other direction), ancient Greece, Victorian London, the mountains of Tolkien's Middle Earth, the surface of Mars. Traditionally referred to as a process of 'suspension of disbelief', this remarkable facility, which arises out of the uniquely (as far as we know) ability of human language to refer to things which are not there, in other words, to refer heteronomously to the abstract, is something which writers should understand and aim to exploit – and should also, as I have already mentioned, be wary of disrupting and/or obstructing unnecessarily. The point bears repetition: it is in advancing understanding of the reader's imaginative process and sensibility that cognitive stylistics has much to offer.

Cognitive psychologists, whose work has had an enormous influence on this kind of literary analysis, research how human experience is represented in the mind. According to schema theory, we construct mental models in analogue form.[19] Thus, we create a kind of mental 'map' upon which are represented recurrent aspects and features of our daily life: memories, faces, locations, names, actions, emotions etc. These aspects are stored with the same level of detail as in the real world; thus, when we are faced with something new, we 'import' information from the world to be stored on our map, much like a video game loads new screens as the player progresses through the game world. Crucially, we can even experience events like this by proxy. Just to be reminded of something we are familiar with by a textual prompt will cause us to experience the emotions associated with that event as if they were 'real' (just as in Borges's story, the boundaries between 'real' and 'fictional' become blurred). As a rough analogy, think of the way in which a particular smell can evoke, very vividly, detailed and textured memories of the past. The features that we focus on are those that are **foregrounded** for whatever reason. Text-world theory homes in on the foregrounded elements of literary discourse, and helps us to see how this conceptual map is put together.

6.4.1   The worlds of Text-world Theory

Text-world Theory is a discourse model, aiming to produce a framework for the study of discourse which attempts to take into account all of the myriad situational, social, historical and psychological factors inherent in language; in other words, the **context** of the discourse, and the ways in which our imaginations interact with it. The model works by dividing discourse into separate levels, which it terms (unsurprisingly enough) **worlds**. We will discuss each of these in turn, and use a poem, Elizabeth Bishop's 'Questions of Travel', in order to illustrate how they work and interact.

Here is the poem in full:

> There are too many waterfalls here; the crowded streams
> hurry too rapidly down to the sea,
> and the pressure of so many clouds on the mountaintops
> makes them spill over the sides in soft slow-motion,
> 5   turning to waterfalls under our very eyes.
> – For if those streaks, those mile-long, shiny, tearstains,
> aren't waterfalls yet,
> in a quick age or so, as ages go here,
> they probably will be.
> 10 But if the streams and clouds keep travelling, travelling,
> the mountains look like the hulls of capsized ships,
> slime-hung and barnacled.
>
> Think of the long trip home.
> Should we have stayed at home and thought of here?
> 15 Where should we be today?
> Is it right to be watching strangers in a play
> in this strangest of theatres?
> What childishness is it that while there's a breath of life
> in our bodies, we are determined to rush
> 20 to see the sun the other way around?
> The tiniest green hummingbird in the world?
> To stare at some inexplicable old stonework,
> inexplicable and impenetrable,
> at any view,
> 25 instantly seen and always, always delightful?
> Oh, must we dream our dreams
> and have them, too?
> And have we room
> for one more folded sunset, still quite warm?
>
> 30 But surely it would have been a pity
> not to have seen the trees along this road,
> really exaggerated in their beauty,
> not to have seen them gesturing
> like noble pantomimists, robed in pink.
> 35 – Not to have had to stop for gas and heard
> the sad, two-noted, wooden tune

of disparate wooden clogs
carelessly clacking over
a grease-stained filling-station floor.
40 (In another country the clogs would all be tested.
Each pair there would have identical pitch.)
– A pity not to have heard
the other, less primitive music of the fat brown bird
who sings above the broken gasoline pump
45 in a bamboo church of Jesuit baroque:
three towers, five silver crosses.
– Yes, a pity not to have pondered,
blurr'dly and inconclusively,
on what connection can exist for centuries
50 between the crudest wooden footwear
and, careful and finicky,
the whittled fantasies of wooden footwear
and, careful and finicky,
the whittled fantasies of wooden cages.
55 – Never to have studied history in
the weak calligraphy of songbirds' cages.
– And never to have had to listen to rain
so much like politicians' speeches:
two hours of unrelenting oratory
60 and then a sudden golden silence
in which the traveller takes a notebook, writes:

'Is it lack of imagination that makes us come
to imagined places, not just stay at home?
Or could Pascal have been not entirely right
65 about just sitting quietly in one's room?

Continent, city, country, society:
the choice is never wide and never free.
And here, or there … No. Should we have stayed at home,
wherever that may be?'

6.4.1.1 The discourse world

The **discourse world** (hereafter, DW) refers to the situation in the **actual world** (the 'real' world; hereafter, AW) in which people communicate with each other. Gavins defines DW as 'the immediate situation surrounding one speaker or writer and one or more listeners or readers, participating in a joint language venture' (2000: 19). Outside of this immediate situation is the AW. The persons participating in this communicative act are referred to, appropriately enough, as **participants**. The discourse could be taking place in a room, a café, either end of a telephone line and so on. If we take the poem (and this is the case with most creative writing), then we are, of course, talking about Bishop as the poet communicating with us, the reader(s), via the text, removed accordingly in time and space. Both the poet and the reader have access to the DW (obviously enough; if not, there could be no communication), hence the DW is termed **participant-accessible**. A further term we need to deal with is **enactor**. To return to Gavins: 'enactors are simply different versions of the same person or character which exist at different conceptual levels of a discourse' (2000: 41).

To represent all this information simply, Text-world Theory (hereafter TWT) uses a special diagrammatic notation. For Bishop's poem, the DW diagram looks like this:

DISCOURSE WORLD
(participant-accessible)
Time: present
Enactors: the poet, the reader(s)

6.4.1.2   The text-world

As the participants in the DW communicate (in our example, as we the readers read Bishop's poem), they construct mental representations of the discourse in their minds according to the analogue schema as discussed in section 6.3 (based on beliefs, prior knowledge, memories, dreams, intentions, expectations etc.). Remember that these schema have a profound effect, and can be as vivid and affecting as experiences in AW. However, to prevent this mass of contextual information from becoming overwhelming TWT asserts that only the information which forms a necessary context, rather than all possible contexts, is used (in a vaguely similar way to Ryan's principle of minimal departure). The means of usage is through the notion of the **common ground** (CG), which is not all knowledge but the totality of information that the discourse participants have agreed to accept as relevant for their discourse. The CG itself shifts and realigns itself during the process as new ideas are introduced and old concepts are discarded as no longer relevant, or fade away due to no longer being mentioned. To refer to Stockwell (2002: 137), TWT is of value because it explains how in the discourse situation:

(1) A specification of contextual knowledge is managed economically.
(2) Text and context (of reading) are placed inseparably together.
(3) Interpretation is founded not on the analysis of sentences but on texts and their cognitive reception.

The cognitive mechanism that is the means of understanding is the **text-world** (hereafter, TW). Discourse participants use the text to construct the TW, the second level of TWT. Look again at the first lines (1–2) of 'Questions of Travel':

> There are too many waterfalls here;
> the crowded streams hurry too rapidly down to sea

As you read the words, your mind begins to formulate a mental picture based on your experience and the incoming linguistic information; this will be based on schema, themselves formed by images you have seen of waterfalls (in real life, in photographs, on screen), of streams, of the sea. You begin to form a corresponding world in your mind, based on the principle of minimum departure (i.e. the water is clear unless the text specifies it should be yellow). This is the TW.

All cognitive approaches to discourse are based on the idea that the mind and the body are linked. Evidence for this comes from the language we use to position ourselves in relation to others and the world around us. This area of language is known as **deixis** (a term we have already encountered in this book). The basic world-building elements of discourse locate us in a particular place, real or imagined, strange or familiar. But deixis is not limited to place – there are also objects and entities. Taken together, deixis and the objects within the TW work together as **world-building elements**. It is these prompts that your reader will be responding to as he or she builds a series of worlds in response to the poem or narrative.

Here is the information presented diagrammatically. The purpose of the diagram is to aid your understanding of the process, so it needs to be as detailed as possible:

> **TEXT-WORLD**
>
> **World-building elements**
>
> Waterfalls→ too many
> Streams→too crowded, rapid
> Clouds→turn to waterfalls
> Mountains→hulls of capsized ships

The horizontal arrows in the diagram signify what TWT terms **relational process**. Relational process can be intensive (x=y); possessive (x has y); or circumstantial (x is on/at/with y). There is also a process termed **material**. Material processes are **function-advancing**; that is, they indicate movement, change or dynamism (relational processes tend to be more static). How we identify the function-advancing elements of the TW depends on how we see the purpose of the text. Thinking of this poem in light of the processes we looked at in Chapter 1 (Halliday's **systemic functional grammar**), we can see that the main emphasis in Bishop's poem is on *perception*. Simply put, it is a poem about seeing, and the reflecting on what is seen.

Look again at stanza 3 by way of example. A feature of this section is **perceptual deixis** and **modality**. By use of the future perfect tense, the speaker speculates on a future possibility anterior to other events related in the present perfect. Future events are not open to observation or memory, so these are modalised, not factive ('it would have been a pity'). There are seven experienced events related in the present perfect, and they all relate to some point in time prior to speech time, that is, they are retrospective. Of the seven types of process encoded in the verbs ('see', 'hear', 'ponder'), all but one are mental processes. The one exception, 'having had to stop for gas', gives rise to all the rest, which are verbs of perception. In the time it takes to fill the tank, she is able to ponder the connections between such disparate objects as 'wooden clogs', 'a fat brown bird that sings', 'a broken gasoline pump', 'a bamboo church of Jesuit baroque'. These details would seem to suggest far more than the objects themselves – the clogs have not been civilised; the church of 'Jesuit baroque' evokes the earlier sixteenth-century colonisers who founded numerous missions in Brazil and are the subject of an earlier poem in the collection, 'Brazil January 1, 1502'. Although the syntax seems ponderous, its repetition serves to frame and foreground these perceptions, which are made even more appealing by Bishop's attention to sound patterning. One example of this is alliteration in phrases such as 'clogs carelessly clacking', the 'bamboo ... baroque' church and the 'calligraphy of songbirds' cages'. Choosing to relate her discoveries in a present tense keeps them very much alive and active, both in the mind of the speaker, and of the reader. Her detailed observation leads her to interrogate the processes of history – a theme of the poem, and arguably its function or objective. So, the 'hindsight' – as it were, the context of the discourse world – available to the creative writer has a very significant impact on the TW that we create in response to the discourse.

6.4.1.3   World-switches

Creative writing will almost always be made up of a series of text-worlds, then, which interact with one another. Each time we move from one TW to another, we talk of a **world-switch** (see exercise 6 as a further exploration of this notion).

Take a look at what happens in stanza 2. The temporal and spatial boundaries of the TW shift (this is indicated linguistically through the use of deictic language: 'Think of the long trip home'), and a new text world is conceptualised. See if you can fill in the gaps in the diagram to indicate how this works:

WORLD-SWITCH	TEXT-WORLD 2
	Time: Location: Objects: Enactors:

World-switches (which can take the form of flashbacks, flashforwards and changes of scene or perception) of this kind are very common in literary narrative and also in poetry. A further world-switch occurs in the poem in stanza 3. Try representing this one diagrammatically too. So far, then, the poem has set up three different text-worlds, moving from one to the next in each stanza.

To return once again to the concept of **empathy**: we as readers are more likely to empathise with humans or animals on the concrete end of a cline between autonomous and heteronomous than with the abstract ideas at the heteronomous end. Where on the scale of empathy would you situate yourself in relation to this poem? The diagrams demonstrate how the present tense translates into the present time for the TW. Because I experience the TW from the point of view of the persona of the poet, Bishop, I feel as if I am there experiencing things along with her. The guide is thus an **enactor**: she *enacts* the TW, and I live in it with her.

TWT can illustrate for us concretely and rigorously the ways in which linguistic elements work to build worlds in our imagination through exploiting, invigorating or reinforcing already acquired schema, and, indeed, altering, switching and extending them. We will explore exactly how this knowledge can be useful to the creative writer in the practice section at the end of this chapter.

6.5   Avoiding inhibition of return

When we write, we rely heavily on the schema of our readers (as TWT demonstrates). To return to the dichotomy between mimesis and diegesis from Chapter 1: it is the *former* (processes of 'showing') that exploit and make use of the reader's capacity to imagine most effectively and scrupulously. *This is why we should aim to show and not tell, to rely on mimesis over diegesis, wherever possible.* The mimetic function of literary discourse leaves enervating space for the reader's imagination to pick up on foregrounded features of the text and interact with them, to create text-worlds in response to them. Where the discourse is overtly diegetic, this process is to some extent already finished; the writer has done it on our behalf. There is less space for schema to be activated, and thus less space for active, vibrant, imaginative engagement with the text. Remember: we create schema from our memories and experiences, and thus, like the interconnected worlds of Borges's story, they have a 'life of their own'. If writing can reactivate these schema, or breathe life back into existing mental 'baggage' and associations, or even radically change them,[20] then it will be more engaging and enjoyable to read.

Relying on mimesis can also help to avoid what cognitive psychology has termed **inhibition of return** (in short, keeping the reader interested and engaged). Mimesis's reliance on existing readerly schema can ameliorate a common problem of beginning writers: overwriting, or overwrought descriptive language. Avoid the temptation to *tell too much*, to set the stage too thoroughly. Cognitive poetics shows us why it is important to learn to trust in the imaginative capabilities of the reader, and to allow them to do their mysterious work.

6.5 Distillation

- Look for internal coherency within text-worlds. Look also for the ways in which they interact with one another.
- Use TWT to ensure consistency of point of view (not just perceptual, or focalised, but also epistemological, i.e. what does a character *know*?).
- Notice how world-shifts can be used to bring out themes (we referred to this in Chapter 3 in terms of complex structure; you can use TWT to explore the effects of complex structure in much more detail).
- Trust the reader's imaginative capabilities, and avoid inhibition of return.
- Avoid excessive diegesis. Remember Hemingway's 'Iceberg Theory': the bulk of a piece of writing's power lies below the surface of the language. A dominant style can itself become **figure** when it should usually be **ground**. (There are some instances where this might be desirable, of course.).
- Manipulation of schema can also be used to unsettle readers through **defamiliarisation** (i.e. taking a situation that the reader will be familiar with, and then turning it on its head).

6.6 Practice

(1) Before you being this exercise, revisit the definitions and discussions of the nature of literary discourse introduced in Chapter 1, as well as the exercise you completed for that chapter (exercise 2). Now write a short piece (this can be prose or poetry, or indeed 'prose-poetry') exploring the idea of defamiliarisation. You should base your piece on one of the keywords from exercise 2 in Chapter 1. This defamiliarisation could take many different forms: a shift of point of view, of perspective, of language, of time and history, or of ideology. When you have finished, you should identify (as rigorously as possible) the linguistic tools you have used in order to defamiliarise your reader and, if possible, compare them with the responses of other students. There are several important questions to be discussed here:

    (a) In what ways are the texts 'literary' in the terms discussed in Chapter 1?

    (b) How does a poem differ from narrative fiction? How do we define a poem? How do we define a 'story'? Does stylistics help us to do this? If other students' work is available for comparison, this discussion could be carried out in comparative terms.

(c) Is it possible, linguistically, to talk of one text being more 'liter-ary' than another, or more poetic than another?

(d) To what extent and in what ways does the process of defa-miliarisation contribute to the imagining of the various text-worlds in your piece?

(2) Write a one-paragraph descriptive passage of prose based on one of the following prompts:

- a farm
- a market square
- a city coming to life in the morning
- the take-off of a jumbo jet.

No rewrite the passage, removing *all* adjectives. What effect does this have in terms of mimesis versus diegesis? When you have considered this, take **one** (only one) of the adjectives previously removed, and put it back in. What changes about your piece? Why?

(3) Carry out exercise 2, but this time focus on a section of an existing piece of work or a longer project.

(4) Focussing on poetry this time: select a piece of your own work which describes something (either physical, like a landscape, or abstract, a mental state, perhaps, or simply a point in time). Now identify the particular linguistic 'mechanisms' of the individual text- and sub-worlds which are being created. If possible, exchange your work with other students and carry out the same analysis, comparing and contrasting your observations in order to highlight how different individual readings can be. In detail: which parts of the individual reader's schema have been used to create different readings? Which aspects of the text lead to different readings, and which aspects to similar ones?

(5) Take a piece of your own writing, either poetry or prose (this could be something produced for one of the other exercises in this book, or something you have written in the past). Now go through the following steps:

(a) Draw a series of TWT diagrams showing all the word-building elements of your piece as appropriate. Which of these ele-ments are foregrounded in your mental representation of the text? Why?

(b) From where in the TW is the scene being described? Which world-building elements are close to the deictic centre and which are further away?

(c) If there is more than one, do you identify with any particular enactor in the TW? Why?

(d) Now identify any sub-worlds in the piece. Now add some more of your own (if there are no sub-worlds, add some). Try writing three different versions of the text:

   (i)   One containing a temporal world-switch
   (ii) One containing a spatial world-switch
   (iii) One containing both.

What expressive effect do these changes have in each case? In what ways could these world-switches be deemed thematically significant?

(6) See if you can find – or write – a piece of creative writing that contains *no* world-switches. Is it coherent? What effect does this 'stasis' have in expressive terms? Does it feel less like a narrative, and more like a moment in time? Is it somehow more intense, more distilled, as a result?

(7) Imagine a building (you could even use one you know) which has been changed dramatically but still bears traces of its former use, for example a pub that was once a church, an old peoples' home that was one a country house, a modern house converted from a barn where animals were kept. Two or more worlds are implicit here, of course. Write about a character who, happily or unhappily, cannot stop being aware of the building's history/previous use. Write no more than 500 words. Think about how the two (or more) worlds of this description inter-relate and interact.

7 Creative Writing: Figurative Language

7.1 Overview

In semantics, **figurative language** is usually defined quite specifically as the extension or augmentation of meaning for a word through the processes of metaphor (i.e. the meaning is transferred from one thing to another). Indeed, cognitive linguistics (and, further, deconstructionists such as De Man and Foucault) would argue that there is *no* genuine distinction between figurative language and literal or non-figurative language; figurative language is universal, both in terms of usage and in terms, even, of its providence. The mind is not at all literal in its methods meaning making, and figurative processes are fundamental to the ways in which we conceptualise experience. We will focus on metaphor as figurative language in the next chapter. The subject of *this* chapter is figurative meaning more generally. To refer to Katie Wales:

> [The term] figurative language sometimes embraces in literary criticism all kinds of devices or features which are semantically or grammatically marked or unusual in some way.

> (2011: 152)

We will be using this general definition of the term for the purposes of this chapter, and then narrow our focus down to metaphor in the next.

By this stage of the book, you should have a reasonably thorough understanding of two core stylistic paradigms sitting at the heart of this approach to creative writing: so-called standard language versus language which is perceived as pulling against such a norm (a process we refer to as **linguistic deviation**), and the accompanying idea of **foregrounding** (the ways in which deviations from the perceived linguistic norm will stand out, or become emphasised against the 'background' of standard language, and draw the reader's attention). You should also be able to see how deviation can be an indicator of the position of a piece of creative writing along a cline between transparency (we see through language into the story or poetic world beyond, in as far as the two can be satisfactorily separated) and opacity (we focus on the language, on the way(s) of *telling*, as opposed to that which is being told – again, and this point really does bear repetition: inasmuch as these two facets of literary discourse are separable). Carter and Nash (1990: 31) summarise the concept as follows:

> According to deviation theory literariness or poeticality inheres in the degrees to which language use departs or deviates from expected configurations and normal patterns of language, and thus defamiliarises the reader. Language use in literature is therefore different because it makes strange, disturbs, upsets our routinized normal view of things, and thus generates new or renewed perceptions.

In other words, degrees of deviation are often associated with 'literariness'. Carter and Nash cite Dylan Thomas's use of the phrase 'a grief ago' as an example of this; it departs from normal semantic selection restrictions, with the result that grief becomes seen as a process connected to time (as in the standard 'a month ago').

To summarise 'the story so far': a common feature of literary language use is its tendency to make use of linguistic deviation for expressive effect. Indeed, simply playing with the forms and shapes of language can be a source of poetic invention in itself – and not just in the writing of poetry. With standard English as 'ground', deviations become 'figure', foregrounded, and thus emphasised in the mind of the reader. A question hovering in the background of this book so far has been whether or not these deviant forms of expression are in and of themselves sufficient to define 'the poetic'. The answer is 'almost certainly not', but the assertion is a good starting point for the discussion of the subject, and for examining its implications for the creative writer.

7.2 Types of linguistic deviation

Stylistics has suggested a system of categorisation for linguistic deviation, which I have adapted for the purposes of this book (based on Short 1996: 37–63). To a large extent, these concepts will be familiar from the sections in Chapter 1 which dealt with levels of style; the focus here will be different, though, in that we will examine the ways in which creative writers can *deviate* from perceived norms which accrue in and around the various stylistic levels. We will now go through each of the categories in turn, taking examples from fiction and poetry by way of illustration. This list of categories is probably incomplete, but it is beyond the scope (or desire...) of this book to go into that level of detail. It should be sufficient for our purposes here to raise your awareness of the kinds of linguistic features that a reader will notice (through their being foregrounded) and respond to, and to give you some ideas as to how these kinds of strategies could be included in your creative practice – or, indeed, how you can work against them.

Linguistic deviation is, as you might expect, a very common feature of poetry. However, it is not uncommon in prose fiction too. The English novelist Martin Amis is a case in point. His narrative voices are full of various kinds of deviation, which stem from a characteristic blend of demotic cadences and 'mandarin' poetic description. There are examples drawn from his writing in the discussion below.

7.2.1 Discoursal deviation

As we saw in Chapter 1, 'discourse' is the highest level of linguistic organisation (above text, clause, lexeme and so on). Associated with different kinds of discourses (say, a conversation in the pub, a university lecture, a short story) are particular kinds of conventions, or norms. Just as in a sentence, we expect discourse to begin at the beginning. Short (1996: 38) quotes a very good example of discoursal deviation using Joyce's *Finnegans Wake*, which opens in mid-sentence ('riverun, past Eve and Adam's') and ends with beginning of the sentence with which it started ('A way a lone a last a loved a long the'):

> From noticing just this one deviant, and hence foregrounded feature, we can begin to understand that Joyce is creating a work which in a sense has no beginning and end. This observation is an important clue to the understanding of a novel where Finnegan observes his own funeral wake and tries to take part in it, thus blurring our commonplace distinction between life and death.
>
> (Short 1996: 38)

Thus, linguistic deviation to some extent provides the key to our understanding of the text. Another example can be found in Italo Calvino's novel *If On A Winter's Night a Traveller*, which begins with the exact words of the title, and on the cover page of the published version of the novel.

Martin Amis's *London Fields* also exhibits a degree of discoursal deviation. It opens as follows:

> This is a true story but I can't believe it's really happening.
> It's a murder story, too. I can't believe my luck.
> And a love story (I think)... (1)

This is an unexpected way for a novel to begin: the story seems to be 'true' (yet the statement opens a work of fiction) and, in some way, out of the control of the writer ('I can't believe my luck'). Amis here is deviating from the expectations of genre, and this has important implications (as was the case with Joyce's novel) for the way the novel's themes are presented.

The common device of *in media res* ('into the middle of things') is an example of discoursal deviation that is often used in literature. Imagine the following as the first line of a story or novel:

> The old man sat in the armchair by the fire. The wind blowing through the open window was making the flames flicker.

Substitute the definite articles for indefinite articles here, and the effect is very different ('**an** old man sat in **an** armchair'). The definite article implies familiarity, or shared knowledge between narrator and reader: 'You know the old man I'm talking about.' This is what creates the effect of *in media res*; the reader arrives on the scene with the action already in train (note the use of the past continuous, 'was making' rather than the past simple 'made', which implies an action already in progress at the time the reader 'enters' the text-world). In the second version, we feel present 'at the beginning' of the world. No shared knowledge is assumed. This second version (with indefinite articles) would be more usual in everyday language, and thus we can characterise *in media res* as deviant, and foregrounded. We realise straight away that, in the terms of Chapter 6, a possible world is being created.

7.2.2 Semantic deviation

Short defines semantic deviation as 'meaning relations which are logically inconsistent or paradoxical in some way' (1996: 43). Look at the unusual use of adjectives in this example from Amis's *London Fields*:

> The *splayed, eviscerated* suitcase' (53)

It is logically inconsistent to describe a suitcase as 'eviscerated', but the effect is clear. Look also at the use of a kind of metaphorical transfer (subsequently extended) in this example from the same novel:

> We passed through the damp dust of the velvet curtain, into *deeper* noise, *deeper* smoke, *deeper* drink. (61)

These instances of figurative language take qualities of depth and apply them to substances that do not usually possess depth: *noise* and *smoke*.

7.2.3   Lexical deviation

This category contains devices like neologism (the invention of new words or compounds, such as 'riverun' in *Finnegans Wake* or large parts of the poem 'Jabberwocky') or deviation from the normal function of word classes such as the deviant use of the noun 'query' in the following example from *London Fields*:

> Selina came at me in *queries* of pink smoke. (37)

7.2.4   Grammatical deviation

This is a very large category indeed, and includes any kind of deviation from accepted norms of word order:

> Yet I'll not shed her blood,
> Nor scar that whiter skin of hers than snow.
>
> > *(Othello*, 5.2.3)

Subject-verb or object-verb inversion are other common examples of this kind of deviation:

> Stopped they must be. On this, all depends... (Yoda, The Empire Strikes Back)

7.2.5   Morphological deviation

As Cureton (1979) discusses in detail, the poet e.e. cummings is a rich source of morphological deviation. There are many examples in the extract presented in Chapter 1.

> tumb
> ling through wonder
> ful sunlight

Other examples can be found in everyday vernacular – 'wonderful- ness', '...' – and from popular culture ('supercalifragilisticexpialidocious').

7.2.6   Phonological and graphological deviation

This type of deviation relies on the norms of phonological organisa- tion and norms of layout convention. In another example from *London*

Fields, Amis patterns the phonemes of the sentence to create an alliterative effect:

> Her *ferociously tanned* hair hung in solid curves over the *vulnerable valves* of her throat and its *buzzing body-tone.* (18)

Here, the pattern creates assonance:

> 'Tuxed fucks'. (18)

This kind of deviation is very characteristic of poetry, and will be dealt with in more detail in Chapter 9. A famous example of graphological deviation can be found in Roger McGough's poem '*italic*':

> ONCE I LIVED IN CAPITALS
> MY LIFE INTENSELY PHALLIC
> but now i'm sadly lowercase
> with the occasional *italic*

7.2.7   Internal and external deviation

So far we have discussed deviations to an external notion of some 'standard' usage. Internal deviation is 'deviation against a norm set up by *the text itself*' (Short 1996: 59). Common examples would be deviation from the formal metrical scheme of a poem in order to emphasise particular aspects of the line (we will return to this kind of deviation in Chapter 9). Can you imagine how this kind of deviation might function in a novel? How might a novel deviate from its own internally established norms?

So: the literary text should aim to 'pull in', to gather, to augment, meaning from as many different directions and methods as possible to create a unique linguistic medium for the work. Deviation from established linguistic norms is one way in which it can do this. Notice, though, as we have implied throughout, that literature is by no means the only form of discourse that does this. To quote Henry Widdowson (1973/2003):

> The meaning of any literary expression is a function of the relationship between the meaning it assumes in conventional discourse and the meaning it assumes as an element of a pattern within a literary text. In other words, because a literary text is deviant as communication the values of communication no longer apply. Consequently

the literary text depends upon a unique patterning of language to provide linguistic elements with new values over and above those which these elements carry with them from conventional use. It is in this sense that literary texts create their own language and thereby necessarily express a reality other than that which is communicated by conventional means. (36)

Is the presence of deviation sufficient in itself as a definition of the 'poetic', or of literary language in general? As I have already proposed: almost certainly not, but the assertion is a good starting point for more detailed discussion of the subject. It is good practice to continually ask yourself not just 'What am I doing *with* language in this piece?' but also 'What am I doing *to* it?'

7.3   Is there a standard language?

As we have seen, the very idea of deviation implies a norm, and thus the idea of linguistic deviation itself must imply that there is a 'normal', or standard, language. The different categories of deviation discussed and illustrated above should amply illustrate the range of norms from which the linguistically attuned (and inventive) creative writer can (perhaps gently) dissent (from conventions of discourse to conventions of textual layout). However, it is difficult to escape or ignore that underlying (and, of course, questionable) assumption of this approach: that there is a linguistic centre which must, in the end, be allowed to hold.

7.3.1   Mikhail Bakhtin and unitary language

An important critic/philosopher of language to dissent from this view (that there is a linguistic centre which must hold) is one already familiar to us from earlier in this book: Mikhail Bakhtin. In 1935 he published an essay, 'Unitary Language', which categorically denied the existence of any such thing. Language, says Bakhtin, is categorised by dissonance and heterogeneity, and without these characteristics it becomes stultified, barren and, worse, dominated by a centralised and dogmatic ideology. When one considers that Bakhtin worked under the shadow of Stalin's regime, these views become even more understandable. The ideas expressed in this essay are also very interesting in terms of the concept of opacity versus transparency of representational discourse.

Bakhtin (2003) asserted that all previous linguistic approaches to understanding discourse hitherto had assumed a 'simple and unmediated' relationship between a speaker and his or her language, and that this language is 'realised' through what he calls the 'monologic utterance of the individual' (269). In other words, linguistics had previously assumed that the individual is in complete control of what he or she speaks and writes, and can present his or her thoughts accurately and without undue evidence of mediation. As we have discussed already, this is not a satisfactory account of how language works; Bakhtin insists that content, sense, meaning etc. are always directly informed by sociohistorical context (i.e. ideology) and also by *purpose* (a kind of linguistic instrumentalism). These remarks are particularly applicable to poetic language.

The very idea of a unitary language, he says, relies for its existence upon centralising forces in language (such as the idea of 'correct' language) which run contrary to the true state of affairs: **heteroglossia** (literally, many languages). By 'heteroglossia', Bakhtin is not referring only to the existence of different national languages (a given) but different languages *within* national languages (dialects, registers, vernaculars, slang, formal registers, journalese, and, yes, literary language). He goes on to castigate the frameworks of classical poetics: Aristotle, Augustine, the Medieval Church, Descartes (neoclassicism), the grammatical universalism of Leibniz, Humboldt's insistence on the idea of 'the concrete' – all give credence, he says, to the myth of standardisation, and ignore the fact that language operates within the context of heteroglossia: of disparateness, difference, change and variety.

The 'authentic' environment of an utterance for Bakhtin is 'dialogised heteroglossia'. This is the context in which it 'lives and takes shape'. The term 'dialogised' comes from 'dialogue', and implies that languages, dialects, registers, voices and so on are in dialogue with one another, and are shaped by each other. **Dialogism** can take place on different levels: between a speaker and listener (where the former anticipates the response of the latter), and between the different *heteroglots* that go to make up language as a whole. Think of the function of parody, ridicule, profanity – all orientated against the so-called official language of the time.

The linguist should not look for 'unity in diversity' (2003: 272), then, and should learn to distinguish between an utterance's *neutral significance* and its *actual meaning*. The former is understood against the background of the sterile system of the language, while the latter is understood in the context of dialogue and heterogeneity.

To *be* means to communicate *dialogically*. We always use another's words in our own language, and every word is a site of struggle, a space where people's voices are perpetually contending with those of others. Every word is directed towards an answer and cannot escape the profound influence of the answering word that it anticipates. There is always some **addressee** projected by every **addresser**. Our dialogues are therefore not only backward-looking (to other people whose words we are using and reacting to) but also forward-looking (to future responses that we expect, fear or desire). There can be no 'unitary language' if these observations are true.

Bakhtin's interest in literature, and in the novel in particular, arose because it was in that genre that he believed writers were most free to experiment with the authentic 'multi-voicedness' (heteroglossia) of human culture. As we write creatively, we imagine an 'other' reading what we write (writingandreading again). Creative writing is intrinsically dialogic. Its energy comes from dialogue (in the broadest sense of that word), interaction and even friction: between you and your implied reader, between your characters, between your narrator and your protagonist, between voices, between registers, between creative writing of the past and creative writing of the now and of the future, between poetic conventions and expectation, between rhyme schemes, between images, between other texts, even between your language and the language of others (dialects, say, or even national languages). It bears repetition: creative writing will not thrive in a vacuum.

7.3.2   A sociolinguistic approach

What does modern linguistics have to say about the idea of a standard language? We should start by insisting that modern linguistics is a **descriptive** activity. It seeks to describe how language *is* rather than prescribe how it should be. From this statement alone, the answer to the question above should be obvious.

In sociolinguistic terms, and indeed in *all* rigorous linguistic terms, there can be nothing intrinsically inferior about any dialect or variety of a language compared to any other member of its language family. Any judgements about superiority/inferiority on aesthetic, moral, expressive or social grounds are simply prejudices, with no empirical basis in truth. All we can talk about are **norms** (see Crystal 1992: 236–7 and Wardhaugh 2002: 33–8) – as we were careful to do in our discussion of deviation above.

So, it would appear that modern sociolinguistics agrees with Bakhtin: language is, by its very nature, diverse and heterogeneous. While accepting these conclusions of twentieth- and twenty-first-century linguistics (that is, in many ways it is meaningless to talk of a standard language), we can still accept the idea of deviations from perceived norms once we focus on the adjective *perceived*. These norms are not set down from on high by the gods of language; rather, they are often local/regional/national in nature, spring from the idea of a linguistic community and are, to some extent, in the eye of the beholder. The sheer variety of language, and especially those languages which push against the notional centre, can in and of themselves be a source of creative invention (as James Kelman does in much of his work, especially the Booker Prize-winning *How Late It Was, How Late*). We can even find examples of invented fictional languages such as in Russell Hoban's *Riddley Walker* (1980), a future projection of an evolved English, based on Kentish and Estuary varieties, the Nadsat language of Anthony Burgess's *A Clockwork Orange* (1962) and the Mocknee of Will Self's *The Book of Dave* (2006).

We look, then, to the multifacetedness of everyday language for inspiration when it comes to writing creatively. To return to T.S. Eliot's (1942) quote from Chapter 5:

> Every revolution in poetry is apt to be ... a return to common speech.

In other words, 'poetic language' is at all times informed by the vernacular (the demotic); further, it is regenerated and reinvigorated by it. If poetry splits itself off from the everyday current of language, it becomes 'rarefied', disengaged and, arguably, irrelevant. As writers, then, we are engaged in a continual fight against tradition, while unavoidably appealing to it and being inextricably connected to it. There is a tension between tradition and originality.

So, if deviation in itself is not enough to 'signal' poetic language, are there certain forms of language which are intrinsically 'unpoetic'? For example: the language of a tax return, a McDonald's menu, the instructions for a washing machine ... This idea has been repudiated during the last century and the early part of this one; poets often delve into all sorts of unlikely sources to find their material (as you will have been doing throughout this book, I hope). In the 1930s, Ezra Pound and Eliot embraced the 'vulgar' and the demotic; in the 1950s, Larkin and others embraced slang and swearing; later, Carol Anne Duffy and Adrienne Rich have made use of quotidian registers; this has been taken even further by writers such as the Scottish poet Tom Leonard (see below). But what happens, then, if 'poetic' language becomes indistinguishable from 'everyday' language? Does it not run the risk of banality?[1]

Take, for example, Wordsworth and Coleridge's *Lyrical Ballads* (1798), which famously attempted to use as far as possible 'the language of the common man'. This excerpt is from the poem 'Simon Lee, the Old Huntsman':

> IN the sweet shire of Cardigan,
> Not far from pleasant Ivor Hall,
> An old man dwells, a little man –
> I've heard he once was tall.
> Full five-and-thirty years he lived
> A running huntsman merry;
> And still the centre of his cheek
> Is red as a ripe cherry.

Note the simplicity of the language, accessible to anyone literate (by no means the whole population at the time it was written, of course, but the poems are to some extent written to be read aloud). Here is a modern example from Tom Leonard, also, quite clearly, asserting that poetry should be reinvigorated by the demotic, not separated from it, and, further, that the language of so-called marginalised or regional varieties of English have every 'right to be written' as literature:

> this is thi
> six a clock
> news thi
> man said n
> thi reason
> a talk wia
> BBC accent
> iz coz yi
> widny wahnt
> mi ti talk
> aboot thi
> trooth wia
> voice lik
> wanna yoo
> scruff. if
> a toktaboot
> thi trooth
> lik wanna yoo
> scruff yi
> widny thingk
> it wuz troo.

Geoffrey Leech (1973) uses the analogy of a canal boat proceeding up a canal through locks: each lock is a poetic revolution, raising the game every now and then towards the level of the land surface of modern language – which is always slightly 'above' (ahead of?) the writing that it gives rise to.

So what does it mean to use language 'creatively'? Is it simply the avoidance of banality? It is something to do with linguistic deviation (doing the unexpected, or 'making fresh')? Leech suggests two definitions of creative language as follows:

(A) Writing which makes use of the established possibilities of the language AND
(B) Writing which goes beyond those possibilities; that is, by creating new communicative possibilities which are not already in the language.

We can find a useful anatomisation of originality here. Leonard's poem above is an example of originality in these terms, and that originality is derived directly from the particular type of language that it uses: the demotic. Look at the following example, again from Joyce's *Finnegans Wake* (1939):

> Eins within a space and a wearywide space it wast ere wohned a Mookse.

Linguists assume that a language such as English, theoretically, has infinite resources: an infinite number of sentences, most of which have never been uttered. Joyce's sentence is original in that, presumably, no one had ever uttered it before. However, it also breaks the 'rules' (deviates from the norms, this case syntactically, lexically, morphologically and grammatically) of English. This is an example of creativity type B, then, in that it goes beyond the existing possibilities of language.

Have we arrived, then, at a definition of the difference between 'creativity' in language and 'ordinary' language use? When we utter an 'ordinary' sentence, we are simply stringing pre-learned blocks of language together in familiar patterns; such 'prefabricated' statements are a part of everyday communication, but are sometimes seen in creative writing as symptomatic of bad style; for example, 'each and every one of us', 'at the end of the day', 'a damning report', 'the storm looks set to hit the city'. Should the mechanical be anathema to the creative writer? Is 'mechanical' the opposite of 'creative'? These are questions that every creative writer needs to engage with, even if they are, of course, very difficult to answer. As we have seen, writing can be invigorated by the 'ordinary'. It can also be invigorated by the 'extraordinary'.

We can agree, then, that it is very difficult to determine the exact limits of what is 'permissible' within the English language. We can finish this discussion, though, by returning to its original premise: that the demotic can enrich the hieratic (the vernacular entering the poetic). The exchange works the other way too, of course; metaphors from literature will sometimes enter general currency (for example, from the work of Shakespeare).

7.4   Is there a literary language?

Throughout this book so far, the vexed question of literariness has haunted the text like Banquo at the feast: what *is* literary language, and is it possible to define it rigorously in relation to so-called everyday language? This is a question central to the discipline(s) of stylistics, and one that it seeks to provide some answers to. I would argue that this question should also be central to the discipline of creative writing. If creative writing is a process of making literary language,[2] then how could it not be? Stylistics certainly provides us with the necessary analytical tools to make rigorous descriptions of the language of literature – in terms of its 'form' (or code) in relation to its 'content' (or message). Stylistics can also highlight the essential interplay between the two (as we saw in our discussion of the interfaces between semantics and the other levels of style), and it is of enormous value to the writer in this sense alone. Linguistic deviation itself has sometimes been cited as signalling that we are 'in the presence of literary language', but even a moment's thought about this will reveal the falsity of such a statement. Media language, especially advertising, makes use of linguistic deviation constantly. We find new words and phrases ('oatgoodness', 'fairy liquid', 'cookability') and also grammatical deviation such as 'A Kwik-Fit Fitter' or 'B&Q it' (Cook 2001: 140).

In short, it is now a generally accepted view within the stylistics and poetics academic community that there is not, or perhaps is no longer, a 'language of literature' which can be definitely excluded from other kinds of language (Jeffries and McIntyre 2010: 61). Indeed, developments within stylistics and linguistics in general, such as the investigation of the effects of metaphor begun by Jakobson and the Prague

Circle (1960, 1990) and extended by Lakoff (1981) and, more recently, Steen (1994), have made it impossible to view literary discourse in isolation from the language of the quotidian or everyday.

How to define 'literature', then? Again, this question should of intense interest to creative writers. Here are some general suggestions, in no particular order, drawn and summarised from the plethora of existing work on the subject. For literature, I'm going to – without apology – substitute the term creative writing.

- Creative writing requires and inculcates a certain readerly competence. We imagine the fictional or poetic world as it develops; the reader of poetry will need an ability to engage with 'non-standard' interventions in the levels of style discussed above (indeed, is it a defining feature of poetry that it blurs the borders between these levels?).
- Creative writing comes about as a *function* of language in its totality, and draws from its resources in totality. Roman Jakobson (1960) envisaged the poetic function as a central aspect of all communication, defining it as focussing on the form of the message for its own sake. He writes: 'Any attempt to reduce the sphere of poetic function to poetry or to confine poetry to poetic function would be a delusive oversimplification.' For example: 'Why do you always say *Joan and Margery*, yet never *Margery and Joan?* Do you prefer Joan to her twin sister?' 'Not at all, it just sounds smoother.'
- Guy Cook (1994) contends that literature (hence, creative writing) changes the way we see the world in that literary discourse is schema-changing (as we discussed in Chapter 6) whereas the discourses of, say, advertising are schema-*reinforcing*. If, as we have seen, it is difficult to define the literary by its stylistic or linguistic features, then we can define it by how a particular culture recognises it (e.g. as an elevated form of verbal art which shows readers an imaginative version of the world (or *a* world) which causes the reader to reflect upon their own views about the world or about the nature of reality). Is this too 'elitist', though? What about the kinds of entertainment provided by popular fiction, TV and drama?
- As with Jakobson, another approach is to describe different types of text by their particular features, and then characterise other text-types according to whether or not they exhibit these features. Those widely perceived as literary, then, will exhibit a particular set of features against which other texts can be compared; for example,
  (A) Formal distinctiveness and a focus on the language of the text (i.e. through foregrounding).

(B) Representational distinctiveness (defamiliarisation through foregrounding).
(C) Specific competence of readers in understanding the fictional world of the text.
(D) High status in the society where it is produced and read.
(E) Focus on the content (message) for its own sake. (Jeffries and McIntyre 2010: 64)

These features should be seen as stops along a cline, however; arguably, A is more typical of poetry, where popular literature might lack D and E.

I hope that you will find one of more of these propositions interesting and energising – even if you draw energy from disagreement with them. However, the key question to ask yourself as a creative writer is: what is it that you do when you manipulate the raw materials of language, and why are you doing it the way that you do?

7.5   Connotative and denotative language

Another key linguistic concept at the heart of the function of figurative language is that of **connotative** versus **denotative** functions. Beyond its 'literal' meaning (its **denotation**), a particular word may have **connotations**. In semiotics (see Chandler 2007), denotation and connotation are terms describing the relationship between the signifier and its signified (in Saussurean terms), and a distinction is made between two types of signifieds: a denotative signified and a connotative signified. 'Denotation' tends to be described as the definitional, literal, obvious or 'commonsense' meaning of a sign (Saussure's model of the linguistic sign focusses on denotation). In the case of linguistic signs, the denotative meaning is what the dictionary attempts to provide. 'Connotation' is used to refer to the sociocultural and 'personal' associations (ideological, emotional etc.) of the sign (a rose means something different in England than it does in Portugal, for example, and these arise from cultural connotations[3]). These are typically related to the interpreter's class, age, gender, nationality, ethnicity and so on. Signs are more open to interpretation in their connotations than their denotations. The denotational meaning of a sign would be broadly agreed upon by members of the same culture, whereas someone's particular connotations of a sign can never be justly criticised, as no inventory (such as a dictionary) of the connotational meanings generated by any sign could ever be complete. 'Meaning' as a whole, then, includes both denotation and connotation.[4]

Figurative language, surely, relies on the connotational capacity of language rather than its denotational aspects, and lays the ground for a richer, more textured and nuanced interaction between reader and text. Instead of following 'well-worn' paths in language, the writer can aim to 'make fresh', and thus to create expressions that are more vivid, and more effective. Awareness of this can also show the way to more innovative exploration of the myriad connections between your writing and its sociocultural contexts and associations.

7.6   Stylistic balance

This leads us to return to a central concept set up in Chapter 1 between writing that aspires to a kind of *transparency* and that which relies upon or exploits the qualities of *opacity*, which we will now term **stylistic balance** (after Boulter 2007: 76–7). Boulter illustrates this using a see-saw metaphor. Style is the pivot under the plank, and on one side is 'the world of the story, or fabula (the world we see through language)' and on the other 'the discourse-world (the world we write)'. The see-saw must compensate for emphasis or weight on one side by lessening emphasis or weight on the other.

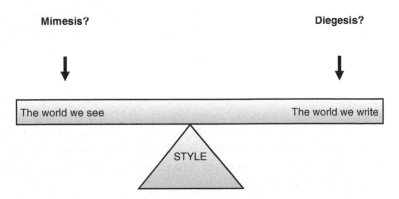

To use another metaphor, the 'canvas' of a piece of creative writing is of a fixed size. Putting more emphasis on one side of this equation (for example, through a strident and overt style which is highly deviant) leads to a change in the nature of the other side (the imaginative world as 'seen' by the reader). At the least, the reader may well focus on it less intently. We should mention and highlight here **the dangers of stylistic inventiveness for its own sake**. As Boulter puts it: 'many texts that strive for novelty do not survive' (76). She also goes on to quote Trevor Pateman (1997):

> Real imaginative achievements – the things that are brilliant, just right and deserve our applause are closer to what might call the banal than the fantastic.

The question of linguistic 'stridency' needs to be borne in mind, then, returning to an earlier issue: the extent to which the very 'effervescence' of such styles can divert attention away from the text-world and lead to undue focus on the text, and thus the discourse-world. Is this more of an issue in fiction than in poetry? Is the reader more accepting of deviation in poetry than in fiction? If so, why?

A further question is implicit here: does emphasis on one side lead to *detraction* from the other? If we are focussing on discourse and not world, is that world less rich? Not necessarily, I would argue, as novels such as F. Scott Fitzgerald's *The Great Gatsby* (1925) and the linguistically deviant poetry of e.e. cummings should show. Furthermore, can the metaphor of the see-saw be applied equally to the relationship between mimesis and diegesis? Does writing oriented towards mimesis (or showing) incline itself *away* from deviation and towards 'norms'? Or can figurative language and deviation in and of itself lead to 'better' and more 'authentic' processes of seeing? Creative writing methodology must, surely, respond to and/or correlate with specific visions of the world, otherwise what is its relevance, and why should we read it? Perhaps the stylistic balance should not draw undue attention to itself (*over*emphasising diegetic process?), but should focus attention on the imagined world (mimesis). In any case, it must always leave plenty of room for the reader's imagination to do its work. There is a fundamental choice for the writer to make here, which stylistics can illustrate: between style that calls attention to itself, and style that calls attention to the imagined world. Where will you aim to position your creative writing along the plank of the see-saw?

7.7 Practice

(1) Write two stanzas of overtly 'poetic' poetry, putting in as many linguistically deviant features as practicable. Examine the results, concentrating on grammatical features that seem expressly

'poetic' in nature. Now re-write the piece, aiming to smooth away those aspects which you think are excessive, and consider rigorously and in stylistic terms why you have deemed them so. What happens if the poem is re-written in as 'standard' a discourse as possible? What judgements have you brought into play to decide whether language is standard or not? How does an awareness of these judgements question the existence of a unitary language?

(2) The same process should then be followed with reference to an extended project or other work in progress. Can you identify those aspects of existing work that could be construed as linguistically deviant? What happens if they are removed/made 'standard'? Is the work improved by this transformation, or is something lost?

(3) Take some examples of narrative voices that you consider to be explicitly deviant (look at Amis's *Money* or Self's *The Book of Dave* for examples, if you like). Re-write some passages in a 'standard', normalised discourse. Is anything gained in terms of effectiveness? Is anything lost?

(4) Consider the suggestion that the very 'effervescence' of some styles can divert attention away from the story-world and lead to undue focus on the discourse-world. Is this more of an issue in fiction than in poetry? Is the reader more accepting of deviation in poetry than in fiction? If so, why?

(5) Here is a single stanza from a poem by Peter Redgrove, 'Old House'. Some of the words have been removed. Fill in the gaps, using the syntactic context to guide you. Then compare your version with original. Reflect upon and account for the differences between the two.

I lay in an _____ of imagination as the wind
_____ up the stairs and _____ on the landings,
_____ through floorboards from the foundations,
_____, withdrew into _____, and _____ the house.

8   Meaning and Play: Metaphor

8.1   Overview

Metaphor is a specific form of figurative language, which we covered in the previous chapter. It is a universal aspect of human communication and, as you should now have realised and predicted, is not confined by any means to literary language. We use metaphor every day. It is often said that metaphor is used to describe something that we don't fully understand in the language of something that we *do* understand. Think of the proliferation of metaphors used to describe loneliness, mystery, love or violence. In this chapter, we will home in on the function of metaphor and explore ways of improving our use of metaphor in our writing. First, we will explore the topic from the perspective of cognitive stylistics in an attempt to define metaphor rigorously and explain how it works. Then, we will look at the universality of metaphor as a fundamental aspect of human communication, and also, briefly, at the ways in which cultural context also plays an important role. After that, some of the pitfalls of writing metaphor as well as guidelines for directing and improving the 'internal logic' of your metaphors will be explored, before we put these ideas into our creative practice at the end of the chapter.

8.2   Defining metaphor

There have been many attempts to define metaphor rigorously and systemically, ranging from Aristotle's discussion of it in *Poetics* to the modern cognitive approach of stylisticians such as Stockwell (2002) and Steen (1994). As you might expect, we will end up by looking at the ideas of the latter school of thought, but it is interesting to look at other approaches to the topic first.

In *Poetics*, Aristotle defined metaphor as giving a thing a name that belongs to something else. The modern dictionary definition of a metaphor is equally straightforward, and will usually be something like this: 'a figure of speech in which a word or expression used to designate one thing is used to designate another and is thus an implicit comparison'. This helps somewhat. Look at this exchange, taken from the script for the US TV Drama *House, M.D.*:

> HOUSE: I'm a night owl, Wilson's an early bird. We're different species.
> CUDDY: Then move him into his own cage.
> HOUSE: Who'll clean the droppings from mine?

House's use of the terms 'night owl' and 'early bird' (and 'species') is metaphorical; the terms designate the differing sleeping patterns of House and his temporary lodger Dr Wilson. He is 'giving a thing a name that belongs to something else'. House likes to stay up late ('designated' by the metaphor 'night owl'), Wilson likes to get up early (he's an 'early bird'). The viewers will have no problem 'decoding' these metaphors; they are familiar and straightforward. Indeed, the term 'early bird' has its providence in a well-known English proverb: 'The early bird catches the worm.' Dr Cuddy, exhibiting excellent metaphorical competence, then extends the metaphor by designating 'apartment' as 'cage'. House continues it further in the last line of the excerpt. Together, these three lines constitute a simple but well-executed extended metaphor (see section 8.4).

A more complex (and, for the creative writer, more helpful) definition of a metaphor was provided by Samuel Johnson in his early version of the English dictionary (1755): 'A simile compressed in a word.' From this definition, we can begin to grasp the idea of metaphor as meaning crossing a gap between two ostensibly unrelated concepts: in the case of our example above, 'House is a night owl.' As we 'decode' this utterance in our minds, we transfer the meaning of 'night owl' across to the word 'House'. Notice the difference if we recast this example as a simile: 'House is like a night owl.' The use of the word 'like' makes the fact that this is a *comparison* explicit, and the meaning has further to travel,[1] in cognitive terms, from 'night owl' to 'House'. Thus, the pure metaphor, as Johnson points out, is compressed in comparison to the simile.

Indeed, we can deduce this process by looking at the etymological roots of the word itself. 'Metaphor' is made up of two morphemes, 'meta' and 'phor'. 'Meta' (from the Greek μετά) is usually defined as 'after' or 'beyond', or 'over' and 'adjacent' (think of 'metamorphosis', which means 'changing shape'; moving from one shape 'over' to another). 'Phor' is derived from the Greek φέρειν (*phérein*, 'to bear' or 'to carry'). Thus, 'metaphor', in terms of its morphological structure, means 'over-carry' – or to 'to carry over' meaning from one thing to another.

We can describe this process more rigorously, though, with an appeal to stylistics. In her *Dictionary of Stylistics* (2011), Katie Wales defines metaphor as follows:

> In rhetoric, a figure or trope that derives from Greek 'carry over'. One FIELD or DOMAIN of reference is carried over or mapped onto another on the basis of perceived similarity.

Introducing the concept of **domain** will be useful to us here (Lakoff and Turner 1989: 2–4). The term 'night owl' carries with it particular associations or 'implicit knowledge' (more formally, *connotations*) which the reader/hearer will use to assemble a mental image (based on pre-existing schema, as we say in Chapter 6). Cognitive linguistics terms these associations a **conceptual domain**. This domain is then 'carried over' to apply, in our example, to the character Gregory House.

Traditional poetics and rhetoric described the different parts of a metaphor as follows: **tenor** is that which is being referred to in the metaphor (i.e. House), and **vehicle** is the domain being carried over to the tenor (so, 'night owl'). The **grounds** for comparison can be found in the proposed similarity between the two separate domains, House and the night owl (obviously enough, both like to be awake during the night). However, these distinctions are purely grammatical, and have nothing to say about the way in which we process metaphor mentally as readers of literature. Cognitive poetics has come up with some interesting alternatives to this traditional model, based fundamentally on the assertion (which is unarguable) that metaphor is a fundamental aspect of human communication, and can be found in *all* types of language, not just the purely literary (we will discuss this in more detail in section 8.3).

8.3   The cognitive roots of metaphor

The universality of metaphor in human communication has been explored and demonstrated by a great many literary and linguistic scholars, most notably Roman Jakobson. Jakobson (Adams and Searle 2004: 1132) viewed all discourse as taking place 'along two semantic lines: one topic may lead to another either through their similarity or their contiguity'. As we speak or write, we select words according to two axes: the syntagmatic and the paradigmatic, in a vertical plane or in a horizontal plane (like a chain).

I'm a(n)	night owl,	Wilson's a(n)	early bird.
	evening person,		early riser
	nocturnal beast,		lark

Thus, our utterances are constructed by a combination of a horizontal movement conjoining words together, and a vertical movement selecting them from the many choices available within the language. Jakobson postulated a parallel here with the processes of metaphor and metonymy (we will discuss metonymy in more detail in section 8.4). Metaphor corresponds to the syntagmatic (vertical) axis (we substitute the domain of one thing for the domain of another across the 'chain' of the sentence; both domains are present in the sentence, i.e. 'House' and 'night owl') while metonymy works on the paradigmatic axis. In metonymy, we substitute a part of the thing for the thing itself, so in 'The night owl is on the wing', the wing means simply 'flying' (wings are a – fairly indispensable – part of the act of flying). 'Wing' replaces 'flying', and the word 'flying' itself is not present in the sentence.

Jakobson identified two forms of a language disorder called aphasia, and found that its two incarnations corresponded to these metaphorical propensities of human language. He called them 'Similarity Disorder' and 'Contiguity Disorder'. In the former, the person has difficulty producing words out of context, and tends to speak metonymically: so 'eat' is substituted for 'toaster' because a toaster helps make toast to eat. In contiguity disorder, the person has problems with context, and the syntactical rules that organise words into higher units are lost. Thus, his or her speech becomes an 'agrammatical' mush of words, often unintelligible. Jakobson's research proves that the metaphorical function of language is a fundamental facet of how we communicate, and also (even more interestingly) that (like narrative and syntax) it is evidence for a physiological truth about the way our brains are constructed.

A fictional exploration of the relationship between mind and metaphor can be found in Mark Haddon's (2004) novel *The Curious Incident of the Dog in the Night-Time*. Christopher Boone, the novel's narrator and protagonist, suffers from a form of autism known as Asperger's Syndrome. Even though sufferers have near-normal language development and average-to-high levels of intelligence, they struggle with particular communicative issues and with social interaction. Christopher speaks here of the problems he has understanding metaphor:

> The second main reason [why I find people confusing] is that people often talk using metaphors. These are examples of metaphors:
>
>> I laughed my socks off.
>> He was the apple of her eye.
>> They had a skeleton in the cupboard.
>> We had a real pig of a day.
>> The dog was stone dead.
>
> [...] I think it [metaphor] should be called a lie because a pig is not like a day and people do not have skeletons in their cupboards. And when I try and make a picture of the phrase in my head it just confused me because imagining an apple in someone's eye doesn't have anything to do with liking someone a lot and it makes you forget what the person was talking about.
>
> (Haddon 2004: 19–20)

While he struggles with metaphor, Christopher is happy with simile, because, in his terms, it is not a lie (22), and indeed often uses complex similes in his narrative, especially when trying to express the workings of his own mind.[2]

So, we have ample testimony to the fact that metaphor is a universal aspect of language use, and, further, our propensity to metaphor can be accounted for psychologically, and even physiologically. How can we put this understanding to use in the crafting of our own metaphors? Here we must turn once again to cognitive poetics, and a branch of it called Conceptual Metaphor Theory (CMT). CMT has proposed a more satisfactory model for the function of metaphor than that provided by traditional rhetoric (section 8.2):

> The central claim in Cognitive Metaphor theory is that pervasive patterns of conventional metaphorical expressions in language (e.g. I need a change of direction in my life) reflect conventional patterns of metaphorical thought, known as conceptual metaphors (e.g. LIFE IS A JOURNEY).
>
> (Semino 2007: 160)

In other words, there are universal metaphorical patterns that all of us are familiar with and make use of. One example, as Semino points out, is LIFE IS A JOURNEY:

> My life is going nowhere.
> She overcame an enormous number of obstacles to get that job.
> We're getting there!

Another is DEATH IS SLEEP:

> George fell asleep on 19th December 1896.
> She's at rest now.

Other examples: PURPOSES ARE DESTINATIONS ('I've nearly reached my target'), STATES ARE LOCATIONS ('I'm in a very bad place right now') and TIME MOVES ('That evening just flew by'). The kinds of conceptual metaphor that a particular culture or language grouping uses can be seen as symptomatic of the world views and ideologies of that culture (Semino and Windlehurst 1996: 147). In addition, particular cultural conditions and contexts will influence the kinds of metaphors that a language group evolves. A good example of this is the plethora of nautical and maritime metaphors in British English, influenced of course by the fact that Britain is an island and has a long maritime history. Some examples:

> My new boss has been showing me the ropes.
> It will be plain sailing from here.
> Let's try a different tack.
> It was all hands to the pumps this morning.

Think also of the numerous metaphors that arrive in the language from popular culture ('I'm feeling spaced out', 'It's a jungle out there', 'He rode off into the sunset'). So, metaphors appear on one hand to be conceptual, and thus in some sense (like syntax and narrative) a fundamental facet of the way we see though language; on the other hand, they are influenced by cultural context. Thus they are of interest to both cognitive linguistics and sociolinguistics – and, of course, to creative writers... Let us now refine the rhetoric model through the insights of CMT. To return to Semino:

> Conceptual metaphors involve systematic sets of correspondences between a **source** conceptual domain (e.g. JOURNEY) and a **target**

conceptual domain (e.g. LIFE), and typically enable us to make sense of abstract, complex, or poorly delineated experiences (such as time and emotions) in terms of more concrete, simple and well delineated experiences (such as movement in space or containers).

(2007: 160, my emphasis)

When we interpret metaphors, we 'map' concepts from the source domain (which corresponds roughly to rhetoric's term 'tenor') to the target domain (roughly speaking, the 'vehicle').

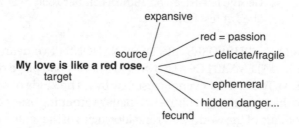

The important difference between the cognitive approach and the traditional literary approach lies in the concept of **blending** (Stockwell 2002: 106–7). In the example metaphor in the diagram, we **blend** the concepts of 'love' and 'rose' by **mapping** the properties of the source domain onto the target domain. The result is a blended conceptual space or domain – an **emergent meaning** (see also Jeffries and McIntyre 2010: 144) created by a combination of two separate domains (the properties we associate conceptually with the rose, shown in the diagram as a kind of spider of associations, and our conception of love; a new meaning emerges). In the best (or most effective metaphors), this emergent meaning will be unique and, crucially, almost inexpressible by any other means. Of course, it could be argued that the example used in the diagram has now become a cliché through overuse. It is a dead metaphor.

Try re-writing the following metaphors *literally* (i.e. without evoking any blend of source and target):

> Dr House is a night owl.
> My new boss has been showing me the ropes.
> My life is going nowhere.
> My love is like a red rose
> Juliet is the sun.
> Why should I let the toad work squat on my life?

This should get progressively harder to do. Presumably, you came up with something like 'Dr House likes to stay up late at night' for the first. However, even that fails to capture the idea of solitude which we glean from the conceptual domain of 'owl'. It also misses the slightly sinister quality that we associate with owls: the silent wisdom we read into their gaze, the spookiness of their hoot and so on. The last two examples are, arguably, impossible to 'translate' into literal language without losing their effect almost entirely. I would argue that the harder a metaphor is to render literally, the 'better' it is. If your metaphor can be easily rephrased literally, why use a metaphor? You could have left 'my love is like a red, red rose' just as it is. It is dead.

What other implications does an understanding of the cognitive roots of metaphor have for us as creative writers? One of the central ideas to grasp is the way in which sophisticated use of metaphor leads to a more active process of text-world building in the mind of the reader by virtue of the fact that the process of semantic cognition 'travels further' in the act of arriving at interpretation. By forcing the reader's mind to arrive at meaning via new routes (in the transfer, or 'carrying over', of meaning from target to source, or, to be more precise, in the act of blending conceptual domains), a text will prove more stimulating, and the reading experience become more vivid. In fact, it might even be possible to argue that the greater the cognitive 'distance' between source and target domain (i.e. the more work the reader's mind has to do in blending the domains and arriving at the emergent meaning), the more effective, rich and interesting the metaphor. The philosopher John Searle writes:

> Although similarity often plays a role in the comprehension of metaphor, the metaphorical assertion is not necessarily an assertion of similarity.
>
> (1979: 88)

I would go further. The less similar the source and target, the more interesting the metaphor. Look at the cognitive 'distance' between 'toad' and 'work', for example. I doubt we would find WORK IS A REPTILE listed as an archetypal conceptual metaphor.

This leads us to a related concept: **cliché**. The following are (in my view; argue with this position if you like) all examples of clichés:

> The night was as black as pitch.
> Your eyes shine like diamonds.
> I cried like a baby.
> I was frozen to the spot.

Three of these are similes, yes, but we will be treating them all under the category of metaphor (see section 8.4). With the help of CMT, we should be able to describe in rigorous terms *why* clichés are examples of bad writing, rather than accepting this as a truism. The answer goes something like this. The reading brain trundles along frequently travelled routes (George Orwell describes these kinds of figurative language as the 'dying metaphor'; another term is **dead metaphor**[3], which we used earlier in this section); in other words, the richness derived from blending dissonant or very separate cognitive domains is dissipated over time and with repeated use. It is almost as if clichés completely lose their metaphorical power. No blending takes place, and the expressions function simply as literal language does. The reader has learned to process them without effort, and without creating an emergent meaning. In the terms of Chapter 7, these metaphors are no longer exploiting the connotative functions of language and have instead become denotative in effect. Sadly, clichés are all too common in published writing; we should aim to avoid them like the plague[4] in our own work.

The final lesson to be drawn from CMT is related to the ways in which we as creative writers represent the minds of our characters and narrators. Semino and Swindlehurst (1996) propose that particular metaphorical habits or 'tics' (as we saw in the excerpt from Mark Haddon's novel) discernible in a character or narrator's habit of speech, thought or writing can be very useful in terms of representing that character/narrator's psychological make-up (or cognitive habits) and world view:

> We suggest that, at an individual level, the systematic use of a particular metaphor (or metaphors) reflects an idiosyncratic cognitive habit, a personal way of making sense of and talking about the world: in other words, a particular mind style. (147)

They go on to cite the example of Bromden in Ken Kesey's *One Flew Over the Cuckoo's Nest* (1973). Bromden is a homodiegetic narrator who makes frequent use of metaphors drawn from the source domain of MACHINERY. Semino and Swindlehurst argue that use of metaphor plays a central role in the ways in which the reader forms an image of Bromden's mind and engages with it. It also sheds interesting light on the mental illness that afflicts him. It gradually becomes apparent that the dominance of machinery imagery in Bromden's mind (as presented by the narrative discourse) is due to his experience as a professional electrician. Further, the reader can relate this to his eventual breakdown and mental illness. He seems to use his understanding of machinery to compensate for his shortcomings in terms of interpersonal communication and, in general, his inability to understand and experience empathy. In short, he cannot relate to other people's minds and emotions, just as he cannot relate to his own.[5] Using particular idiosyncratic metaphorical logic or patterns can allow the writer to represent mimetically not only mental illness, of course, but also a character or narrator's particular obsessions, preoccupations, ideologies and, in general, their 'habitual ways of conceptualising reality' (Semino 2007: 161). Deft representation of metaphorical habits can add authenticity to both dialogue and narration.

8.4   Types of metaphor

We have already hinted at some of the different forms of metaphor. It will now be useful to list and define each one individually, with examples.

8.4.1   Simile

At school you will have been taught about the difference between metaphor and simile. You will have been told that a simile is a figure of speech that directly compares two different things, usually by employing the words 'like' or 'as', and that it is different from a metaphor, which compares two unlike things by saying that the one thing *is* the other thing. I would like you instead to think of simile as a *kind* of metaphor, rather than as separate from metaphor. So, we will talk about *pure* metaphor versus simile. The reasons for this, as you may have predicted, arise from the fact that both pure metaphor and simile exploit the same cognitive concepts of blending, where a source and target domain come together to create an emergent meaning. The difference between them lies in the 'conditionality' imparted by the use of 'like' and 'as' (or even explicit conditional structures such as 'as if').

> My love is like a red, red rose
>
> That's newly sprung in June.
>
> Boats on clear water look as if they float in air.
>
> They are as gentle
> As zephyrs, blowing below the violet,

Not wagging his sweet head; and yet as rough,
Their royal blood enchaf'd, as the rud'st wind,
That by the top doth take the mountain pine,
And make him stoop to th' vale.

Bob was as perplexed as a hacker who means to access
T:flw.quid55328.com\aaakk/ch@ung but gets
T:\flw.quidaaakk/ch@ung by mistake.

I raise my head like a snare.

The second example illustrates how simile can function by setting up an alternative text-world through the deictic shift of 'as if'. Rather than the conceptual domains found in pure metaphor, it is perhaps helpful to the creative writer to picture the function of simile in text-world terms. The simile creates two text-worlds that seem to co-exist and interrelate, rather than blend (as would be the case in pure metaphor). A distance between target and source is maintained.

8.4.2   Synecdoche

A synecdoche is formed by substituting a physical part of the thing being described (the target) for the thing itself. Think of it as the substitution of a part for the whole, or vice versa.

Come and have a look at my new set of wheels.

The suits are all in a meeting.

And did the countenance divine
Shine forth upon our clouded hills?
And was Jerusalem builded here
Amongst these dark, Satanic mills?

Can you spot the synecdoche in each case? What is the 'larger part' that forms the absent target of the metaphor? The answer is particularly interesting in the case of William Blake's 'Jerusalem'.

8.4.3   Metonymy

In contrast to synecdoche, metonymy occurs in the substitution of one term for another with which it is commonly associated; if you prefer, an *attribute* of the thing is substituted for the thing itself: the Crown (for the Monarchy), the White House (for the Presidency of the United

States), 'on the bottle' (for having a drink problem). Jacques Lacan was of the opinion that our dreams function through metonymy; the things that you dream about are really just aspects or attributes of the *real* focus of the dream. This is a troubling idea...

8.4.4 Extended metaphor

Extended metaphors are metaphors in which the source domain is extended and drawn upon in more detail, often sustained throughout a text or through a significant part of it.

> You with your snout, your seams, your stitches and your sutured youth. You, you with your smocked mouth are what your songs left out.

> He gave the appearance of a man who can count angels on the head of a pin, but is at a loss to notice when the pin is skewering him.

Do you need to know all this – to distinguish rigorously between metonymy and synecdoche, for example – to be able to write good metaphor? Almost certainly not. Do you need to know all this to be able to analyse, say, poetry with insight and precision? Almost certainly yes. Somewhere in between these two positions lies the subject's relevance to creative writing. I would argue that it is helpful (at the very least) to the creative writer to be able to spot where his or her metaphorical thought processes and logic are going awry. I would also argue that the concept of cognitive distance between source and target is a helpful one in guiding the writer towards the creation of rich and exciting figurative language. See the exercises in section 8.7 for more detailed exploration of the application of these concepts to creative practice.

8.5 Pitfalls: the mixed metaphor

The mixed metaphor is a paradigmatic example of poor writing, and it can be found all the time, even in published work. Look at these examples:

> A lot of success early in life can be a real liability – if you buy into it. Brass rings keep getting suspended higher and higher as you grow older. And when you grab them, they have a way of turning into dust in your hands. Psychologists . . . have all kinds of words for this, but the women I know seem to experience it as living life with a gun

pointed to their heads. Every day brings a new minefield of incipient failure: the too-tight pants, the peeling wallpaper, the unbrilliant career.

If not, the quagmire of self destruction in which societies have placed themselves will run its course until nothing of the former civilization is left, but a rotting shell of its former self. This is another natural law which will not be denied.

Can you see where these metaphors go awry? Look for the ways in which the source of the metaphor becomes confused and entangled with a different conceptual domain (brass rings, dust, guns, wallpaper, quagmire, rotting shell...). Why do you think a mixed metaphor should be seen as 'bad writing'?

What has gone wrong in this example (from a recent edition of a well-known newspaper)?

The Tory rebellion tells us nothing we didn't know: even among those voting with Cameron, fanaticism over Europe runs through the party like a stick of rock.

8.6   Why use metaphors?

- Metaphors enliven the language.
- Metaphors encourage readers to think and to come up with their own interpretations of your writing. They encourage the active, creative use of schema and imagination.
- Metaphors give a great deal of meaning with a minimum of words; they are economical.
- Metaphors create new meanings; they also allow you to write about feelings or thoughts or experiences for which there are 'no words'.

8.7   Practice

Exercises:

(1)   Look at the following prompt:

Your eyes are...
I cried...
Love is...

That Autumn was...
The journey was...

Continue each of these as a short metaphor. The challenge is to avoid cliché at all costs. When you are happy with the results, try extending the metaphor with one line. You should then aim to refine and distil the results, referring again to issues raised in previous chapters about diegesis versus mimesis and trust of the reader's imaginative capabilities.

(2) Think of a hobby or pastime that you are familiar with and, ideally, partake in (e.g. photography, playing or watching sports, dancing etc.). Now use the lexical field associated with that hobby to create an extended metaphor from prompt nouns taken from Lakoff. 'Love' combined with 'football', 'Time' with 'role playing games', 'Death' with 'graffiti art' – the more disparate the two, the more interesting the exercise. Is it true also that the more disparate the target and source, the more effective the results? If so, why?

(3) Find two examples of haikus (see Chapter 9). These are examples of tight, compact metaphors – distilled almost to their bare bones. First try to anatomise them according to the model of source, target and grounds. Then, try writing your own haikus centred on a 'distilled' metaphor.

(4) Take an abstract concept like 'neglect', 'absence' or 'joy'. Write an x = y metaphor. Then see if you can change it grammatically, using it as a verb, an adjective/adverb, or in a prepositional or appositive phrase. Which version do you think is more effective?

(5) Write a 20-line poem in which you use similes and/or metaphors to convey a feeling, an idea, a mood, or an experience you have never been able to communicate to anyone before because each time you tried it seemed that you were being untrue to the experience; say, you left out something essential or you couldn't convey how mixed your feelings were. No matter how hard you tried, the feeling or the experience slipped through the sieve of language. In your poem use as many similes and metaphors as you want, but don't use fewer than five. Otherwise, there are no restrictions, so the lines can be of any length and you don't have to use rhyme.

9 Creating Soundscapes: Rhythm and Meter, Sound and Sense

9.1 Overview

I.A. Richards makes the following assertion in his *Practical Criticism* (1929: 15):

> The effects of *technical presuppositions* have to be noted. When something has once been done in a certain fashion we tend to expect similar things to be done in the future in the same fashion, and are disappointed or do not recognise them if they are done differently. Conversely, a technique which has shown its ineptitude for one purpose tends to become discredited for all. Both are cases of mistaking means for ends. Whenever we attempt to judge poetry from outside by technical details we are putting means before ends, and – such is our ignorance of cause and effect in poetry – we shall be lucky if we do not make even worse blunders. We have to avoid judging pianists by their hair.

He sounds a cautionary warning in the direction of the enterprise this chapter is about to undertake. Is he right to do so? As we have discussed elsewhere, is it possible to take issue with Richards's separation of means and ends, especially when it comes to a genre where (assuming we understand 'means' to signify 'language' and 'ends' to signify 'expression') the two are so inextricably entwined? This question should be uppermost in your minds as we approach perhaps the most difficult and wide-ranging topic addressed in this book so far. Indeed, this relatively short chapter can only ever scratch the surface of the complex interrelationships between rhythm, sound and sense in language (especially when it feels duty bound to take in at least some of the vast amount of research on the topic generated within modern linguistics) – but it is hoped that this overview will give you enough material with which to experiment in your own creative writing. It should also be noted that large parts of the material in this chapter (with the sections on phonology being a notable exception) are explored also by literary criticism in general, and should not be seen purely as insights gleaned from stylistics or literary linguistics per se (although I maintain that these latter disciplines shed far more powerful light on the topic). However, it should be obvious that a book aspiring to approach creative writing from the perspective of the study of language must take account of them.

Although many of the ideas discussed in this chapter are most obviously applicable to poetry, writers of narrative fiction too have an enormous amount to learn about control, accuracy of expression and the correspondence between 'sound' and 'sense' from the processes involved in writing poetry (just as poets can learn from traditionally fictive disciplines such as narrative structure; see Chapter 3).

9.2   Phonology: a brief overview

If this chapter has a central point to make, then, it is this: that meaning can come about not only through the conventional correspondence between what Saussure (1995) called the signifier and signified,[1] but also through **phonological** reinforcement. Briefly, phonology (a huge area of research) is the study of how sounds are organised and used in natural languages. The phonological system of a language includes an inventory of its sounds and their features as well as rules which specify how sounds interact with each other to produce meaning. A **phoneme** (like a morpheme and a lexeme) is a linguistic unit, this time of sound, which may indicate meaning. A useful way of grasping how phonemes can indicate meaning is by imagining what would happen if we replace one phoneme with another in a word. So, take the word 'bad'. If we replace the middle phoneme we can make 'bawd', 'bed', 'bid', 'bird' and 'bud' – or 'bod'.[2] In all cases, it is just a single vowel sound that changes (even if two letters are used graphologically to represent that vowel sound, as in 'aw' or 'ir'), but the word's meaning alters fundamentally.

The other significant aspect of phonology for us to bear in mind here is related to what are called **prosodic features** – to do with emphasis in pronunciation. Broadly, we can talk about:

- *Stress or loudness*
  Increasing volume is a simple way of giving emphasis, and this is a crude measure of stress. It is usually combined with other things like changes in tone and tempo. We use stress to convey various

meanings (semantic and pragmatic) such as urgency or anger (in imperatives, say: 'DON'T do that').

- *Intonation*
  We use varying levels of pitch in sequences to convey particular meanings. Falling and rising intonation in English may signal a difference between statement and question. Younger speakers of English may use rising (question) intonation without intending to make the utterance a question. Think also of the difference intonation can make to meaning in certain words: 'to re**lay** information' versus 'a **re**lay race'.
- *Tempo*
  We speak more or less quickly for many different reasons and purposes. Occasionally it may be that we are adapting our speech to the time we have in which to utter it (as, for example, in a horse-racing commentary). However, mostly tempo reflects some kind of meaning or attitude. For example, we might give a truthful answer to a question, but do so rapidly to convey our distraction or irritation.
- *Rhythm*
  Patterns of stress, tempo and pitch together create a rhythm. Some kinds of formal and repetitive rhythm are familiar from music, rap, and even the chants of football fans. However, the crucial point to grasp is that *all* speech has rhythm; it is just that in spontaneous utterances we are less likely to hear regular or repeating patterns.

The relevance of phonology (in terms of sounds and rhythms) to literary language, especially poetry, should be obvious. We as creative writers exploit phonological reinforcement and correspondence through sound and rhythm to create particular effects in our writing. There is an important connection, then, between sound and sense which a knowledge of phonology can help make clear.

9.3   Musical or meaningful?

Following on from the previous section's very brief overview of phonology, I will try to distil these insights into a paradigm that we can work from for the rest of the chapter. The insights into sound and sense below come from two practising poets, Don Paterson and J.H. Prynne, and a practising poeticist, Gerald Bruns.

> In English poetry, the feeling that a piece of writing is 'musical' usually means that it quietly exhibits two kinds of phonetic bias. ... The first

is the deliberate variation of vowel sounds; the second is consonantal patterning.

(Paterson 2007: 58)

So, we get a sense of musicality from language when it shows evidence of conscious phonetic 'ordering' (or, if you prefer, mediation), as I attempted to demonstrate at the end of the last paragraph. This sense of ordering, of crafting, comes from patterns on one hand and variations on the other. To quote from Alexander Pope's 'Sound and Sense':

> True ease in writing comes from art, not chance,
> As those move easiest who have learn'd to dance.

Combine Paterson's view with that of Bruns and J.H. Prynne:

> Poetry is made of language but is not a use of it – that is, poetry is made of words but not of what we use words to produce: meanings, concepts, propositions, descriptions, narrative, expressions of feeling and so on. ... Poetry is language in excess of the functions of language.
>
> (Gerald Bruns, quoted in Prynne 2009: 144)

> It is indifference to the alterative effect of textuality that causes Derek Attridge to write, following the consensus, that 'poems are made out of spoken language'. I believe this statement to be decisively not true, unless it is also to be believed that tables and chairs are made out of living trees.
>
> (Prynne 2009: 144)

Paterson implies that poetry can and should exploit the sound symbolism (the phonological reinforcement of meaning) which is inherent in language. His concept of the function of poetry insists that it relies fundamentally on *spoken* language, and thus is drawn from normal speech. This is entirely in keeping with the premises of stylistics, with which you will be more than familiar by now. Prynne refers instead to what he calls 'mental ears', and a more complex correlation between sound and meaning, focussing on phonology and the history of the word. In other words, the correspondence between sound and sense is sociocultural, and not inherent to language itself. There are patterns in language that we recognise and respond to through learning to understand what they signify over time.

This is a fascinating and complex debate which is of enormous relevance to creative writers in terms of the ways in which we work with and manipulate the sounds of language, whether writing poetry or prose. Unfortunately, we do not have the space to explore it in the detail it deserves here.[3] These are the two concepts, though, which I wish to draw from it and then use throughout this chapter: the tension between **musicality** and **meaning** which exists in language. As creative writers, we should be attuned to the ways in which our work can gain 'expressive capital' from this tension. In short, we should aim to replace the 'or' of the title at the head of this section with the word 'and'.

9.3.1   Trying it out

Before continuing, it is worth putting these ideas into practice through stylistic analysis. To start with, I would like to return briefly to the breakdown of linguistic/stylistic code described in Chapter 2. When approaching poetry, both reading it and writing it, or, indeed, any piece of creative writing that aims to exploit the music of language, we need to think about all of these levels of style in order to see how they interact. Indeed, it is in the genre of poetry, arguably, that the interaction between the various linguistic levels is most mixed. To reiterate, we can arrange linguistic levels as follows:

Meaning	Lexis (word meaning)
	Semantics (sentence meaning)
Grammar	Syntax and morphology (the 'shapes' of sentences and words)
Sounds/Writing/Shapes[4]	Phonology (speech)
	Graphology (writing)

When it comes to stylistic analysis of poetry, we home in on each of these linguistic levels in order to see how they interact. As one might expect from the focus of this book, we are going to reverse the usual method of working by applying this stylistic toolkit to a piece of our own work rather than someone else's.[5] The reason for bringing this practical exercise in earlier on in the chapter rather than at the end is that I hope it will 'make concrete' some of the rather (unavoidably) abstract speculation of the previous two sections. It is also to get you used to a method of working when writing poetry that could be summed up as 'close re-reading', for which we have used the term writingandreading).[6] Another reason is that we will return to this list at the end of the chapter, in a much more detailed form (augmenting it with the concepts that we introduce in the rest of the chapter). So, think of it as a 'before and after' exercise. What do you gain from carrying out this analysis now (with the knowledge of stylistics you already have), compared to what you gain from carrying it out at the end of the chapter?

So, take a poem that you have already written, or perhaps one that you are currently working on, or, perhaps, something from a friend, colleague or fellow student. You could, equally, try this with a short piece of creative prose. Go through the following list:

(a) First, read for **general understanding**. Read your poem (or prose) through several times and then summarise it in a couple of sentences. What is it about, in as few words as possible? The idea is to try and split yourself in two, to separate (for the moment) reader from writer. (We will be putting you back together again shortly.).

(b) Now, try a **semantic** analysis. Look at each stanza (or sentence, or line) in turn. Look for semantic deviation (anything that strikes you as odd) and relate this to your overall understanding as summarised in (a).

(c) Next, focus on **grammatical** patterning. Isolate the sentences or clauses of the poem, and then look for grammatical and syntactical patterns (structures that repeat themselves). Look also for structures that are deviant, both from 'perceived linguistic norms' and the norms set up by the poem itself. Explain how these work, again in terms of (a).

(d) Next comes **phonology**. Are there any patterns of rhyme, alliteration ('**P**eter **P**iper **p**icked a **p**eck of **p**ickled **p**epper'), assonance ('**sou**nd gr**ou**nd', 'the w**e**st is the b**e**st') or other sound elements that are fairly obvious and can be related in an interesting way to (a), or, indeed, to more localised aspects of meaning?

(e) Lastly, focus on **graphology** – the look on the page. Does the text deviate in any obvious way from norms of presentation, punctuation, layout or typeface? Again, can these be connected back to (a)?

What you should have by the end of this process is a relatively detailed overview of the way the 'sense' of your poem is reinforced, augmented or otherwise affected by its constituent linguistic elements (above and beyond the 'purely' semantic, if that is not an oxymoron). If you tried this with a piece of prose, we would (presumably) expect the results to be less detailed and less interesting. We would expect to find a less obvious relationship between sound and sense, in other words. Are we approaching (one of) the Holy Grail(s) of literary criticism here: a definition of poetry? Probably not. However, we are on safe enough ground, I think, when we suggest that poetry usually foregrounds language, its structures, and, particularly, its *sounds* to a greater extent than prose. This stylistic exercise should prove that point rigorously.

We will now return to the concept of musicality and go into more detail on the various phonological aspects of language (including sound and prosody) that are important to the writer. We will split the concept of 'musicality', then, into **sound** and **rhythm**, focussing on each in turn.

9.4   Sound and sense

Saussure (1995) postulates that the relationship between a word and its meaning (the signifier and the signified, 'tree' and the idea of 'tree-ness') is arbitrary. In other words, there is no reason why we call a tree a tree, and no reason – contrary to popular opinion – that we should call a spade a spade. A moment's thought will demonstrate the sound-ness of this proposition (to common sense, at least). 'Tree' in French is '*arbre*', 'spade' is '*pelle*'. These different linguistic signs are no 'righter' than their English counterparts, and have evolved out of a particular set of historical, sociocultural and linguistic circumstances to signify what they signify today. Just a moment, though. What about words like 'hiss' and 'cough'? To some extent, these words in their phonetic make-up mimic the actions which they signify; they are mimetic rather than purely referential (or diegetic, perhaps). Here, it could surely be argued, the connection between sound and sense is no longer simply incidental. This is a very simple example, then, from everyday language of how meaning can come about not only through the conventional correspondence between signifier and signified, but also through phonological reinforcement.

9.4.1   *Phonological parallelism*

These reinforcements of meaning through sound occur, as we have seen, not just at the level of the individual word but also across clauses, sentences, paragraphs and complete texts. In other words, we make use of what Paterson called 'phonetic bias': patterns of sound. Stylistics categorises these patterns as examples of **parallelism** (a 'balance' between two or more instances of words, clauses, sentences or, as here, *sounds*; we will look at other kinds of parallelism in section 9.5). Parallelism occurs whenever there is a partial, not full, correspondence between two or more pieces of text at some linguistic level (see section 9.3.1); a full correspondence would, of course, be repetition.

Phonological parallelism can be found between two or more phonemes. There are six possible ways in which one or the other 'halves' of the parallel structure can vary, and these lead us to neat definitions of all of the most common poetic effects that rely on sound patterning:

great/**gr**ow	C-v-c	send/**s**it	alliteration
great/f**ai**l	c-V-c	send/b**e**ll	assonance
great/mea**t**	c-v-C	send/han**d**	consonance
great/**gra**zed	C-V-c	send/**sel**l	reverse rhyme[7]
great/**gr**oa**t**	C-v-C	send/**s**oun**d**	pararhyme
great/b**ait**	c-V-C	send/**end**	rhyme

c = consonant; v =vowel.
Adapted from http://raid.layliturgy.org.

This list, as you can see from the second column, covers all the possible options for phonological patterning of vowels and consonants (for creating music from language, in Paterson's terms). It is worth noting, too, that in poetry generally, sound is more significant than spelling. As a result, we can also talk about eye-rhyme (e.g. *cough/bough*), which exhibits a pleasing parallelism on the page if not to the ear when enounced. Eye-rhyme is an example of graphological parallelism, then. In terms of the differences between reading aloud and reading text 'silently': many poets, the performance poet Patience Agbabi included (see Swann et al. 2011: 32), see poetry as something that has to be performed rather than read on a page to reach its full expressive potential. This is certainly something for the creative writer to bear in mind. Reading work aloud (even if you are happy for it to be disseminated fundamentally as text) is a very good way of spotting phonological parallelism (often where you least expected it to be) and honing or developing it further. Remember: these patterns will often evolve spontaneously in the act of writing; it is up to you during the process of re-reading and editing to hone and to shape them as you see fit. It is also worth pointing out, finally, that the act of reading silently can also involve the silent articulation of the sounds we are reading. It is not necessary to hear language spoken aloud to recognise and appreciate the phonological patterns being set up and exploited.

The examples of phonological parallelism discussed above can also be discerned through sounds which are *similar* as well as identical; in other words, the pattern can be 'looser' than the fairly strict categories identified above would suggest. One example of this would be 'loose alliteration', as in this example:

> Stasis in darkness.
> Then the substanceless blue
> Pour of tor and distances.
> (Sylvia Plath, *Ariel*, 1968)

The foregrounded consonants of this excerpt (/p/ /d/ /t/) are all examples of what phonetics terms **plosive** sounds (characterised by the 'explosion' or gush of air expelled to make the sound). These plosive sounds are further sub-divided according to the actions we perform with our lips and tongues in order to make them. So –/d/ and /t/ are **velar** sounds (produced by arching the blade of the tongue up and pushing it against the soft palate at the back of the roof of the mouth); the /p/ is a **bilabial stop** – the sound is produced by pressing the lips together and then opening them as the air passes through.

For the sake of completeness, here is a list of the characteristics of consonants in English (it is not exhaustive by any means, but should be enough to give you an overview). Think of these as the bricks from which you are able to build your patterns.

(1) Liquids and nasals: e.g. /l/, /r/, /n/, /m /
(2) Fricatives and aspirates: e.g. /v/, /f/, /h/, /s/
(3) Affricates: e.g. /tch/ (as in church), /dz/ (as in judge)
(4) Plosives: e.g. /b/, /d/, /g/, /p/, /t/, /k/.

So, how do the sounds we make with our tongues and lips as we read these lines above (or hear internally if we read them silently) augment or reinforce the 'meaning' of the lines (bearing in mind the complexities of this idea of poetic meaning as explored in section 9.3.1)? It could be argued that the loose alliteration in these lines is in many ways equivalent to the lexis; in this case, to the features of the landscape being described (look at the line 'Pour of tor and distances' and imagine the undulations of the landscape mapped onto – or under – the undulations of the words' sounds). The lines also link together the three elements of air, water and earth, and the phonological patterns shared across the three lines reinforce this connection.

9.4.2 Onomatopoeia

As we have already mentioned, onomatopoeia refers to the *mimetic* power of language: its (presumed) ability to imitate other (mostly non-linguistic) sounds. We mentioned 'hiss' and 'cough' above. Other fairly obvious examples are 'buzz', 'whisper', 'clatter' and, of course, 'cuckoo'. Look at the following examples:

(a) Calm was the day, and through the trembling air
Sweet-breathing Zephyrus did softly play. (Edmund Spenser, *Prothalamion*, 1596)
(b) Wild thyme and valley lilies whiter still
Than Leda's love, and cresses from the rill. (John Keats, *Endymion*, 1818)
(c) There lies a vale in Ida, lovelier
Than all the valleys of Ionian hills. (Alfred Lord Tennyson, *None*, 1833)

How do the sounds of the language reinforce the lines' sense in each case? In (a), the sibilants represent the sound of the wind, perhaps. All the consonants in (c), except the 'd' of 'Ida', belong to the 'soft' end of the scale. Moreover, each one of them is a voiced consonant, rather than unvoiced which further suggests softness. Also, placing the plosives between vowels as in 'Ida' makes it less vigorous than if it was placed at the beginning of a word, say 'Dia' for example. The repetition of the /l/, /v/, /n/, and of the diphthong /ai/ in 'lies', 'Ida' and 'Ionian' gives (c) a richness in sound texture. What about (b)? However easy it is to yield to the vague suggestiveness of sounds, you also need to make sure you associate the sound carefully to its particular linguistic context. In short, beware **the phonoaesthetic fallacy** (Simpson 2004: 68–9), which comes about when trying to connect a phonetic feature of a text with non-linguistic phenomena outside it.[8]

9.5 Rhythm and meter

Prosodist (prǫ·sǒdist). 1779. [f. as prec. +-IST.] One skilled or learned in prosody.

Prosody (prǫ·sǒdi). 1450. [ad. L. *prosodia* the accent of a syllable, a. Gr. προσῳδία, f. πρός to + ᾠδή song, ODE.] **1.** The science of versification; that part of the study of language which deals with the forms of metrical composition; formerly reckoned as a part of grammar, and including also *phonology* or *phonetics*, esp. in relation to versification.

Having dealt with the sounds of words, we now move on to look at their rhythm (termed **prosody** in phonology), and how the fact that English is an accentual language with a high percentage of monosyllabic words can be exploited by creative writers to add to the effect of musicality. Indeed, it is useful (and intuitive) to borrow some terminology from music and speak of the **measure** (or 'bar' in British English) as a basic unit of rhythm, just as we divide musical scores into bars for the same reason. Think of each measure beginning with a stressed syllable. So, the line '**Half** a league, **half** a league, **half** a league **on**ward' by this reckoning contains four measures, and the foregrounding of the stressed syllables against the background of the unstressed ones is what creates the phonological pattern, or, in this case, rhythm. A number of unstressed syllables (varying from 0 to 4) can occur between one stressed syllable and the next. In this example, we have two unstressed syllables between each stressed syllable. In any ten syllables there tends to be 4–6 stresses, depending on whether the lexis is Latinate or Germanic. Iambic pentameter (e.g. 'If **I** should **die** think **only** **this** of **me**'), of course, takes existing stresses and orders them into a pattern of 5 per line (count them). These patterns also provide cohesion (holding the poem together as a text across its lines), and a **ground** against which variations can be used to foreground particular parts of the poem for various effects (for example, to create extra emphasis, a phonological correspondence with an actual-world event – the thundering of horses' hooves, for example – or even humour).

A useful rule of thumb to bear in mind here is that 'proper' nouns (names) and lexical words (nouns, verbs, adjectives and adverbs) tend to be stressed in speech, whereas grammatical words (prepositions, auxiliaries, articles, pronouns) are usually unstressed. So:

The **present King** of **France** is **bald**.
Oh my **word**, I've **left** the **gas** on.
Someone must have been **telling lies** about **Joseph K**.

(Note that all three of these sentences would conventionally be identified as prose, and yet have clear rhythmic structures; rhythm is a fundamental quality of language.) Syntax also has a bearing on syllable quantity. An unstressed syllable is especially short if it closely relates in syntax to the stressed syllable following it ('the **gas**'; we barely enounce 'the' if speaking this sentence quickly – as presumably we would be). Remember too that syllables within the same measure will not necessarily have the same length, even if they all count as one syllable. Some vowel groups, especially diphthongs, tend to be longer, as in: *bite, bait, beat, bought* (all longer than *bit*). Others tend to be short: *bit, bet, bat, but*. Furthermore, the type of final consonant influences the length of the vowel: *beat* is shorter than *bead*, *bead* is shorter than *bees*. If there is more than one final consonant, this contributes to the length of the syllable: *bend* is longer than *bed* or *Ben*. All of these features contribute to the effect of the rhythm of your writing, and phonological features that your writingandreading ear should be attuned to.

There is a formal system of prosody which is used to describe and classify the rhythmic effects of poetic language. We call this **meter**. Each unit of meter in traditional poetic prosody is called a **foot** (as if things were not confusing enough already). The bold type in the list below indicates stress, the backslash indicating the boundary between one foot and the next.

Iamb (e.g. re**fuse**, dis**miss**, for**get**)
If **I** /should **die** /think **on**/ly **this**/ of **me**

Trochee (e.g. **fan**cy, **ear**wig, **Lon**don)
Peter /**Pe**ter /**Pum**pkin/ **Ea**ter

Anapest (e.g. debon**air**, inter**vene**, disa**gree**)
The Assy/rian came **down**/ like a **wolf** /on the **fold**

Dactyl (e.g. **mag**ical, **won**derful, **Jer**emy)
Half a league, /**half** a league, / **half** a league/ **on**ward.[9]

Spondee (e.g. **football**, **hairbrush**, **climax**)
Rocks, caves, / **lakes, fens**, /**bogs, dens**, / and **shades** of **death**.[10]

The metrical patterns set up in each case, then, play some role in mirroring/augmenting the sense of the line. The trochee, for example, has a child-like air about it due, presumably, to its rhythmic simplicity and march-like qualities (**dum** da **dum** da **dum** da **dum** da, 1–2–1–2–1–2–1–2), and is often found in children's poetry and nursery rhymes ('**Incy win**cy **spi**der', '**Old** Mac**Don**ald **had** a **farm**'). Its mirror image, the iamb, is the classic foot of English poetry, largely because rhythm in English, as we have mentioned, is characterised by patterns of alternating stressed and unstressed syllables. It is also tempting to speculate that another attraction of the iamb is the way it mirrors the heartbeat as well as the beat of the language (da **dum** da **dum** da **dum** da **dum**). We find the iamb (as a **pentameter**, arranged in patterns of five iambs per line as in the example above) at the heart (pun intended) of English poetry from Chaucer through to Shakespeare through to Wordsworth and beyond.

In the poetic contexts from which they are drawn, the dactyl and anapest seem to gallop, like the hooves of the horses and the feet of the warriors in Tennyson's 'Charge of the Light Brigade' (a dactylic tetrameter; four feet) and Shelley's 'The Destruction of Sennacherib' (an anepestic tetrameter), while the spondee mimics the tolling of a bell and seems to signal portentousness, even doom (think of King Lear's desperate cry 'Blow winds and crack your teeth' – a spondaic trimeter, if you are still counting – where each monosyllable is stressed equally).

The point of all this, of course, is not simply to learn the various prosodic names from 'classical' literary criticism and apply them to your own work (although you may wish to do so, and to do so is, in fact, a very worthwhile exercise in control and poetic discipline[11]), but rather to realise, once again, the importance of pattern in terms of poetic effect. For example, an extension of a previously established pattern can increase tension (adding extra feet to subsequent lines); reducing the number of stresses, correspondingly, reduces pace and tension. Look at the opening lines to Wordsworth's 'Ode: Intimations of Immortality' (below) for a very good example of how varying meter can influence tension, pace and texture. (The number of feet per line is given in brackets at the end.) The stanza combines dimeter, trimeter, tetrameter, pentameter and hexameter, while the rhythm throughout is iambic.

There **was**/ a **time**/ when **mead**/ow, **grove**,/ and **stream** (5)
The **earth**,/ and **ev**/ery **com**/mon **sight**, (4)
To **me**/ did **seem** (2)
Ap**par**/elled **in**/ cel**est**/ial **light**, (4)
The **glor**/y **and**/ the **fresh**/ness **of**/ a **dream**. (5)
It **is**/ not **now**/ as **it**/ has **been**/ of **yore**; (5)
Turn **where**/soe'**er**/ I **may** (3)
By **night**/ or **day** (2)
The **things**/ which **I**/ have **seen**/ I **now**/ can **see**/ no **more**. (6)

The prosodic 'scaffolding' of a line also provides a background against which carefully manipulated deviations can foreground themselves, adding emphasis and, often, augmenting or complementing sense.

> To **be** /or **not**/ to **be**/, **that** is/ the **ques**/tion.

The heartbeat of the iambic pentameter is pointedly interrupted by the trochaic substitution which occurs in the fourth foot (**that**). This deviation, in tandem with the sense of the lexis, stresses the monosyllable 'that'. (Note also the weak ending, which adds an extra syllable to the five two-syllable feet preceding it.)

9.5.1   Forms ...

Often, the kinds of formal meter described above are combined into particular patterns that constitute classical poetic forms. It is worth looking briefly at some of these (once again, this list is by no means exhaustive) before we move on. In all of these examples, form itself is foregrounded, and it is the conventional structure that lends shape to the poem. The poem situates itself within a genre, and that genre is characterised by a structured form in just the same was as, say, an iambic pentameter or trochaic hexameter, but over the scale of the whole text rather than just one line. Once again, these forms provide backgrounds against which deviations can foreground themselves to great effect.

9.5.1.1   Sonnet

The **sonnet** is a lyric poem of 14 lines of equal length, traditionally in iambic pentameter. The rhyme scheme follows two patterns: in the Italian sonnet, there is an eight-line octave of two quatrains (four lines long) rhymed *abbaabba*, followed by a six-line sestet, rhymed *cdecde*. The English sonnet comprises three quatrains and a final couplet, rhyming *ababcdcdefefgg*. Here is a famous example of an English sonnet (note the trochaic substitution in the first and second feet of the first line before the traditional iambic rhythm begins):

> Let me not to the marriage of true minds (a)
> Admit impediments, love is not love (b)
> Which alters when it alteration finds, (a)
> Or bends with the remover to remove. (b)
> O no, it is an ever fixèd mark (c)
> That looks on tempests and is never shaken; (d)
> It is the star to every wand'ring bark, (c)

Whose worth's unknown although his height be taken. (d)
Love's not time's fool, though rosy lips and cheeks (e)
Within his bending sickle's compass come, (f)
Love alters not with his brief hours and weeks, (e)
But bears it out even to the edge of doom: (f)
If this be error and upon me proved, (g)
I never writ, nor no man ever loved. (g)[12]

9.5.1.2   Ghazal

The **ghazal is** another type of lyric poem, much shorter than the sonnet and written in couplets using a single rhyme which creates a cohering parallelism across the lyric as follows: *aa, ba, ca, da*. It is usual (but by no means a 'rule') to find the poet's name mentioned in the last couplet. The form originates, it is believed, in Arabic verse, and was often sung as opposed to simply being recited. Once again, the link between pattern/form and musicality in language is explicit. Look at this example by Nancy Gaffield:

> **Belle Isle**
> Sweltering heat so they withdrew to the river
> Love under the bridge within view of the river
> It was always there in the middle, whispering
> Through the long night, a sigh they knew as the river
> In unreliable light, motor city murk,
> Man in khaki learns to make do by the river
> A woman who's never alone, her arms enfold
> The baby inside who is used to the river
> You could see the USA from your Chevrolet
> Then the city of Detroit outgrew the river
> In the red and green blink of the light everything
> Changed as migrating birds flew over the river
> At the end of summer the roads doze in the haze
> Today nothing remains of you, or the river
> ©Nancy Gaffield 2012

9.5.1.3   Sapphic verse

These lyrics are written in four-line stanzas originating from the classical Greek tradition, and, again, the pattern of the form is strictly proscribed by convention and a long tradition. The first three lines have 11 syllables, and the last have five. Although in Greek the meter is fixed (the first three lines use a sequence of five metrical feet of trochee; trochee or spondee; dactyl; trochee; trochee or spondee and the fourth line is a dactyl followed by a trochee or a spondee), it is difficult to adapt these stress patterns to lyrics in English.

9.5.1.4 Sestina

Sestinas, believed to be a medieval French lyric form originally, are poems of six six-line stanzas followed by a three-line stanza known tradition-ally as an *envoi* or *tornada*. The sextets and the envoi are lent cohesion through an intricate pattern of repeated line-endings. The established pattern of repetition is as follows: 1 ABCDEF, 2 FAEBDC, 3 CFDABE, 4 ECBFAD, 5 DEACFB, 6 BDFECA. The envoi uses all six words, line of them as line-endings. See Kathryn Maris's poem 'Darling, would you please pick up the books?'[13] for a wonderful modern example of the form.

It is worth leaving this section on rhythm, meter and form with a direct piece of advice. Creative writers who are coming to poetry afresh, or those who approach it with some trepidation, will find the idea of meter and rhythm, and, of course, the classic forms discussed briefly above, a useful scaffolding against which to lean and gain support when they first begin to construct poetry. It is, of course, a scaffolding that you are free to dismantle and pack away, piece by piece if neces-sary, as you gain confidence. Or it may well be that you wish to keep working within it, find the stability and framework it provides inspir-ing, and notice that it has a stark beauty all of its own. I will leave the last word on this distinction between so-called formal and free verse to a much better crafted extended metaphor than mine by W.H. Auden and to another poet, Robert Hass; it is up to you to take these pieces of advice or discard them with the bottles on the floor:

> The poet who writes 'free' verse is like Robinson Crusoe on his desert island: he must do all his cooking, laundry and darning for himself. In a few exceptional cases, this manly independence pro-duces something original and impressive, but more often the result is squalor – dirty sheets on the unmade bed and empty bottles on the unswept floor
>
> (Auden 1962: 22)

Hass (1984: 107–8)) writes about meter and rhythm as follows, con-trasting it with poems that do not adhere to it:

> Every metrical poem announces a relationship to the idea of order at the outset, though the range of relationships to that idea it can suggest is immense. Free-verse poems do not commit themselves

so soon to a particular order, but they are poems so they commit themselves to the idea of its possibility, and, as soon as recurrences begin to develop, an order begins to emerge. The difference is, in some ways huge; the metrical poem begins with an assumption of human life which takes place in a pattern of orderly recurrence with which the poet must come to terms, the free-verse poem with an assumption of openness of chaos in which an order must be discovered.

The central point to take from this as that *all* poetry, regardless of whether it adheres to a meter or a rhyme scheme, sets itself against the background of rhythm in language. Free verse poems 'commit themselves to the idea of [meter's] possibility', but in some sense work against it. To be glib for a moment: metered poems *impose* order on chaos, free verse poems *find* order in chaos.

9.6   Parallelism revisited: repetition

In the terms of stylistics, we should place most of the remarks made so far about sound and rhythm under the umbrella of parallelism (as defined in 9.2.1) in as much as they are all examples of establishing and then working from (or against) patterns, whether simply binary or more extended. However, **repetition** as a form of parallelism in poetry is so common a device as to be worthy of a section of its own.

Repetition is one of those poetic elements that plays, I would argue, on our basic, most atavistic instincts. Human beings love to find patterns (just witness the way we manage to find a face on the surface of the moon and the shapes of animals in the patterns of clouds). Repetition, of course, is the most obvious form of pattern, and as readers we look for it, home in on it and find it pleasing. Repetition also allows anticipation, and gives us something to work from in poetry that can often be conceived of as 'difficult'.

Free repetition (exact copying of some previous part of a text – whether word, phrase or even sentence) is a deliberate rhetorical effect. These different sorts of repetition have their own taxonomy.[14] However, the taxonomy itself is not particularly important; it is much more important that you understand the particular effect or concept that each term denotes. Repetition, skilfully handled, can add a great deal to your poetry (or, indeed, prose), for example, by suggesting an intensity of feeling or through reinforcement. Repetition can add force to emotion – by suggesting an intensity of feeling, for example, in this instance from The Bible:

> O my son Absalom, my son, my son Absalom! Would God I had died for thee, O Absalom, my son, my son!

What are the functions of verbal parallelism? One argument for it might be that we need to express ourselves 'super-abundantly' on matters which deeply affect us. There is also a connection with ritual, and liturgy. The repetition hammers home the message, and as such could be seen as an example of sound reinforcing sense.

9.7 Free verse

The kinds of 'formed' writing that we have looked at in section 9.5 should now be contrasted with contemporary free verse and prose-poetry. The first point to make is that, despite Auden's protestations above, writing free verse should not be like playing tennis with the net down. It is just as formally demanding as metrical verse (if not more so, since the order lent by the presence of the net and the chalk lines on the grass has been removed), and it should have aural and visual rhythms of its own which, when manipulated with skill, should augment or in other ways interact with the 'semantic' capacity, or sense, of the writing. The second point to make, which is in some ways contrary to the first, is that all the concepts and ideas discussed so far in relation to phonology and to formed verse can (and often should) also be applied to free verse. The idea is *moderation*. In other words, the parallelism and patterning lent by phonological reinforcement and prosodic features will be less ostensible, less explicit, in free verse. You should, in short, still be looking for these patterns in your writing (either as part of creative practice itself or during later editorial rewrites and reappraisals, through writingandreading) and augmenting or developing these patterns if they seem promising, however subtle or understated the final result. To emphasise: these patterns can, of course, be phonetic or prosodic in orientation – or both. Having said all that, of course, there is nothing to stop you writing free verse which eschews all such patterning (as far as that is ever possible, given the way English works phonologically; that is, through the alternation between stressed and unstressed syllables).

This raises that troublesome question again which I have tried to dismiss already but which keeps returning like a boomerang: can we formulate a rigorous linguistic definition of 'literariness', or, to be more specific for the purposes of this chapter, the *poetic*? As we have seen already, stylistics in general eschews any such distinction between literary and 'everyday' language, and Roman Jakobson's communication model (see Chapter 7) explicitly and definitively located the poetic function of language within the scope of language as a whole, including its quotidian manifestations. Is the following poetry, then?

> Two all-beef patties, special sauce, pickles, cheese and onions, all wrapped up in a sesame-seed bun.[15]

What about now?

> Two
> all-beef patties, special
> Sauce,
> Pickles, cheese and onions,
> all wrapped
> Up in
> A sesame seed bun.

I will shy away from providing a detailed answer to this question, but you could (if you so wished) discover plenty of phonetic and prosodic patterning across the line. The second version makes use of the kinds of graphological and typological deviations discussed in Chapter 7, as well as a range of different line-endings and pauses. At the risk of ducking the question, I leave its answer up to you, and to that great poet of the objectivist school George Oppen:

> Prosody is a language, but it is a language that tests itself. Or it tests itself in music – I think one may say that. It tests the relations of things: it carries the sequence of disclosure.

> (2008: 49)

9.7.1 Pauses...

A further instance of patterning that we need to address is represented in the line break, which constitutes a graphological (and thus an interpretive) pause in the poem. This is particularly important in free verse; in formed verse, the metrical structure itself (and, indeed, the formal limitations imposed on the line length) will to some extent determine the position of pauses and line breaks, although of course there is still plenty of scope for artful manipulation. You can exploit the position of line breaks in free verse (and for that matter in formed verse) to great effect, once again augmenting the overall sense of the writing.

We can define a line of poetry as a unit of verse ending in a typographical break. This break usually represents a slight hesitation or pause, so that the word at the end of the line and the beginning of the next line receives added emphasis; in other words, they are foregrounded against the background of the poem's graphological scheme.

There are two kinds of break described in classical literary criticism. The first is the **caesura**, another musical term, which refers to a pause or halting that occurs in the course of a line rather than in between one line and another ('To err is human; to forgive, divine' – Alexander Pope, 'An Essay on Criticism', 1711)). The second is enjambment, which describes a link break where the running-on of sense continues from one line to another ('It woz in April 1980-wan/doun inna di ghetto af Brixtan/dat di babylan dem cause such a frickshan' – Linton Kwesi Johnson, 'Di Great Insohreckshan', 1999)). If there is no running-on of sense from one line to another (i.e. there is a pause in sense at the end of the line, or the line-end coincides with a major syntactic boundary, that of sentence or clause, then we refer to the line as **end-stopped** ('They fuck you up, your mum and dad. / They may not mean to, but they do./' – Philip Larkin, 'This Be the Verse', 1971)).

We can also add some more kinds of line break to this list, more typical of free verse. One example is **extension**. As the reader comes to the end of a line, they think that the linguistic unit is completed (there is a syntactic boundary, or the sense seems complete). However, the next line continues the sentence. This creates a surprise effect: for example, 'And everyone young going down the long slide / To happiness, endlessly.' Note also that the meaning across this particular extension works in contrast; the end of the preceding line seems tragic in tone, but the following line contradicts this impression (or does it...?).

Another is **arrest-release**. Sometimes upon reaching the end of the line the reader knows from the preceding structure that it is grammatically incomplete: 'Silence, and space, and strangers – our neglect /Has not had much effect.' As the reader gets to 'our neglect' he or she knows that there is more to come due to innate expectations of grammar. So far, we have only been given the subject of the clause. The arrest-release, which is of course a variety of enjambment, tends to produce two instances of foregrounding, one at the end of the line where the arrest occurs ('our neglect'), and one at the later point, where the arrested structure is released ('Has not').

9.7.2   Some features of free verse

While accepting that the sub-title of this section is, arguably, an oxymoron, there are still some linguistic and stylistic features that we can associate with free verse. The following list is *descriptive* rather than prescriptive, of course, and is in part made up of a series of observations about the kinds of stylistic features that are often seen in free verse writing. The other points in the list are to do with issues surrounding it rather than specific linguistic features associated. The aim should, again, be to combine creative practice with editorial acumen through writingandreading. These concepts can, of course, be in the forefront of your mind as you write, but, equally, you may prefer to let the work flow on its own terms during the draft stage and then read it through with the following suggestions and concepts in mind. Finally: remember that everything we have discussed regarding prosodic features and phonological reinforcement (as well as parallelism in general, line-endings, repetition) also applies to free verse. This cannot be stressed enough: be on the lookout for interesting patterns in your writing, and develop those that look promising.

These ideas will be explored more fully in the practice section of this chapter.

- Remember, as Auden implies and Hass insists, that so-called free verse is in fact foregrounding itself against the background of stricter forms (for example, from the canon of classical poetry) just as formal or lyric poetry foregrounds itself against the 'freer' phonetic and prosodic patterns of everyday language. Herein lies the musicality of both. Both imply conscious, artful mediation. The opposition between 'free' and 'formal' verse is in fact a binary one, just like 'darkness' and 'light'. The one would be inconceivable, and physically impossible, without the existence of the other.
- Explore and probe at the liminal zone between 'poetry' and 'prose'. As we have seen, it is difficult to say with any certainty where one form ends and the other begins. The **prose poem** is indeed an important genre in its own right.[16] There is no formal verse, stanza or line arrangement, but the language draws attention to itself, often through prosodic and phonetic patterning, or through a kind of *distillation* of sense, in a manner in excess of that which we normally expect from prose. The prose poem is, generally, shorter too, of course. An absence of narrative is also characteristic of this kind of writing. To return to Bruns, prose poetry is also 'language in excess of the functions of language'.

- Syntax and its innate structures provide an essential background against which to foreground aspects of your writing. Your knowledge of functional grammar gained from Chapter 2 will help you as writers of poetry to consider the ways you can use grammatical construction to special effect. However, it is particularly important to examine syntax in relation to the line break, to structure, and to semantic issues. Note any unusual features of syntax relating to semantics or to the line break, and think about the ways in which syntax and the line interact to create poetic meaning. In particular note how syntax and the line together control what Oppen calls the 'sequence of disclosure'.

- When you have completed a draft of the poem, think about the following syntactical features, adapted, once again, from one of the checksheets in Short (1996: 352). Short's checksheet provides a comprehensive and extensive list of syntactic features to look out for in your work. Revealingly, this one was designed by Short for analysis of style features in *prose*...

  o **Sentences**: Does the poem contain sentences? If so, are they statements, questions, commands, etc., or are they like 'speech sentences', e.g. without a finite main verb? Are they simple, compound or complex? How long are they? Are there any striking contrasts in sentence length or structure at any point in the poem? If the sentences are long, is their length due to the embedding of clauses inside one another, coordination of clauses, long phrases acting as single clause elements (like subject or object), or other reasons?

  o **Clauses**: What types of clauses are noticeably favoured (e.g. relative, adverbial, noun clauses etc.)? Is there anything special about the clauses, e.g. a frequent and unusual placement of adverbials, or 'fronting' of object or complement? Are there clauses with 'dummy subjects' (i.e. 'there', 'it')?

  o **Phrases**:

    □ *Noun:* Are they simple or complex? If complex, is this due to the frequency of pre-modifiers (adjectives, noun-modifiers, etc.) or is it due to post-modification (prepositional phrases, relative clauses, complement clauses, etc.)? What is the nature of the nouns: abstract, concrete, simple, complex? Are pronouns used, and if so, who do they identify? Speaker? Addressee?

    □ *Verb*: What is the tense? Present or past? Are there sections where the tense is other than simple, or where modal auxiliaries occur? What is the relation of verb tense to movement? Look for interesting transitivity relations.

☐ *Other*: Are there any remarkable features about other phrases (i.e. prepositional, adverbial, adjectival)?

- Consider the following graphological deviations in your work, commonly found in free verse. You should be at all times mindful, of course, of their impact on meaning and effect. Avoid being 'tricky' just for the sake of it, though. The deviations should always do good expressive work.
  - ○ abandoning the capital letter to start each line;
  - ○ non-standard punctuation;
  - ○ use of '&' or other symbols (J, xxx, lol???);
  - ○ non-standard spellings and neologisms;
  - ○ use of dialect and slang.

If you need a poem to practise applying these concepts to as you do not have one of your own, use this one: 'Thing Language', by Jack Spicer (1998). It should go without saying that not all of the features mentioned in the list above will be present here.

> This ocean, humiliating in its disguises
> Tougher than anything.
> No one listens to poetry. The ocean
> Does not mean to be listened to. A drop
> Or crash of water. It means
> Nothing.
> It
> Is bread and butter
> Pepper and salt. The death
> That young men hope for. Aimlessly
> It pounds the shore. White and aimless signals. No
> One listens to poetry.

9.8   Practice

(1) Here is a poem re-written as a paragraph of prose. Re-write it as poetry, trying out different line lengths and line breaks until you arrive at a version you are satisfied with. You should work toward a sense of line and break that operates consistently throughout the poem, rather than shifting from one rhythm or principle to another every few lines. In other words, look for and establish *patterns* (if this chapter had a forehead, that sentence would be tattooed across it). If you like, you can compare your results with the original (available online).

Night Toad
You can hardly see him – his outline, his cold skin almost a dead leaf, blotched brown, dull green, khaki. He sits so quietly pumping his quick breath just at the edge of water between ruts in the path. And suddenly he is the centre of a cone of light falling from the night sky – ruts running with liquid fire, cobwebs imprinted on black, each grass-blade clear and separate – until the hiss of human life removes itself, the air no longer creaks, the shaking stops and he can crawl back to where he came from. But what *was* this if it was not death? (Susan Wicks 2003)

This exercise should demonstrate the truth of one of the central tenets of this chapter: that writing free verse is just as formally demanding as writing metrical verse. You could also use a paragraph of prose from a newspaper, magazine or novel as a source for this exercise, and pay attention to the various kinds of semantic effects created by breaking sentences into smaller line units.

(2) The poem below is 'What is Poetry' by John Ashbery. Write a replacement poem. That means you will retain all the syntactical choices, but replace all the open-class words (nouns, verbs, adjectives and adverbs) with other words that are your own (you will be venturing along the paraidgmatic axis). For the closed-class words – conjunctions, prepositions, articles – you may use the same words if you choose. So for the first stanza below, you might write:

> The autumn garden, with topiary
> Of elephants from Kenya? The Welshman
> Who crafted it when his hedge had overgrown?

What Is Poetry?
> The medieval town, with frieze
> Of boy scouts from Nagoya? The snow
> That came when we want it to snow?
> Beautiful images? Trying to avoid
> Ideas, as in this poem? But we
> Go back to them as to a wife, leaving
> The mistress we desire? Now they
> Will have to believe it
> As we believed it. In school
> All the thought got combed out:
> What was left was like a field.
> Shut your eyes, and you can feel it for miles around.

Now open them on a thin vertical path.
It might give us – what? – some flowers soon?

What do you make of the results?
Are they nonsense?
Or do patterns emerge?
What does this exercise teach you about creative process?

(3) Write a poem which makes deliberate and highly ostensible use of syntactic deviation. You might, for example choose to write:
    (a) a poem without any verbs;
    (b) a poem which suppresses its syntactic subject;
    (c) a poem in which the tense of the verbs changes in the final stanza;
    (d) a poem which is a single sentence.

(4) Building on the work on line endings, try using line endings to create small surprises in a poem you have already written or are working on. Experiment with different arrangements of the poem on the page. Is it a long, 'river'-shaped piece, or does it divide into regular, or irregular, sections? Consider the ways in which the shapes and sounds of the poem interact with its effect. Finally, choose a title that adds to the poem, heralds it, or encompasses it in some way.

(5) Take a short extract (say, 500 words) from a piece of prose fiction you are currently working on. Go through it very carefully using the checksheet from exercise 6 below. What do you find? Does the exercise tell you anything about the differences between poetry and prose? Are you inclined to introduce *more* of these kinds of patterning into the piece? Why? See what happens if you do so.

(6) As promised at the opening of the chapter, we should now return to an augmented version of the list given there to see how far the themes and topics of this chapter have impacted upon the way you approach the writing of poetry. What do you gain from carrying out this analysis now compared to what you gained from the exercise at the beginning of the chapter? Again, you should try and use an example of your own work in progress for this exercise or, perhaps even more usefully, the work of a friend, colleague or fellow student. You could exchange work and compare the results, for example.

    The list of questions is adapted from both Short (1996), Rachel Blau Du Plessis's list of 'Poetry Questions', and the teaching materials of my esteemed colleague Nancy Gaffield. In all cases, you should be relating your answers to all subsequent questions as far as possible to your answer to question (a). I think it is fair to say that in nearly all of the questions, you are looking for examples of **deviation** and **parallelism**.

(a)   **Describe the poem, as succinctly as possible. What are its overall themes and concerns? How does it affect you?**

(b)   Comment on the form. Is it an existing form (lyric poem, sonnet, free verse, etc.) or an invented form?

(c)   What about its appearance on the page? Is it unusual in any way?

(d)   Comment on the organization. How is the poem divided into segments? What motivates the stanzas? Line breaks? Is the dominant pattern of line breaks end-stopping, arrest-release, or extension? Are they related to prosody? Is it a question of meter? Rhyme? Semantic hinges? Syntax?

(e)   Comment on the lexis. Are there any words that are unfamiliar, or neologistic? What is the relation of abstract to concrete language/lexis? The nature of the imagery used? Are there any dominant semantic fields? What are the key words in the poem, the particular words that seem foregrounded? Why are they foregrounded? Is there any use of non-standard lexis or idioms? Any metaphors? Any transformation of idioms? Any examples of playful language? What about invented or found language? Denotative or connotative? Is there evidence of intertextuality, i.e. the use or echoing of documents or other texts?

(f)   Think about semantics. How are meaning connections made? By repetition? By use of words from the same semantic field?

(g)   Comment on issues of phonological patterning (e.g. alliteration, assonance, rhyme). What sound patterns/parallelism do you observe? Are there any examples of sound symbolism?

(h)   The tradition and the canon are also important. We write with them, or against them, but we never ignore them. Are there allusions to other poems or poetic practices?

(i)   Comment on syntactical issues – syntax in relation to line break, to structure, to meaning. How are pronouns used? What is the nature of nouns (abstract, concrete, simple, complex)? Verb tenses and movement (transitivity)? Phrases, clauses, modifiers? How do syntax and the line interact to create meaning? Comment on the 'sequence of disclosure'.

(j)   Comment on notions of subjectivity displayed in the poe⸱ Is the 'I' used, and if so is it narrative, meditative, drama⸱

lyric? Are interlocutors or listeners evoked? Who are the characters/personae in the poem?

(k)   Comment on the layout of the page and its significance. How is white space employed? Typography (letter size, fonts, capital letters, punctuation, etc.)?

(l)   Does the poem constitute a narrative to any extent? If so, can you separate discourse from 'fabula'? Are they integral, or in some sense distinct? Who tells? Who sees?

(m)   What issues are raised by the title? Is it introductory? Does it claim authority? Does it say something about the poem? Is it integral to the poem? Is it summative, or somehow abstract?

If you find it difficult to make links between your answers to each of these questions and question (a), or the links you make seem unduly tenuous or even forced, focus carefully on the particular stylistic feature in question and ask yourself: 'Does is need changing, or does it even need to be there?' The goal is to inculcate a certain – perhaps even artificial and forced, at first – stylistic discipline and control. Feel free, of course, to wrench yourself out of this straitjacket at any point once you feel its lessons have been duly absorbed.

(7)   This exercise involves working with a draft. Choose three rough drafts of poems that you feel are the most promising of the current batch you are working with. If you possibly can spare the time, spend about a day with each, reading it aloud, and altering its phonological and prosodic patterning in the light of exercise 6, the insights of this chapter and any other work that you have been doing. Try loosening the rhythm and meter a little. Try cutting the poem down – drastically. Look for internal rhymes, alliteration, puns, paradox and doubleness of any kind. Play with the form. Should it be a prose poem, rather? Does it need a tighter meter? Would it work better decanted into one of the formal lyric forms discussed in 9.5.1? Should it really be a short story? Is there action or a movement of meaning within the lines? Put each poem away as long as you can (ideally, weeks, even months, rather than days), then take it out again and read it again. The idea is that it should feel as though you have never seen it before, and thus are reading it as a reader would (you have located yourself at the far end of the cline encapsulated in Oatley's writingandreading). Whereas prose is always double-spaced, poetry is not. Try to produce it on the page the way it would be printed. Single spacing achieves this better. Centre the title above the poem, and put your name at the top. If your poem goes onto a new page, make sure the new page begins with a new stanza, and that the stanza break is clear. Submit it.

Appendix: A Stylistic Sandbox

Look at the following short story. Go through it carefully, bearing in mind as many of the themes and concepts we have looked at throughout the book as possible. You also need to look out for spelling and punctuation. What works well in the story? What doesn't work well?

The Christmas Present[1]

by

Cassandrina Dustworthy

Emily Cartwright was a widow in her late fifties. Emily had grey hair and blue eyes and stood about five foot three inches tall. Emily wore her hair in little curls along her forehead, and her features were sharp, and aquiline nose with high cheekbones and thin lips. But despite her appearance Emily was a kindly, unassuming sort of person, who always kept her home neat and tidy. It was a bungalow, in a non-estate position, in a pretty village in the Cotswolds.

Since her husband had died in tragic circumstances five years ago, Emily had been alone in the world except for her son, James, now eighteen. He had been a lovely little boy, quite and kind, polite and well-manered, he had been his mother's pride and joy. He was good at school, too, always got good reports and the teachers always said what a quite, polite, well-manered boy he always was. And he was an excellent tennis player.

So how, Emily wondered to herself musingly, had it all changed so drastically? The lovely little boy had somehow, over the years, become a difficult teenager who had got completely and utterly out of control and fallen in with a bad lot. Since his father was tragically dead and he got his motorbike it had got even worse. She had never wanted him to have a motor-bike. She had hated them ever since her brother was so tragically killed during the blackout when he had been a messenger on the staff of the famous Monty. Now, he had been a fine young man, one of the best. It was a tragedy that Fred had been taken so young, Emily sighed to herself. She had always thought young Jim might take after his uncle, but it was not to be, sad to say. He had turned out more like his drunken father.

One day, James and his friends met up at there usual meeting place, 'the pub', naturally. There bikes roared into the car park, disturbing those who had gone for a peaceful drink just to quench there thirst on a hot day.

'Well, Jim, what shall we do this evening', enquired big Mick the Irishman? 'Sure and there are a couple of Proddies I should very much like to make sorry they were ever born, begorrah'.

No, that's boring stuff', replied Jim ironically. 'I vote we have a burn-up down the shopping precinct and see what's happening down there. There are a few old ladies we could mug and if not we can smash a shop window or two. It will be super fun'.

Off they went with a very great deal of noise and petrol fumes, causing an innocent motorist to break sharply and almost have a nasty accident.

'What a crowd of terrible yobs', said one of the men sitting in the sunshine at one of the tables outside 'the pub'. 'What are the police doing, I should like to know'.?

Emily sat watching Coronation Street and wondering what James was doing. He always stayed out so late every night and she never knew where he was, but how could she stop him, he was an adult now. He was eighteen, so the law said, even though to her mind a lad of eighteen was still only a child, even if he was full-grown his emotions were still childish.

Come on, lads', yelled James loudly as he drove his Cowasaki at high speed down the pedestrian precinct, which was filthy with litter and dog mess, as usual. 'Why didn't people every clean up after themselves?', Emily always said. Jim felt a surge of exhilaration as the powerful machine surged past shops like the wind, sending paper flying and kicking up dust in the faces of the poor people going about there lawful business.

The bikers all laughed and hooted there horns as people jumped out of the way of the really very noisy and dangerous machines.

They came to a particularly well-dressed window of a large emporium. It was brightly lit and had a magnificent display of gifts all wonderfully arranged at various heights on fat pedestals all draped with thick black velvet to set off the colourful goods and tempt the eager shopper into parting with there hard-earned cash. There were lacquered fans of exquisite design, terra-cotta pots with silk flowers arranged in them very tastefully indeed, silk scarves of very hue under the sun, and a dazzling host of other most delightful and attractive goods ideal for Christmas presents for close friends and family. They were all cleverly set out with glittering tinsel and shiny baubles in a masterful display of the window-dresser's art.

James slammed on his brakes and reversed his machine, gazing with greedy eyes at a particularly beautiful brooch. 'Mum would like that for Christmas', he thought with an unusual moment of thoughtfulness for the woman who had brought him up and been so good to him and it was time he appreciated all her unselfish love for him down the years. He pictured her by the fire with her knitting, her grey hair and her shawl.

'Oh James', ejaculated pretty Fiona, who he had on his rear seat. 'I would so love to have a necklace like that, only Ma hasn't got two halfpennies to rub together since our dad ran off with his fancy woman.'

That was enough to goad him into action. He reversed his machine a few yards, so that he was facing the great big window and jammed his foot on the accelerator. The bike leapt forward at great speed and smashed right through the window and landed on its side in the middle of the display amid showers of broken glass and pottery.

Jim leapt off. 'Come on lads! Help yourselves!', he shouted with a grin as he snatched up the necklace for Fiona and the brooch for his mother. She was jumping up and down in delight, but looking a bit scared in case the police might come along at just that wrong moment in time.

The other had all climbed in through the hole in the window and were making the most of the unexpected windfall. Eventually, there pockets stuffed with ill-gotten loot, they revved up there machines to a deafening pitch, enough to wake the dead, rousing all the elderly people in a nearby old folks home from there beds with there thoughtlessness. What a racket in the dead of night, enough to give you a heart attack.

As they left, the burglar alarms were jangling ineffectively behind them, to add insult to injury.

Then suddenly a dog ran out. Jim slammed on his brakes but sadly hit him and he was dead before he hit the ground. The motorbike skidded and he felt it getting completely out of control so that he couldn't hold it. It was smashed up against the wall with terrific force. Jim was knocked unconscious and fell to the ground with a terrible pain all through his body.

When Jim came round after several awful days when his poor mother had been driven nearly frantic with worry, he was in bed with a nurse beside him, who told him sadly with tears in her eyes that poor Fiona was dead.

'That's tragic', thought Jim sadly to himself. It will teach me to mend my ways, And it did.

It was the best Christmas present Emily Cartwright ever had.

Now, rewrite it. You can approach this exercise in any way you like. You can stick as close as possible to the original, correcting the stylistic foibles and errors as best you can while trying to bring the author's original vision to fruition. Or, you can rip it up and start again. There *is* a story, a fabula, here, however deeply it is buried beneath the discourse. See if you can find it, then plot it out according to the model from Chapter 3. Where is the climax? How should tension be built? Is it worth reorganising the discourse and using a complex structure to mediate the story? What might be a better or more interesting way of mediating it? Try rewriting it as a poem. Or from the perspective of 'The Lovely Fiona' (now dead…). Write it as a play script. Write it from the perspective of Emily Cartwright herself, or in a heterodiegetic voice using Jim's fixed focalisation.

See what happens.

Good luck.

Then do the same with your own work.

Notes

Introduction: Style, Composition, Creative Practice

1. As any writer knows, if we wait around for inspiration to strike, then little work will get done...
2. Another discipline closely related to stylistics, narratology, also has a great deal to offer the writer, and will be referred to on several occasions throughout the book. See Shen (2007) for a detailed discussion of the interfaces between stylistics and narratology.
3. A key conference paper that has been influential in the development of stylistics is by Roman Jakobson (1960): 'Concluding Statement: Linguistics and Poetics'.
4. The concept of foregrounding will be of central importance to us as we explore the applications of stylistics to creative practice.

Chapter 1: Seeing Through Language

1. In keeping with the traditions of stylistics, this book will be democratic in its application of the term 'literary', a position that the range of examples used will demonstrate (and justify).
2. We will return to this notion of reading as performance in Chapter 6. We accept intuitively that writing is a performance; we are less eager to accept that reading is a performance too. But it is an intriguing hypothesis to present the two processes as equivalent.
3. Again, we will discuss this concept in more detail in Chapter 6.
4. As will be discussed in Chapter 6, reading and writing (for our purposes) are two different sides of the same coin.
5. Derrida's work, and the work of poststructuralism in general, takes this assertion to some fascinating (but controversial) extremes.
6. Warner, Alan (1999) *The Sopranos*. London: Vintage.
7. Mievill, China (2000) *Perdido Street Station*. London: Pan Macmillan.
8. Cummings, e.e. (2003) *73 Poems*. New York: W.W. Norton and Co.
9. Joyce, James (1939/1971) *Finnegan's Wake*. London: Faber and Faber.
10. I have deliberately used a small 's' here. Sociolinguists maintains that here is no single Standard English; only standard Englishes.
11. We will be introducing more rigorous terminology for point of view in Chapter 4.
12. Yes, this is a slightly problematic pronouncement – but it can surely be agreed that the vast majority of third-person narratives of literature in

English make use of a standard English written idiom, albeit with various nuances depending on a context that is British, American, Irish, Australian or whatever.

13. A useful term for texts of this kind – ergodic literature – was coined by Espen Aarseth in his (1997) book on cybertext: 'In ergodic literature, nontrivial effort is required to allow the reader to traverse the text.' While Aarseth focusses on hyperfiction, online literature and games, the term could perhaps be usefully applied to poems such as this; the effort required to read them is certainly non-trivial, as they do not conform to textual norms in terms of cohesion, narrative linearity, syntax and so on.

14. We will return to this concept in Chapter 3 when we discuss *overt* and *covert* modes of narration.

15. Ideas established and developed in cognitive linguistics have found their way into literary analysis through cognitive poetics (see Stockwell 2002, for example).

16. We will return in Chapter 5 to how the distinction between mimesis and diegesis can shed light on methods of discourse presentation.

17. Lodge's work has been shortlisted for the Booker Prize twice, once in 1984 for the novel *Small World* and again in 1988 for *Nice Work*.

18. See, among others, Toolan 2001; Short 2007; and Semino and Short.

19. As always, there will be exceptions to this general rule.

20. As Caliban declaims in Shakespeare's *The Tempest*: 'You taught me language, and my profit on't is, I know how to curse.'

21. To be italicised no longer …

Chapter 2: Building Blocks I

1. But see Nash (1980) for a notable exception; while focussing on the writing of prose in general, the book does have a great deal to say of relevance to creative writing.

2. A morpheme is the smallest meaningful unit in the grammar of a language; so, in the word 'morpheme' there are two morphemes: 'morph' (which means 'form' or 'shape') and 'eme' (meaning, in fact, 'emic unit' – an abstract object studied in linguistics). A lexeme is a distinctive unit in a semantic system; so 'walks' and 'walking' would both be variants of the lexeme 'walk'. 'Lexeme' is essentially just a more careful and precise definition of 'word': that which is listed in the dictionary in each separate entry. A morpheme can sometimes be the same thing as a word (say, 'critic') but a word may contain more than one morpheme ('criticise').

3. See De Beaugrande and Dressler (1981) for detailed discussion of this concept, as well as an overview of critical discourse analysis in general.

4. See Stanley Fish's (1980) criticisms of early stylistic methodology.

5. But for ease of reference: 'subject' is that which performs the action, 'predicator' is the part of the sentence that contains the verb or verbal group, the 'complement' is a general term for the word or phrase that is required to complete the sense of the clause, and the 'adjunct' is

modifying part of the clause which augments its meaning in some way and can be removed without rendering the clause 'ungrammatical', for example, an adverb or an adjective.

6. To be strictly correct and fair to Saussure, we should distinguish between negative and positive value in meaning. Negative value comes about through difference as described here; positive value comes about through 'association'. So, the synonyms of 'doctor' above belong to the latter category.

7. See Chapter 6 on cognitive poetics for more detailed discussion of this notion.

8. In Chapter 3 we will discuss more rigorous terminology for these different aspects of the literary text. Form and content are troubling terms, to say the least – but they will do for now. (Incidentally, their very slipperiness points to the need for the kinds of more rigorous approaches to creative writing that this book argues for, and, it is hoped, constitutes.).

9. The study of semantics has often focussed on how meaning arose in a decontextualised fashion, trying to arrive at an objective account of meaning generation (see, for example, Cruse 1986). Modern linguistics, especially pragmatics, has attempted to demonstrate that meaning is generated throughout the whole system (and, especially, by context) and not just by one aspect of it.

10. This excerpt probably needs no introduction, but it is, of course, the first verse of Lewis Carroll's 'Jabberwocky' (excerpted in *The Norton Anthology of Poetry*, pp. 1032–3). The poem is here deliberately taken out of context, for reasons which should be obvious given the themes of this chapter.

11. The response to this question among students has often been 'What about the tropes of environmentalism? They are "green ideas", surely?' Yes, but 'green' in that case is being used figuratively, and so is an instance of Jakobson's poetic function of language, and thus a little beside the point of an example where 'green' is a colour – a physical property erroneously applied to an abstract notion: 'ideas'. Can you have 'green empathy'?

12. We will discuss more rigorous terminology for this in the next chapter, looking particularly at narratology's use of the terms **discourse** and **fabula**, with the former, broadly, referring to the language of the text and the latter to the imaginary world of the poem or story.

13. Indeed, Jeffries and McIntyre refrain from treating it as a linguistic level in its own right (2010: 58).

14. Transitivity is a way of describing that facility of grammatical structure to capture experience in language. See Simpson 2004: 22–6 for a comprehensive overview of transitivity.

15. An iambic tetrameter consists of four feet with a marked stress on the second syllable of each, so da-DUM–da-DUM-da-DUM-da-DUM. More on meter in Chapter 9.

16. We will be engaging with more rigorous terminology for these different aspects of voice in Chapters 4 and 5.

7. There will be more detailed discussion of sound and sense in Chapter 9.

3. See Scott (2009) for detailed discussion of this type of writing.

Chapter 3: Building Blocks II

1. For a detailed discussion of the interfaces and tensions between stylistics and narratology, especially in terms of their respective appropriations of the term *discourse*, see Dan Chen's essay 'What Narratology and Stylistics Can Do For Each Other' in Phelan and Rabinowitz, 2005: 136–49. Also, Manfred Jahn (2002) writes as follows: 'To the extent that narratology ... focuses on the ways, means, and effects of telling narratives, narratology is part of, or intersects with, stylistics in the sense that the tools of narratology can be used for the purposes of stylistic analysis. ... In set-theoretical terms, imagine two intersecting circles, one large, one small. The large one is stylistics, the smaller one is narratology.'

2. This isn't a facetious point. It is at the very least arguable that creative writing discourse, especially poetry, *creates* the world of the tale rather than merely mimetically representing it. The latter stance implies an anterior relationship between the two which is often questionable. As I argue elsewhere in this book, creative invention can arise in and through language itself. See Semino (1997) on Possible World Theory for a fascinating exploration of the relationship between fiction and truth.

3. Note: a world, not necessarily the world. More on this shortly.

4. A term which encapsulates the many modes we now have for transmitting meaning across channels.

5. To reiterate the material in Chapter 1: this concept depends on whose perspective you are looking at things from. The implied reader is the reader as perceived (imagined) by the author, who, normally, will not be speaking or reading to the reader face to face. The implied author is the author from the perspective of the reader; he or she is the 'agency' which the reader imagines behind the text and its narrator. Again, usually the reader will not have met this author in person (a common feature of literary narrative in comparison to, say, everyday oral narrative).

6. We will develop these ideas in a little more detail in Chapter 6 when we examine cognitive poetics.

7. Read chapter 8 of Toolan (2001) for a detailed discussion of media narratives and their relationship to ideologies.

8. Gaiman et al. (2004) *The Sandman: Endless Nights*. London: Titan Books.

9. See Semino (1997, chapters 4 and 5) for an excellent overview of possible-world theory as applied to fiction and poetry.

10. We will look at an even more extreme example of this effect in the next chapter.

11. From the Greek ἔλλειψις, meaning 'omission' or 'falling short'.

12. See Chapter 6.

13. Note a world, not necessarily the world.

14. Indeed, looking at sport through the prism of narrative structure could well explain why it can become boring for the spectators/audience the same team or individual continually wins competitions. We 'hard-wired' to expect upheaval in narrative.

15. Angel cake originates in England, and consists traditionally of three layers of sponge, typically coloured pink, yellow and brown.
16. Now *there's* a question to ponder.
17. There is some good software available that will help you do this if you prefer working electronically. Take a look, for example, at *Scrivener 2.0*, by Literature and Latte, or apps such as *Index Card* by DenVog.

Chapter 4: Through the Looking Glass

1. Chapter 5 deals with another aspect of discourse narratology: the presentation of speech and thought.
2. 'Thought experiment' is a term used often in scientific discourse to describe the process of *imagining* a particular set of circumstances and their outcome which may not be physically possible in the real world. I intend no definitive answer to the question of whether or not it is possible to separate discourse and fabula, though; but let us assume for the purposes of this chapter that it is sometimes desirable to do so.
3. See Genette (1983), *Narrative Discourse: An Essay in Method*.
4. It could be argued, in fact, that this extract is an extended example of free indirect discourse (see Chapter 5), combining character thought and narrative voice.
5. See my own short story *Eucharist (or the Lark Ascending)* (2010) for an example of extended second-person narration.
6. See Toolan (2001: 68–76) for a thorough overview of these models. It is also worth looking at Simpson (1993) for a comprehensive exploration of linguistic indicators of perceptibility in point of view, and also of the relationship between point of view and ideology.
7. Based, again, on Genette (1980).
8. Again, see Rimmon-Kenan (1984: 71–85) for in-depth discussion of narrative focalisation.

Chapter 5: Writing Voices

1. The entity who speaks and the entity who tells may, of course, be one and the same, as is the case in intradiegetic narration (see p. 000).
2. This is another example of the effect discussed in Chapter 4: the importance of levels of mediation in enhancing the expressive effect of narration.
3. The difference between the conscious asking of this question and the unconscious asking of it is a crucial point that will be returned to in some detail when we consider creative versus 'editorial' practice.
4. The discourse presentation scale used here has, since its proposal, been revised and updated following extensive corpus-based studies of English writing (see Semino and Short 2011; Short 2007). However, I have opted to use this earlier incarnation as, first, it is a little simpler and

more flexible and, second, is in my view more directly applicable to the craft of creative writing (the reasons for this are complex, but are connected to the new version's roots in corpus analysis and to the fact that the scale is still undergoing embellishment, discussion and revision as research continues).

5. Toolan (2001) refers to this as Pure Narration, a term you may prefer as being more self-explanatory.

6. The different modes of narrative presentation available to the writer – homoediegetic, heterodiegetic and so on – in NRA (dominated, of course, by the voice of the narrator) have been discussed more fully in Chapter 4, where we explore points of view and focalisation.

7. Notice, too, how Rimmon-Kenan homes in on the problems associated with applying the word *mimesis* to creative writing, seeing *all* creative writing as, essentially, in the end, rooted in diegesis. It can only ever represent through language, she says. However, in order to be more rigorous with the term, I have fallen back on Aristotle, seeing mimesis as associated with character discourse, and diegesis with narrator discourse. We will return to this issue at the end of this chapter, and (hopefully) arrive at a workable definition for the creative writer to reflect on in practice.

8. See Scott (2009) for in-depth discussion of the relationship between character and narrator voice in terms of authenticity and levels of mediation.

9. See Wardhaugh (2002: 25–56) for a detailed sociolinguistic perspective on the issue.

10. See my own *The Demotic Voice in Contemporary British Fiction* (2009), London: Palgrave Macmillan.

11. See also section 5.8.

12. Again, certain writers working in this way would claim the status of a distinct *language* for their narrative voices (Scots, say), and would not view them as dialects. The ideological complexities of this debate are beyond the scope of this book, but are well worth investigating and thinking about.

13. The tendency is common in American writing too. See, among countless examples, the work of William Faulkner, Mark Twain, Charles Bukowski and Zora Neale Hurston.

14. See section 5.4.2.

15. Incidentally, this has the effect of making the speech operate on the same level as the narrator's discourse; it removes the orthographic barriers between the two, implying equality of status. It was out of revulsion at this artificial separation of narrative voices from character speech that James Joyce referred to quotation marks, or inverted commas, as 'perverted commas'. The same effect can be seen at work in Kelman's refusal of quotation marks as discussed in sections 5.4.2 and 5.8.

16. The same applies to use of NRA/NRT; see section 5.6.

17. Note that Joyce uses a dash instead of quotation marks in DS; see note 15 for a brief discussion of why.

18. Notice how writers prefer to avoid inverted commas in thought presentation.
19. I need to add a caveat to this assertion: that modern stylistics research (again, see Short 2007; Toolan 2001; Semino and Short 2011) has attempted to distinguish more rigorously between these forms. However, for our purposes the term FDT will suffice for both, with due reference to terms drawn from literary criticism.

Chapter 6: Creating a World

1. For an excellent introduction to this fascinating subject, see Evans and Green (2006).
2. See particularly Stockwell (2002); Gavins (2007); Semino (1997); and Gavins and Steen (2003). The pioneering work of Paul Werth (1999) has also been crucial in the development of the field.
3. Loosely, the posited relationship is similar to that between, say, England and C.S. Lewis's Narnia or Tolkien's Middle Earth, except that Tlön is less 'authored', more intrinsic to Uqbar's history and culture.
4. See Flew (1979: 160).
5. For further reading on these topics, see Lavine (1985) and Blackburn (2001), particularly chapter 11 in the former and chapter 7 in the latter.
6. The tenets of cognitive poetics are applicable to any kind of text, not just literary ones. It is often used, for example, to analyse the effects of media writing. However, for the purposes of this book we will of course confine our attention to creative writing.
7. Indeed, Borges's story is published in a collection entitled *Labyrinths* (2000).
8. This is a vast topic, of course, and, again, beyond the scope of this book to explore in detail. The reader is referred to Pinker (2008) for an excellent and recent overview of the research. In keeping with the premises of this book, Pinker here describes language as a 'window' into human nature.
9. The particular image you see will depend on your past experience, or pre-existing mental scripts. Cognitive scientists refer to this 'baggage' as *schema* (see Bartlett 1995 for the first experimental exploration of this ideas). Perhaps you were once entranced by a particular moon rising over a particular lake in Lapland as the sun set. This may well be the image which is prompted by the sentence. Or it may be more generic, a non-specific image.
10. Essentially, the Sapir–Whorf Hypothesis proposes that the structure of one's language can strongly influence one's view of the world. 'World view' could be described as a consistent and integral sense of existence, as well as a characteristic framework for generating, sustaining and applying knowledge. For example, the number and type of words in one's language for describing colours determine how one sees a rainbow, the fact that Finnish has only one ungendered pronoun (i.e. no

'he' and 'she', just 'it': *han*) means that there is greater equality between females and males in Finnish society.

11. The situation which would have to pertain in the 'real world' for the world expressed in the sentence to be deemed as true.

12. We can, of course, conceive of a situation in which a badger might be used as a spade. And this is precisely the point (believe it or not…). Language can be used to create worlds other than the world that is, but these worlds must be similar enough to be recognisable.

13. See Semino (1997) for detailed discussion of world creation and compatibility, especially chapter 4.

14. If you're really paying attention, you'll have noticed that Dubrovnik doesn't have a central station. No trains run to the city at all. The truth conditions of the utterance don't match the actual world, and so we have to create a possible world for them to be deemed true.

15. These ideas are drawn from the framework of possible world theory, another aspect of cognitive poetics and narratology. For further reading, see Semino (1997) and Dolezel (2000).

16. Marie-Laure Ryan (see Semino 1997) has proposed a useful scale to measure the relationship between language and a fictional world, which allows us to describe rigorously degrees of compatibility or incompatibility between the two. This is worth exploring if you would like to take these ideas further.

17. In semantics, truth conditions are what obtain precisely for a proposition to be deemed true. (See Saeed 2003: 293 for a good definition of this concept.)

18. It is way beyond the scope of this book to deal with text-world theory in the detail it deserves, and this can only ever be a brief – and necessarily simplified, even simplistic – overview. The reader is referred to Gavins (2007) for proper exploration of the topic.

19. Here, the term 'analogue' is used in the sense which is derived from 'analogous', that is, parallel or equivalent.

20. We have all, I'm sure, had the experience of reading a piece of creative writing that has fundamentally altered our view of the world. This is the gold at the end of creative writing's rainbow surely: to write the book or poem that will, literally, change someone's life.

Chapter 7: *Creative* Writing: Figurative Language

1. If you worked through exercise 11 in Chapter 5, return to the results now and re-examine them in the light of this discussion. Could the poem be accused of banality? If so, why? How might this be remedied? If not, why not?

2. If not, then what is it?

3. The rose is a national emblem of England, derived from the royal crest of the Tudors.

4. Bakhtin and Volosinov (1973) argue that no meaningful division can be made between denotation and connotation because referenti* meaning is always shaped first and foremost by ideology (and is th*

to some extent based on subjectivity, or dependent on sociocultural context).

Chapter 8: Meaning and Play: Metaphor

1. Is my use of the word 'travel' here metaphorical too? Arguably not, as we shall see.
2. I'm indebted to both Scarlett Thomas and Elena Semino (2007) for this example.
3. See Wales 2011: 151.
4. Well spotted. That's a cliché.
5. See Semino 2006 for a more detailed discussion of this method.

Chapter 9: Creating Soundscapes

1. Simply put, a *sign* (or word) and its meaning.
2. For reasons of simplicity, I am deliberately avoiding the phonetic alphabet or any other typographical conventions for representing the sounds of language. I may occasionally – and reluctantly – resort to bold type for stress and attempt to render sounds through the standard alphabet.
3. The interested reader is referred to Derek Attridge's forthcoming (at the time of writing) book on the subject, *Moving Words: the Forms of English Poetry*.
4. By 'shapes' I mean the 'look' of a text on the page, for example.
5. Of course, you could try the method out on someone else's poem if you prefer – ideally, a colleague or classmate's, but if none is available, then by all means use a published poem. The idea, though, is to look at your own work through this particular analytical lens and see what it reveals.
6. In fact, we could easily include this process under the heading of writ-ingandreading.
7. Essentially, reverse rhyme is an extended from of alliteration.
8. See Simpson 2004, section B4 for a detailed discussion of the pitfalls inherent in the interpretation of patterns of sound, including the dreaded phonoaesthetic fallacy: 'impressionistic labels have no place whatsoever in the systematic study of speech sounds' (68).
9. The last foot here is a trochee.
10. Here the line ends with two iambs.
11. If you are interested, a simple Google search will provide you with lots of sites giving overviews of these classification systems.
12. 'Shakespeare's Sonnet 116' in Burrow (2008).
13. You can find the poem online, and on *The Guardian* newspaper's website.
4. For a detailed exploration of poetic prosody from a practical perspec-tive, see Stephen Fry's wonderful book *The Ode Less Travelled* (2007), which makes exactly the same assertion.

15. This is an old 'jingle' for the McDonald's Big Mac hamburger, common currency when it was first 'released'. If you could go into an outlet and recite it in less than ten seconds you would get a free burger. Perhaps this story is apocryphal, though.
16. See the work of the prose poet Patricia Debney for some wonderful examples of this kind of writing.

Appendix: A Stylistic Sandbox

1. Taken from Mackie (1995), with thanks.

References and Selected Further Reading

[Author unknown] 'Sound Restrictions: Generic Rhyme'. http://raid.layliturgy.org [accessed 20 October 2012]

Aarseth, Espen (1997) *Cybertext: Perspective on Ergodic Literature*. Baltimore, MA: Johns Hopkins University Press.

Abrams, Meyer H. (1953) *The Mirror and the Lamp: Romantic Theory and the Critical Tradition*. Oxford: Oxford University Press.

Adams, Hazard and Leroy Searle (2004) *Critical Theory since Plato*. Boston, MA: Heinle and Heinle.

Anderson, Linda and David Neale (2005) *Creative Writing: A Workbook with Readings*. London: Routledge.

Attridge, Derek (1995) *Poetic Rhythm: An Introduction*. Cambridge: Cambridge University Press.

Auerbach, Erich (1953/2003) *Mimesis: The Representation of Reality in Western Literature*. Princeton: Princeton University Press.

Bakhtin, Mikhail (1984) *Problems of Dostoevsky's Poetics*. Trans. Caryl Emerson. Minneapolis: University of Minnesota Press.

Bakhtin, Mikhail (2003) 'Unitary Language'. In Lucy Burke, Tony Crowley and Alan Girvin (Eds) *The Routledge Language and Cultural Theory Reader*. London: Routledge. 269–279.

Baldwin, Michael (1986) *The Way to Write Short Stories*. London: Elm Tree Press.

Barthes, Roland (1977) *Image – Music – Text*. London: Fontana.

Bartlett, F. C. (1995) 2nd ed. *Remembering: A Study in Experimental and Social Psychology*. Cambridge: Cambridge University Press.

Beck, Heather (2012) *Teaching Creative Writing*. London: Palgrave Macmillan.

Behn, Robin and Chase Twichell (Eds) (1992) *The Practice of Poetry: Writing Exercises from Poets Who Teach*. New York: HarperCollins.

Bell, Julia and Andrew Motion (2001) *The Creative Writing Coursebook*. London: Macmillan.

Bennett, Alan (2010) 'The Greening of Mrs Donaldson'. In *London Review of Books* 32(17). 6–8.

Berkeley, George (1710) *A Treatise Concerning the Principles of Human Knowledge*. http://www.earlymoderntexts.com/pdfbits/bp.html_[accessed 2 August 2010]

Bishop, Elizabeth (1965) *Questions of Travel*. New York: Farrar, Straus and Giroux.

Blackburn, Simon (2001) *Think: A Compelling Introduction to Philosophy*. Oxford: Oxford Paperbacks.

Booth, Wayne C. (1983) *The Rhetoric of Fiction*. Chicago: The University of Chicago Press.

Boulter, Amanda (2007) *Writing Fiction: Creative and Critical Perspectives*. London: Palgrave Macmillan.

Brady, Catherine (2010) *Story Logic and the Craft of Fiction*. London: Palgrave Macmillan.

Bremond, Claude (1964) 'Le Message Narratif'. *Communications* 4. 4–32.

Burroway, Janet (2003) *Writing Fiction: A Guide to Narrative Craft*. London: Longman.

Butler, Paul (2009) *Style and Rhetoric in Composition*. Boston, MA: Bedford/St Martin's Press.

Carter, Ron (2004) *Language and Creativity: The Art of Common Talk*. London: Routledge.

Carter, Ron and Walter Nash (1990) *Seeing Through Language: A Guide to Styles of English Writing*. Oxford: Blackwell.

Carter, Ron and Peter Stockwell (2008) *The Language and Literature Reader*. London: Routledge.

Carver, Raymond (1998) *Where I'm Calling From: The Selected Stories*. London: The Harvill Press.

Casterton, Julia (2005) *Creative Writing: A Practical Guide*. London: Palgrave Macmillan.

Chandler, Daniel (2007) *Semiotics: The Basics*. London: Routledge.

Chomsky, Noam (1957/2002) *Syntactic Structure*. 2nd ed. The Hague: Mouton.

Chomsky, Noam (1964) *Current Issues in Linguistic Theory*. The Hague: Mouton.

Cobley, Paul (2001) *Narrative (New Critical Idiom)*. London: Routledge.

Cook, Guy (1994) *Discourse and Literature: The Interplay of Form and Mind*. Oxford: Oxford University Press.

Cook, Guy (2001) *The Discourse of Advertising*. London: Routledge.

Cox, Alisa (2005) *Writing Short Stories*. London: Routledge.

Cruse, D.A. (1986) *Lexical Semantics*. Cambridge: Cambridge University Press.

Crystal, David (1992) *A Dictionary of Linguistics and Phonetics*. 3rd ed. Oxford: Blackwell.

Crystal, David (1996) 'Language Play and Linguistic Intervention'. In *Child Language Teaching and Therapy* 12(3). 328–344.

Cureton, Richard D. (1979) 'e.e. cummings: A Study of the Poetic Use of Deviant Morphology'. In *Poetics Today* 1(1/2) Autumn. 213–244.

Davidson, Chad and Gregory Fraser (2008) *Writing Poetry: Creative and Critical Approaches*. London: Palgrave Macmillan.

Dawson, Paul (2004) *Creative Writing and the New Humanities*. London: Routledge.

De Beaugrande, Robert and Wolfgang Dressler (1981) *Introduction to Text Linguistics*. London: Longman.

Derrida, Jacques (1976) *Of Grammatology*. Baltimore, MD: Johns Hopkins Press.

Deutscher, Max (2009) 'Some Friendly Words for the Postmodern'. In *Crossroads: An Interdisciplinary Journal for the Study of History, Philosophy, Religion and Classics* 4(1). 5–12.

Dobyns, Stephen (2011) *Next Word, Better Word: The Craft of Writing Poetry*. London: Palgrave Macmillan.

Dolezel, Lubomir (2000) *Heterocosmica: Fiction and Possible Worlds*. Baltimore, MD: Johns Hopkins University Press.

DuPlessis, Rachel Blau. *Poetry Questions*. http://writing.upenn.edu/library/DuPlessis-Rachel_Poetry-Questions.html [accessed 18 October 2012]

Dvorak, Kevin and Shanti Bruce (2009) *Creative Approaches to Writing Center Work (Research and Teaching in Rhetoric and Composition)*. New York: Hampton Press.

Eliot, T.S. (1932) *Selected Essays*. London: Faber and Faber.

Eliot, T.S. (1942) *The Music of Poetry*. Glasgow: Jackson, Son and Company.

Evans, Vyvyan and Melanie C. Green (2006) *Cognitive Linguistics: An Introduction*. Edinburgh: Edinburgh University Press.

Evenson, Brian (2010) 'Across the Curriculum: Creative Writing'. In David Herman, Brian McHale and James Phelan (Eds) *Teaching Narrative Theory*. New York: Modern Language Association of America.

Ferguson, Margaret, Mary Jo Salter and Jon Stallworthy (Eds) (1996) *The Norton Anthology of Poetry*. 4th ed. New York: W.W. Norton and Company.

Fish, Stanley (1980) *Is There a Text in this Class? The Authority of Interpretive Communities*. Cambridge, MA: Harvard University Press.

Flew, Anthony (Ed.) (1979) *A Dictionary of Philosophy*. London: Pan.

Fludernik, Monica (2009) *An Introduction to Narratology*. London: Routledge.

Fry, Stephen (2007) *The Ode Less Travelled: Unlocking the Poet Within*. London: Arrow.

Gavins, Joanna (2007) *Text World Theory: An Introduction*. Edinburgh: Edinburgh University Press.

Gavins, Joanna and Gerhard Steen (Eds) (2003) *Cognitive Poetics in Practice*. London: Routledge.

Genette, Gerard (1980) *Narrative Discourse: An Essay in Method*. Ithaca, NY: Cornell University Press.

Graham, Robert (2006) *How to Write Fiction (And Think About It)*. London: Palgrave Macmillan.

Graham, Robert, Helen Newall, Heather Leach, Julie Armstrong and John Singleton (2004) *The Road to Somewhere: A Creative Writing Companion*. London: Palgrave Macmillan.

Grice, Paul (1975) 'Logic and Conversation'. In P. Cole and J. Morgan (Eds) *Syntax and Semantics, 3: Speech Acts*. New York: Academic Press. Reprinted in *Studies in the Way of Words*, ed. H.P. Grice, pp. 22–40. Cambridge, MA: Harvard University Press (1989)

Halliday, Michael (2003) 'On the "Architecture" of Human Language'. In *On Language and Linguistics, The Collected Works of M.A.K. Halliday*, Vol. III. Ed. Jonathan Webster. London: Continuum.

Halliday, Michael and Christian Matthiessen (2004) *An Introduction to Functional Grammar*. 3rd ed. London: Hodder Education.

Harber, Ralph and Maurice Hershenson (1980) *The Psychology of Visual Perception*. 2nd ed. New York: Holt, Rinehart and Winston.

Harmon, William (2012) *The Poetry Toolkit: For Readers and Writers*. Oxford: Wiley-Blackwell.

Harper, Graeme (2006) *Teaching Creative Writing*. London: Continuum.

Harper, Graeme (2008) *Creative Writing Guidebook*. London: Continuum.

Harper, Graeme (2012) *Inside Creative Writing: Interviews with Contemporary Writers*. London: Palgrave Macmillan.

Harper, Graeme (2013) *A Companion to Creative Writing*. Oxford: Wiley-Blackwell.

Harper, Graeme (2014) *The Future for Creative Writing*. Oxford: Wiley-Blackwell.

Hass, Robert (1984) 'Listening and Making'. In his *Twentieth Century Pleasures*. New York: Ecco Press.

Herbert, W.N. (2009) *Writing Poetry*. London: Routledge.

Herman, David (2009) *Basic Elements of Narrative*. Oxford: Wiley-Blackwell.

Jahn, Manfred (2002) *Poems, Plays, and Prose: A Guide to the Theory of Literary Genres*. www.uni-koeln.de/~ame02/pppq.htm. [accessed 12 April 2012]

Jakobson, Roman (1960) 'Closing Statement: Linguistics and Poetics'. In T.A. Sebeok (Ed.) *Style in Language*. Cambridge, MA: MIT Press. 350–359.

Jakobson, Roman (1990) *On Language*. L.R. Waugh and M. Monville-Burston (Eds). Cambridge, MA: Harvard University Press.

James, Henry (1957) *The Principles of Psychology*. New York: Dover.

Jeffries, Lesley and Dan McIntyre (2010) *Stylistics* (Cambridge Textbooks in Linguistics). Cambridge: Cambridge University Press.

Keith, William M. and Christian O. Lundeberg (2008) *The Essential Guide to Rhetoric*. Boston, MA: Bedford/St Martin's Press.

Kenner, Hugh (1978) *Joyce's Voices*. Berkeley, CA: University of California Press.

King, Stephen (2012) *On Writing: A Memoir of the Craft*. New York: Hodder.[1]

Köhler, Wolfgang (1992) *Gestalt Psychology: An Introduction to New Concepts in Modern Psychology*. New York: W.W. Norton and Sons.

Kroll, Jeri and Graeme Harper (2012) *Research Methods in Creative Writing*. London: Palgrave Macmillan.

Labov, William (1973) *Sociolinguistic Patterns*. Philadelphia, PA: University of Pennsylvania Press.

Lakoff, George (1987) *Women, Fire and Dangerous Things: What Categories Reveal About the Mind*. Chicago: The University of Chicago Press.

Lakoff, George and Mark Johnson (1981) *Metaphors We Live By*. Chicago: The University of Chicago Press.

Lakoff, George and Mark Turner (1989) *More Than Cool Reason: A Field Guide to Poetic Metaphor*. Chicago: The University of Chicago Press.

Lavine, T.Z. (1985) *From Socrates to Sartre: The Philosophic Quest*. New York: Bantam.

Leech, Geoffrey (1973) *A Linguistic Guide to English Poetry*. London: Longman.

Leech, Geoffrey and Mick Short (2007) *Style in Fiction*. 2nd ed. Harlow: Longman Pearson.

Leitch, Vincent B. (2001) *The Norton Anthology of Theory and Criticism*. New York: Norton.

Lodge, David (1990) *After Bakhtin: Essays on Fiction and Criticism*. London: Routledge.

Lynn, Steven (2010) *Rhetoric and Composition: An Introduction*. Cambridge: Cambridge University Press.

Mackie, Mary (1995) *Creative Editing*. London: Weidenfeld & Nicolson.

May, Steve (2007) *Doing Creative Writing*. London: Routledge.

Michaels, Leonard (2007) *The Collected Stories*. Danvers, MA: Farrar, Straus and Giroux.

Mills, Paul (2005) *The Routledge Creative Writing Coursebook*. London: Routledge.

Morrison, Matt (2010) *Key Concepts in Creative Writing*. London: Palgrave Macmillan.

Nash, Walter (1980) *Designs in Prose*. London: Longman.

Oppen, George (2008) *Selected Prose, Daybooks and Papers*. Berkeley, CA: The University of California Press.

Pateman, Trevor (1997) 'Space for the Imagination'. In *Journal of Aesthetic Education* 31(1). 1–8. www.selectedworks.co.uk/imagination.html. [accessed 7 June 2009]

Paterson, Don (2007) 'The Lyric Principle'. *Poetry Review* 97(2) (Summer). 56–72.

Phelan, James and Peter J. Rabinowitz (Eds) (2005) *A Companion to Narrative Theory*. Oxford: Blackwell Publishing.

Pinker, Stephen (2008) *The Stuff of Thought: Language as a Window into Human Nature*. London: Penguin.

Pope, Rob (1994) *Textual Intervention: Critical and Creative Strategies for Literary Studies*. London: Routledge.

Pope, Rob (2002) *The English Studies Book*. London: Routledge.

Propp, Vladimir (1928 [1968]) *The Morphology of the Folktale*. Austin: University of Texas Press.

Prynne, J. H. (2009) 'Mental Ears and Poetic Work'. *Chicago Review* 51(1). 126–157.

Richards, I.A. (1929/1991) *Practical Criticism: A Study of Literary Judgment*. New ed. London: Routledge.

Rimmon-Kenan, Shlomith (1989) *Narrative Fiction: Contemporary Poetics*. London: Routledge.

Robinson, Howard (Ed.) (2009) *George Berkeley: Principles of Human Knowledge* and *Three Dialogues*. Oxford: Oxford World Classics.

Ryan, Marie-Laure (1980) 'Fiction, Non-factuals and the Principle of Minimum Departure'. *Poetics* 9. 403–22.

Ryan, Marie-Laure (2003) 'On Defining Narrative Media'. *Image and Narrative*. Issue 6: *Medium Theory*. www.imageandnarrative.be. [accessed 10 September 2011]

Saeed, John I. (2003) *Semantics*. Oxford: Blackwell.

Saussure, Ferdinand de (1995) *Course in General Linguistics*. London: Duckworth.

Scott, Jeremy (2009) *The Demotic Voice in Contemporary British Fiction*. London: Palgrave Macmillan.

Searle, John (1979) *Expression and Meaning*. Cambridge: Cambridge University Press.

Semino, Elena (1997) *Language and World Creation in Poems and Other Texts*. London: Longman Pearson.

Semino, Elena (2006) 'Metaphor and Fictional Minds'. In R. Benczses and S. Csabi (Eds) *The Metaphors of Sixty*. Budapest: Eötvös Loránd University Press.

Semino, Elena (2007) 'Mind Style 25 Years On'. *Style* 41(2). 153–203.

Semino, Elena and Jonathan Culpeper (2002) *Cognitive Stylistics: Language and Cognition in Text Analysis*. Amsterdam: John Benjamins.

Semino, Elena and Mick Short (2011) *Corpus Stylistics: Speech, Writing and Thought Presentation in a Corpus of English Writing*. London: Routledge.

Semino, Elena and Kate Swindlehurst (1996) 'Metaphor and Mind Style in Ken Kesey's *One Flew Over the Cuckoo's Nest*'. *Style* 30(1). 143–66.

Shklovsky, Victor (1965 (1917)) 'Art as Technique'. In L. Lemon and M. Reis (Eds) *Russian Formalist Criticism: Four Essays*. Lincoln: University of Nebraska Press.

Short, Mick (1996) *Exploring the Language of Poetry, Plays and Prose*. Harlow: Longman Pearson.

Short, Mick (2007) 'Thought Presentation Twenty-five Years On'. *Style* 24(2) Summer. 225–41.

Simpson, Paul (1993) *Language, Ideology and Point of View*. London: Routledge.

Simpson, Paul (2004) *Stylistics: A Resource Book for Students*. London: Routledge.

Singleton, John (2001) *The Creative Writing Workbook*. London: Palgrave Macmillan.

Singleton, John and Mary Luckhurst (1999) *The Creative Writing Handbook*. London: Palgrave Macmillan.

Spicer, Jack (2008) *My Vocabulary Did This to Me: The Collected Poems of Jack Spicer*. Middletown, CT: Wesleyan University Press.

Stacey, Robert, Graeme Harper, Marion Lomax, Rob Pope and Robyn Bolam (2008) *The Writer's Reader: Ways of Writing, Ways of Reading*. Oxford: Wiley-Blackwell.

Stanzel, F. K. (1986) *A Theory of Narrative*. Cambridge: Cambridge University Press.
Steen, Gerard (1994) *Understanding Metaphor in Literature: An Empirical Approach*. London: Longman.
Steinberg, Edwin R. (1973) *The Stream of Consciousness and Beyond in* Ulysess. Pittsburgh, PA: University of Pittsburgh Press.
Stockwell, Peter (2002) *Cognitive Poetics: An Introduction*. London: Routledge.
Strunk, William and E.N. White (1999) *The Elements of Style*. London: Longman.
Swann, Joan, Rob Pope and Ronald Carter (2011) *Creativity in Language and Literature*. London: Palgrave Macmillan.
Toolan, Michael (1998) *Language in Literature: An Introduction to Stylistics*. London: Arnold.
Toolan, Michael (2001) 2nd ed. *Narrative: A Critical Linguistic Introduction*. London: Routledge.
Volosinov, V.N. (1986) *Marxism and the Philosophy of Language*. Cambridge, MA: Harvard University Press.
Wales, Katie (2011) *A Dictionary of Stylistics*. Harlow: Longman Pearson.
Wandor, Michelene (2008) *The Author is Not Dead, Merely Somewhere Else: Creative Writing Reconceived*. London: Palgrave Macmillan.
Wardhaugh, Richard (2002) *An Introduction to Sociolinguistics*. 4th ed. Oxford: Blackwell.
Werth, Paul (1999) *Text Worlds: Representing Conceptual Space in Discourse*. London: Longman.
Whiteley, Sara (2011) 'Talking about "An Accommodation": The Implications of Discussion Group Data for Community Engagement and Pedagogy'. *Language and Literature* 20(3). 236–256.
Widdowson, Henry (1973) 'On the Deviance of Literary Discourse'. In Carter, Ronald and Peter Stockwell (Eds) (2003) *The Language and Literature Reader*. London: Routledge.
Young, Johnnie (2011) *Resources for Teaching Creative Writing*. London: Continuum.

Primary texts

Amis, Martin (1989) *London Fields*. London: Penguin.
Amis, Martin (2003) *Time's Arrow*. London: Faber and Faber.
Ashbery, John (2007) 'What is Poetry?' http://www.writing.upenn.edu/~afilreis/88/what-is-poetry.html. [accessed 3 October 2012]
Auden, W.H. (1962) *The Dyer's Hand and Other Essays*. New York: Random House.
Banks, Iain (1993) *The Crow Road*. London: Abacus.
Barker, Pat (1991) *Regeneration*. London: Penguin.
Bennett, Alan (2010) 'The Greening of Mrs Donaldson'. *London Review of Books*. 32(17). 9 September 201. 9-22.
Borges, Jorge L. (2000) *Labyrinths: Selected Stories and Other Writings*. London: Penguin Classics. *Tlön, Uqbar, Orbis Tertius*. http://en.wikipedia.org/wiki/Tl%C3%B6n,_Uqbar,_Orbis_Tertius [accessed 22 June 2012]
Brown, Dan (2010) *The Lost Symbol*. London: Random House.
Burgess, Anthony (1962) *A Clockwork Orange*. London: William Heinemann.
Chaucer, Geoffrey (1483/2003) *The Canterbury Tales*. London: Penguin Classics.

Conrad, Joseph (1895/1989) *Heart of Darkness*. London: Penguin Classics.

Cummings, e.e. (2003) *73 Poems*. New York: W.W. Norton and Co.

Dickens, Charles (1837/2000) *Oliver Twist*. London: Wordswoth Classics.

Dickens, Charles (1839/1995) *Nicholas Nickleby*. London: Wordswoth Classics.

Dickens, Charles (1850/1992) *David Copperfield*. London: Wordsworth Classics.

Duffy, Carol Ann (1999) *The World's Wife*. London: Picador.

Faulkner, William (1989) *The Sound and the Fury*. London: Picador.

Fitzgerald, F. Scott (1925) *The Great Gatsby*. New York: Charles Scribner.

Fowles, John (1969) *The French Lieutenant's Woman*. London: Jonathan Cape.

Gaffield, Nancy (2011) *Tokaido Road*. London: CB Editions.

Gaiman, Neil, P. Craig Russell, Frank Quitely, Glenn Fabry, Bill Sienkiewicz and Milo Manara (2004) *The Sandman: Endless Nights*. London: Titan Books.

Haddon, Mark (2004) *The Curious Incident of the Dog in the Night-time*. London: Vintage.

Hemingway, Ernest (1927) *Men Without Women*. New York: Charles Scribner's Sons.

Hemingway, Ernest (1932/2003) *Death in the Afternoon*. New York: Charles Scribner's Sons.

Hoban, Russell (1980) *Riddley Walker*. London: Jonathan Cape.

Ishiguro, Kazuo (1989) *The Remains of the Day*. London: Faber and Faber.

Joyce, James (1916) *A Portrait of the Artist as a Young Man*. London: The Egoist.

Joyce, James (1916/1990) *Dubliners*. London: Penguin Classics.

Joyce, James (1939/1971) *Finnegans Wake*. London: Faber and Faber.

Joyce, James (1986) *Ulysses*. London: Penguin.

Joyce, James (1991) *Stephen Hero*. London: Paladin.

Kafka, Franz (1925) *The Trial*. Berlin: Verlag Die Schmiede.

Kelman, James (1994) *How Late It Was How Late*. London: Minerva.

Kelman, James (1995) *Not Not While the Giro*. London: Minerva.

Kesey, Ken (1973) *One Flew Over the Cuckoo's Nest*. London: Picador

Mamet, David (1993) *Oleanna*. London: Methuen.

Mieveille, China (2000) *Perdido Street Station*. London: Pan Macmillan.

Plath, Sylvia (1968) *Ariel*. London: Faber and Faber.

Salinger, J.D. (1951) *The Catcher in the Rye*. New York: Little, Brown and Company.

Scott, Jeremy (2010) 'Eucharist (or the Lark Ascending)'. *New Writing* 7(2). July. London: Routledge. 107–22.

Self, Will (2006) *The Book of Dave*. London: Viking.

Sillitoe, Alan (1958) *Saturday Night and Sunday Morning*. London: Pan Books.

Swift, Graham (1996) *Last Orders*. London: Picador.

Warner, Alan (1999) *The Sopranos*. London: Vintage.

Welsh, Irvine (1994) *Trainspotting*. London: Vintage.

White, Patrick (1966) *The Solid Mandala*. London: Eyre and Spottiswoode.

Wicks, Susan (2003) *Night Toad: New and Selected Poems*. Tarset: Bloodaxe Books.

Williams, William Carlos (1963) *Paterson*. New York: New Directions.

Woolf, Virginia (1927) *To the Lighthouse*. London: Hogarth Press.

Wordsworth, William and Samuel Taylor Coleridge (1798/2005) *Lyrical Ballads*. London: Routledge.

References and Selected Further Reading

If you only ever read one book from this list, let it be this one.

Index